David Rae

entrepreneurship

from opportunity to action

palgrave
macmillan

First published 2007 by
PALGRAVE MACMILLAN
Houndmills, Basingstoke, Hampshire RG21 6XS and
175 Fifth Avenue, New York, N.Y. 10010
Companies and representatives throughout the world

PALGRAVE MACMILLAN is the global academic imprint of the Palgrave
Macmillan division of St. Martin's Press, LLC and of Palgrave Macmillan Ltd.
Macmillan® is a registered trademark in the United States, United Kingdom
and other countries. Palgrave is a registered trademark in the European
Union and other countries.

ISBN-13: 978-1-4039-4175-6
ISBN-10: 1-4039-4175-0

This book is printed on paper suitable for recycling and made from fully
managed and sustained forest sources.

A catalogue record for this book is available from the British Library.

Library of Congress Cataloging-in-Publication Data
Rae, David, 1960–
    Entrepreneurship : from opportunity to action / by David Rae.
      p. cm.
    Includes bibliographical references and index.
    ISBN-13: 978-1-4039-4175-6 (pbk.)
    ISBN-10: 1-4039-4175-0 (pbk.)
     1. Entrepreneurship. 2. Creative ability in business. 3. Business planning. I. Title.
    HB615.R33 2007
    658.4'21–dc22

                                                   2006051453

10   9   8   7   6   5   4   3   2   1
16 15 14 13 12 11 10 09 08 07

Printed and bound in China

contents

figures

tables

What does this book do?

Creating, recognising and exploiting opportunities are at the very heart of entrepreneurship. This book aims to help you to develop the skills, awareness and mindset to find, create and develop opportunities. Taking 'opportunity for life' as its central idea, it proposes that entrepreneurship is a skill-set which can be learned, so that everyone can learn and develop enterprising skills and behaviours, if they wish to.

Whilst not everyone wishes to become an entrepreneur, the book does propose that enterprising skills are valuable for everyone, whether their life goals are concerned with business venturing, building a career in employment or in other areas. We all need to be able to find, select and work on opportunities, whether at work or in other aspects of our lives. The book provides ways of seeing the world which generate opportunities, ways of developing a wide range of enterprising skills which can be applied in many different environments, and tools and techniques which can be used to create, select, plan and make opportunities happen. It also includes stories and examples of entrepreneurial people and organisations which show what can be achieved.

What is Opportunity-Centred Entrepreneurship?

Opportunity-Centred Entrepreneurship describes the human activities which we use in thinking, learning, decision making, working and managing in entrepreneurial ways. Thinking and acting as an entrepreneur are real-world learning processes through which people can develop the skills and confidence to recognise, create and act effectively on opportunities.

Opportunity-Centred Entrepreneurship is an active learning process which is stimulated by such basic motivations as curiosity, desire, and the intentions to find out and achieve results. People may use this approach intuitively, without being aware of it, yet it can be learned consciously and the abilities enhanced. Opportunity-Centred Entrepreneurship enables people to identify, discover and explore opportunities, to select and make decisions on them, to relate them to their personal and social goals, and to plan and work with others to act on and accomplish them. This is active learning through discovery, achieved through working with other people.

Opportunity-Centred Entrepreneurship is an integrative approach which connects entrepreneurship with creativity and innovation, because through it people can recognise their world as an opportunity-rich environment. In this world we all face the constant challenges of investigating, making sense of, responding creatively to, selecting and acting on opportunities. Opportunity-Centred Entrepreneurship helps people create new reality by doing new things and acting as innovators: to create new ventures, experiences, products, services and value in the broadest sense.

This approach to entrepreneurship is innovative, in several ways. This book makes a distinctive contribution by focusing on people at the centre of entrepreneurial action. It concentrates on the human interaction in generating ideas, opportunities and business ventures. It is not dominated by academic subjects such as business studies, economics or psychology, although these are used as important resources to help explore and act upon opportunities and business ventures.

Who is the book for?

The book is written for you, if you wish to enhance your knowledge and skills in entrepreneurial thinking and working, either from an academic or practitioner perspective. It is especially intended for use in entrepreneurship and enterprise teaching, at undergraduate (especially final year) and postgraduate levels. It is designed to be useful in courses and modules including, for example, enterprise, entrepreneurship, new venture creation, creativity and innovation, small business management, social enterprise and corporate entrepreneurship. It also aims to help practitioners such as managers in business ventures or larger organisations to develop their entrepreneurial skills.

Students from non-business subjects such as sciences, creative and applied arts, design, technology, tourism and sports are increasingly opting to study an enterprise, entrepreneurship or small business management course or module, and the book is intended to appeal to their interests too. It does not require prior knowledge of other business subjects. So if you are in one of the groups described below, the book is intended for you:

- students, especially on final-year undergraduate entrepreneurship courses
- students on postgraduate and post-experience courses in entrepreneurship
- start-up entrepreneurs in university and other business incubators
- people changing career or in mid-career (roughly mid-30s to mid-50s) who are considering self-employment
- managers and personnel within organisations (including corporate and public sector organisations) focusing on innovation, new opportunity and business development
- social entrepreneurs and community activists developing new forms of economic and social activity
- readers with a general interest in opportunity creation and exploitation.

The book is specifically intended to appeal to an international readership, both students who are studying in the United Kingdom and those studying in other countries.

What can you get from reading the book?

Why might you want to read this book for your personal direction, interest and motivation? In addition to its role as an academic course text, these are the aims of the book.

First, to enable you, the reader, to consider yourself as an entrepreneurial person, and to enhance your skills, confidence and capacity to act in entrepreneurial ways. It aims to build skills, confidence and entrepreneurial ambition in your career. Enterprising skills can be applied in employment as well as in creating new business ventures, and there are strong links between being enterprising and being employable, so you can definitely benefit from the book if your initial goals are to gain a foothold in employment. The book can help you to be conscious of the boundaries within which you can be most effective, and to challenge and go beyond them, which might include exploring new frontiers of skills, confidence, culture, types of business, technology, resources or geography.

Second, by taking a 'practical theory' approach, the book aims to connect the theory and practice of entrepreneurship in useful ways which can be applied in the real world. So you are encouraged in the practical activities to try out and explore 'what works' for you, how and why.

Third, to use the concept of Opportunity-Centred Entrepreneurship as an approach which enables you to accomplish the first two aims, and to access and use a range of ideas, tools and techniques, skills and insights in a structured yet flexible way.

Fourth (probably the most important) to enable you, the reader, to achieve your personal objectives, which may be concerned with passing a course module successfully, planning an entrepreneurial project and making it happen, or gaining a new career direction. Hopefully you will take away from the book more than you anticipated.

Note for enterprise tutors

Your role is vital in helping readers to gain the maximum benefit from the book. It is designed to help you as a teaching resource, and can be used very flexibly to support your course or module. The tutor website provides guidance on using Opportunity-Centred Entrepreneurship as an educational approach, with reference to the related methods of teaching and learning. This emphasises an active and discovery-based approach to learning, in which students 'feel the enterprise experience' through practical activities, supported by tools and techniques, concepts, frameworks, examples and case studies. This is broadly similar to such approaches as problem-based, inquiry-based and action learning, with which you may well be familiar. The website includes a range of learning, teaching and support resources and materials, including a set of presentations for a full course on entrepreneurial management.

acknowledgements

Thanks are due to the many entrepreneurs and students who have contributed to this book, often unknowingly providing inspiration. To the experts, scholars and colleagues who have provided many intellectual foundations and challenges. To my family and Roz, for allowing me the time.

opportunity-centred entrepreneurship

chapter contents

introduction to the book

This chapter introduces you, the reader, to the approach taken in this book. It connects entrepreneurship with related subject areas, also providing a plan of the book and a 'routemap' of how to get the best from reading it or using it as a resource. By reading the chapter you should be able to accomplish these learning goals:

● to become familiar with the basic terms, concepts and definitions used in the book
● to identify your learning goals of what you want, and can expect, to learn from the book
● to become familiar with the structure of the book, and how to use it to achieve your goals.

what you will find in the book

The book will help and urge you to find, explore, develop and try out ideas, opportunities and techniques for working on them. You will be able to select and make decisions on opportunities, to plan and act on them, and accomplish your aims. You will be able to relate them to your own goals, interests and motivations, and by doing this to enhance your skills, confidence and experience as an entrepreneurial person.

Each chapter of the book starts with learning goals which suggest what you can expect to learn from the chapter, and help you decide how relevant this is to your study needs or the course you are following. The chapters all include activities – short questions and practical exercises. These are designed to help you accomplish the learning goals for the chapter. They will help you to 'feel the enterprise experience' and to develop your enterprising skills and thinking patterns. It is easier to skip past the activities and just read on – but this will not develop your skills and awareness, because enterprise requires *learning by doing*, not just reading. The activities can be done by self-study, by working on your own, or as small group activities in a class.

At the end of each chapter there are critical questions to help you review and consolidate what you have learned and how you could apply it, so that you are consciously aware of your learning, or that 'you know what you know.'

Wealth warning

Some of the activities will ask you to do things which may be new and unfamiliar. Being enterprising is about 'going into the unknown' and trying new things.

Some activities ask you to work on real life opportunities which you will choose. So there is a risk that … you may enjoy and have fun with some of these activities! … you may even make some money or possibly lose a little money!

The aim overall is that you learn and gain confidence in your enterprising skills. None of the activities should place you at any personal risk to your safety, and all can be carried out entirely within the law.

definitions

It is important to understand the key ideas and concepts used in this book, so that we know what we are talking about when we use them. For this reason, here are short definitions to introduce and explain the main concepts in the book.

- *Enterprise*: if people display enterprise, it means they are using the skills, knowledge and personal attributes which are needed to apply creative ideas and innovations to practical situations. These include initiative, independence, creativity, problem solving, identifying and working on opportunities, leadership, and acting resourcefully to effect change. These are explored more fully in Chapter 3. The term enterprise is also used to describe a small or new business venture.
- *Entrepreneur*: this is the person who acts in an enterprising way, and who identifies or creates and acts on an opportunity, for example by starting a new business venture.
- *Entrepreneurship*: this is the subject of enterprise and entrepreneurs, encompassing both the practical and academic knowledge, skills and techniques used in being an entrepreneur.
- *Entrepreneurial management*: the application of enterprise to the organisational environment, including self-employment, new venture creation and small business management, and managing in enterprising ways in corporate, public and social organisations of all types and sizes.
- Enterprise is a generic capability, since everyone is capable of being enterprising, and entrepreneurial management is considered to be the application of those capabilities in different organisational settings and at differing levels.
- *Opportunity*: we can define an opportunity as: 'the potential for change, improvement or advantage arising from our action in the circumstances'.

  Casson (2003) defined entrepreneurial opportunities as 'those situations in which new goods, services, raw materials and organising methods can be introduced and sold at greater than their cost of production'. Shane (2003) defined them as 'a situation in which a person can create a new means–end framework for recombining resources that the entrepreneur believes will yield a profit'. Both of these are only definitions of profit opportunities. This book takes a broader definition, in that the pursuit of profit is important but not the sole determinant of entrepreneurial opportunity. Improvements in social, cultural, health and environmental arenas are also important, especially for social entrepreneurs and entrepreneurial managers in public sector organisations, as well as 'mainstream' entrepreneurs.

  The opportunity may be a situation which already exists, or one which we create and which would not otherwise have occurred. An opportunity may be one which we can actually recognise now, or one which will arise in the future. Types of opportunity may include, for example,
  - a 'gap in the market' for a product or service
  - a mismatch between supply and demand
  - a future possibility which can be recognised or created
  - a problem that can be solved, for example by applying a solution to a need
  - a more effective or efficient business process, system or model
  - a new or existing technology or approach which has not yet been applied
  - the transfer of something that works in one situation to another, such as a product, process or business concept
  - a commodity or experience people would desire or find useful if they knew about it.
  These types of opportunity will be expanded in Chapter 5.

Enterprise involves using creative thinking, behaviour and skills to come up with new ideas and concepts. To innovate is then to translate those ideas into practical solutions such as products or business models and to implement them, thus acting on the opportunity and causing change. Entrepreneurs recognise problems and unsatisfactory situations, then find ways of changing them, by seeing the potential of 'what could be' and acting to make it happen. Every person has this innate capacity for thinking and acting creatively, and as they grow up this may be encouraged and developed, or it may be stifled and constrained. Creative skills are explored further in Chapter 3.

The first activity asks you to think about your approach to enterprise. The aim is to relate examples from your own experience to the key ideas in the book.

activity

1. Do you see yourself as an enterprising person? Can you recall examples from any situation when you have acted in enterprising ways?
2. When have you used creative skills to invent or do new things? Think of one of these occasions.
3. Have you ever 'spotted an opportunity'? What did you do about it? Did you act on it? If not, what stopped you?

You may come up with quite 'small' examples from your experience or major ones; the scale does not matter, but the realisation that you are an enterprising person, in your own way, is important.

why do we need to get better at creating and working on opportunities?

Being aware of opportunities is central to developing and learning entrepreneurial behaviours. This focus on opportunity at the heart of entrepreneurship is important, because opportunity recognition has only been the subject of serious academic research in recent years (e.g. Shane, 2003; Stevenson and Jarillo, 1990). The entrepreneurship literature increasingly views the subject as being connected closely with the concept of opportunity, as will be discussed in Chapter 2. The recognition, creation and exploration of opportunities in practical ways will be analysed in depth in Chapters 4–5.

There is a need for people to become more skilled in selecting, assessing and working on opportunities for the following eight fundamental reasons.

● At a worldwide, macro level, there is a growing list of social, health, economic and environmental problems, including shortages of water, food, energy, materials and other resources. Opportunity-oriented thinking and innovation are required to generate and implement new, workable approaches which can help to address the challenges of growing populations and their expectations when faced with limited resources. These can create economic growth and more efficient means of production and resource management to increase wealth and employment, such as moving from subsistence farming to commercial production. The alternatives are resource grabbing, conflict, poverty and famine.

- There is a need to re-energise societies to overcome economic disadvantages, at national government and international levels, as well as at regional, local and community levels. It is significant that multinational organisations such as the European Union (EU), Organisation for Economic Co-operation and Development (OECD) and the New Partnership for African Development (NEPAD) all emphasise the development of entrepreneurial societies and culture as a means of creating economic growth, change and social renewal. However as Chapter 2 will argue, there is often a gap between the policy rhetoric and its ability to effect change.

- Regional economic development in both urban and rural areas is a priority in many countries, where challenges such as de-industrialisation, the closure of old or uncompetitive industries, agricultural decline and poverty result in the need to grow economic activity and employment from new businesses and social enterprises.

- The rate at which new knowledge is translated into business innovations and practical solutions is both lower and slower than it could be, because there is a lag between the creation of new knowledge and the rate at which it is adopted. For example, Europe has lower and slower rates of productivity of its science and knowledge base, and conversion of research into commercial technology and innovation, than the United States.

- The failure and closure rates of small business ventures within three years of starting remain consistently high, for example within the UK. This suggests that entrepreneurs often do not develop the skills to identify the optimal business opportunities or to manage their response to opportunities so that the venture is able to survive and grow.

- The continuing decline in employment and career opportunities within big organisations, including state-owned firms, increasingly requires people to achieve their social and career aspirations through self-employment, entrepreneurship or working in small firms. This affects the growing number of graduates looking for 'corporate' career opportunities who need to develop skills of personal enterprise to get started, increasingly in smaller companies.

- Demographic changes create the need for people to extend their working lives, to establish new careers, and to find ways of caring for the increasing ageing populations in many developed countries.

- Many groups of people in all societies experience inequality of opportunity, disadvantage and even discrimination, resulting from such factors as ethnicity, disability, geographical location, gender and family responsibility, including motherhood and age. This represents 'human capital' which is an underused resource.

These are examples of the reasons why identifying, creating and developing opportunities is a concern of strategic importance in economic and social development. They are 'macro' issues, but they affect all of us, and are worth exploring in more detail than has generally been the case in entrepreneurship literature. All of these challenging issues actually present opportunities for change, because they show gaps between the current reality and future potential. They open up possibilities for innovation and entrepreneurial action to provide solutions to the problems. First they require definition of the problems or unsatisfactory current situations, and creative thinking to develop new initiatives and solutions. These solutions can create employment, reduce waste or conserve resources, improve the quality of lifestyles and generate financial income.

activity

1. Choose an aspect of one of the eight macro issues listed above that concerns you most or in which you have a direct personal experience or interest.

2. Define one small or specific aspect of the problem as you see it. Try using the following questions to do this:
   - What is the problem? What is the difference between the current situation and what you think the situation should be?
   - What factors cause the problem? How does it occur, what events take place?
   - What results or effects is this having?
   - What is the scale or measure, e.g. the numbers of people affected?
   - Who is causing, and who is affected by, the problem? How do those causing the problem benefit from it?

   Just defining the problem in this way is a useful first step, in order to identify the scope and scale of the problem, and parameters for solving it. It is too simplistic to claim that such macro problems are capable of being solved easily, permanently or by one initiative. Rather than attempting to devise a solution yourself, the next step is to find out what is already being done to solve or cope with the effects of the problem. For this you require Internet access to gather information on the problem.

3. Carry out an Internet search on the problem. Aim to find examples of innovative actions, projects or initiatives which are taking place to act on it. These might be by government, business, research or community organisations for example. Start by using search tools such as Google or Yahoo. You may also find the social and 'not-for-profit' entrepreneurship websites shown in the further reading section useful.

   www.ashoka.org Ashoka social enterprise network
   www.drucker.org Peter Drucker Foundation for Non-profit Management
   www.socialentrepreneurs.org US National Center for Social Entrepreneurs
   www.sse.org UK School for Social Entrepreneurship
   www.globalideasbank.org Global Ideas Bank

4. Read and review the information you have gathered. What are the strengths and limitations of the initiatives you have discovered?

5. What opportunities can you see for initiatives to address and help

activity continued

to solve the problem you have identified? This may include learning from, replicating or expanding small-scale initiatives which already exist.

6. What benefits could one of these initiatives provide? How would these counteract the negative effects of the problem?

This activity has asked you to define one aspect of a problem, and to research what is currently being done to address it. This investigation shows you can learn about the problem and also about current solutions. There is almost certainly more activity out there than you imagined. Once you know what is already being done, you can be more creative in extending, transferring or improving on these.

example

Rising fuel costs

During 2005–6, the world price for crude oil rose past $60 per barrel to over $70 after Hurricane Katrina disrupted oil supplies in the US Gulf Coast, with no sign that prices would fall quickly. Demand from Western and developing countries remained strong, with political instability in the Middle East and oil-producing countries accompanying a realisation that oil production would deplete known oil reserves over the following 50 years.

Potential opportunities

- more economic oil use, e.g. through smaller engine sizes and lean-burn technology
- improved energy conservation, lower emissions and better building insulation
- alternative energy sources, e.g. solar, wind and wave power
- increased nuclear power generation
- hydrogen fuel cells
- bio-diesel production
- increased taxes such as road pricing and fuel duty to contain demand
- advanced logistics systems to gain greater efficiency and productivity from road, sea and air transportation by 'filling empty spaces'.

All of these are practical steps, although clearly none on its own is sufficient to resolve the problem. All involve innovation, by combining technology, resources and public policy in new ways to reduce energy use. Entrepreneurship is required to apply the innovation to the real-world problem, to produce both economic and other benefits.

How do we connect learning with opportunities?

The normal way of learning about subjects at school or college is curriculum-based. You may have had little choice about the way it was taught, the curriculum itself, the books, coursework or assessment method: it was imposed learning.

Now think of something you are interested in. Remember how you passionately learned all about it, by practical experience, reading, friends, TV and radio, the Internet and so on. People can become self-taught experts in subjects and skills such as sport, music, fashion, computers, gaming, technology applications or almost anything. This kind of self-motivated, self-directed informal activity we can think of as curiosity-inspired learning.

If we connect the ideas of opportunity and of learning about it, we can create this kind of inspired learning. This is a natural and social process which is stimulated by motivations of curiosity and desire to find out and accomplish things. This type of learning centres on recognising an opportunity, finding out about it, immersing ourselves in it, relating it to our personal and social being, planning intentionally to act on and accomplish it. We may use this much of the time, without realising it.

Recognising an opportunity is an act of learning. We may not be aware of this at the time, yet it creates new meaning, the moment of discovery or the 'ah-ha' factor. People

example

CRT recycling

The shortage of basic resources, coupled with the need to improve recycling of manufactured materials to reduce waste disposal, is providing increasing opportunities for environmentally oriented businesses. In the UK and Europe, strict regulations to restrict the dumping of electrical and electronic equipment have been introduced to prevent land and water pollution. However, as old-style cathode ray tube (CRT) televisions and computer monitors come to the end of their lives and are replaced by flat-screen technology, there will be a need over the next ten years for environmentally sound methods of disposing of millions of glass screens, which contain heavy metals. Most of these methods are labour intensive and costly.

However an entrepreneur realised that a government-funded CRT manufacturing plant had closed, and that this had included an automated recycling facility for defective screens produced during the manufacturing process. Local authorities were keen to find a cost-effective means of disposing of life-expired screens without the additional costs of transporting them to mainland Europe. He recognised the opportunity to combine this redundant yet efficient facility with the recycling need, and prepared a plan to reopen the plant for a limited lifespan to meet the peak in demand for recycling before the site was redeveloped by its new owner. This would create jobs in an unemployment black spot and produce sand from the recycling process which could be used in golf bunkers and other applications.

tend to be curious about opportunities because they are novel, they may involve creative or unusual activity, they are future-oriented and positive, and they offer the possibility of personal advantage, gain or growth. Learning about opportunities is similar to the instrumental learning people do to accomplish a desired goal or state. It recognises that achievement is an important motivation to learn, often more so than the desire to 'learn for its own sake'.

By using opportunity-centred learning, we can recognise the world as an opportunity-rich environment, in which we face the constant challenge of investigating, making sense of, selecting and acting on opportunities. We can learn to become more aware of existing opportunities and of how to create new ones. We can also learn to be more effective in selecting which opportunities to work on, and in developing these into real ventures or projects. Opportunity is at the heart of entrepreneurship and of developing enterprising skills. It means working in conditions of speed, uncertainty and competition, so learning to be effective in managing or adapting to these is vital. It means learning to think as an entrepreneur.

an outline of the opportunity-centred entrepreneurship concept

Opportunity-Centred Entrepreneurship is a learning process which focuses on four interconnected themes. These themes, shown in Figure 1.1, are essential to exploring and understanding an opportunity by relating it to personal (individual and group) interests and goals, planning to realise it, and acting to make the opportunity happen. The book takes an action-based approach to these themes, introducing tools for thinking, planning and learning, and

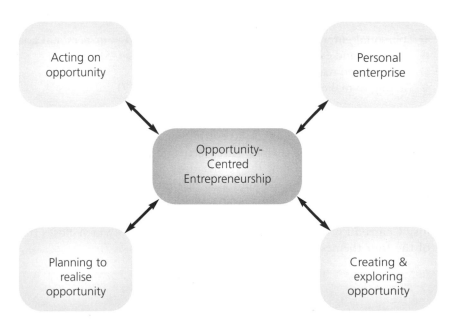

FIGURE 1.1 **Opportunity-Centred Entrepreneurship**

using case studies and connections with related conceptual material. The action-based approach means that the book will encourage you to identify a range of opportunities and apply decision-making skills and techniques to select and work on developing the most promising opportunities.

The reason for taking an action-based approach is that other texts inform people and help them to learn about entrepreneurship, enterprise and small business management. Allan Gibb, who pioneered new thinking in enterprise education in the UK, distinguished between learning *for* and learning *about* enterprise. To learn *for* enterprise it is necessary to learn through direct, practical, hands-on experience of doing it. This book will urge you to find, explore, develop and try out ideas, opportunities and techniques for working on them, and by doing this to enhance your skills, confidence and experience as an entrepreneurial person. In doing this you will also become more knowledgeable about enterprise. An important aim of the book is to enable the reader to relate theory to practice, using principles which work in real situations. This is accomplished partly by encouraging activity, or practice, and partly by prompting you to reflect on 'what works', how, and why, in given situations; this approach is called *practical theory*.

Developing and managing opportunities requires skills of creative thinking, planning, managing human relationships, marketing and selling, and project and resource management. These management skills must be deployed and in many cases learned through experience. We can term these the skills of *entrepreneurial management*. Opportunity-Centred Entrepreneurship is an integrative approach which connects with the broader subjects of business and organisational management, creativity, innovation and learning.

The learning process of Opportunity-Centred Entrepreneurship focuses on the identification, development, planning and implementation of an opportunity, from idea to realisation. In developing the opportunity, we work and learn through four interconnected processes. These are shown in the simple mind-map in Figure 1.1. This is the starting point for you in using the book, which will guide you to focus on each of the four arms, or quadrants, in turn:

● personal enterprise – relating the opportunity to your personal goals (Chapter 3)
● creating and exploring the opportunity (Chapters 4–5)
● planning to realise the opportunity (Chapter 6)
● acting to make the opportunity happen (Chapter 7).

This provides the structure for the book, which is designed to be used as a handbook in developing opportunities by using entrepreneurial approaches. This can be accomplished within an academic or a work-based learning process, or simply as a personal project. However it is essential that the reader does identify and work on a real opportunity in order to engage with the action-based learning approach and thereby to gain full value from the book, rather than reading it simply to learn 'about entrepreneurship'. This opportunity can be of any type and any scale. The fully detailed activity map of Opportunity-Centred Entrepreneurship is shown at Figure 1.3 which closes this chapter, and each of the four themes are explored in turn in Chapters 3–7.

how can the book increase your understanding of entrepreneurship as a subject?

This book provides a new perspective on the subject by concentrating on opportunity as a defining concept at the heart of entrepreneurship. This moves away from considering

example

Opportunity-Centred Entrepreneurship in action: William Chase – Tyrrell's Potato Chips

Personal enterprise

William Chase grew up in rural Herefordshire in a potato-farming family. His mother died while he was young, and William raised the money to buy the family farm from his father. He was keen to be a farmer, but struggled to meet the debt repayments on the farm and the 1992 recession led to his own bankruptcy. As a result of this he evaluated his life, 'grew up', and subsequently bought back the farm a second time from the receiver. He grew potatoes successfully for a few more years, but realised that the major supermarkets were constantly forcing down farmers' prices and profit margins. He concluded that there was no future in growing potatoes as a commodity: 'I had to change direction or go out of business.'

Creating and exploring the opportunity

William needed to consider other options to use the farm and the high-quality potatoes he could grow. He sold potatoes to a crisp manufacturer and realised that the profit margin was around 35 per cent, far higher than on potatoes, with crisps being sold for thousands of pounds per ton. Visiting the United States, he found sales of gourmet hand-produced chips were growing by 15 per cent each year, and discovered that farm-based production was feasible.

Assessing the UK snack food market, he concluded that whilst there were potato crisp brands which were perceived as 'premium', there was an opportunity in the market for a genuine top-quality brand of potato chips aimed at premium customers. He decided that making hand-produced chips from potatoes grown on his own farm, aimed at the gourmet end of the market, would be unique and this was where he wanted to be. He knew nothing about making chips but realised from his experience with the supermarkets that 'you have to find a niche.'

Planning to act on the opportunity

Initially he produced and successfully test-marketed batches of crisps using an adapted chip-shop fryer. This, together with market research, proved that demand existed. On the strength of this, William prepared a business plan to invest £1m of a bank loan, a small grant and personal equity in buying chip-manufacturing equipment from the United States, converting a potato storage shed into a production plant and training the farm staff to become chip makers, 'starting off as you mean to go on, with good people and equipment'.

Chase also invested in creating the Tyrrell's brand, named after the farm. The identity, packaging and marketing materials are carefully produced to 'sell the story' and convey the 'magic' of the farm-grown, hand-produced chips with a distinctive range of 'natural' flavours, and even root vegetable and apple chips. Having experienced downward price pressure from supermarkets, he refused to supply these and instead targeted the product at up-market retailers, independent stores and gastro-pubs, which enabled Tyrrell's to offer a premium-priced product with a good profit margin and avoid the pressure to discount: 'I decided to be the little guy who took the supermarkets on.'

Acting to make the opportunity happen

After starting full production in 2002, Tyrrell's grew rapidly through successful marketing, product innovation and distribution to achieve over £7m turnover by the end of the fourth year. The brand involved customers and retailers closely from the beginning, continually gaining customer feedback and giving excellent support and service to retailers with independent distribution.

However, William felt that ' there are no rules, no limit to keeping the magic going' and aimed to grow to be a £50m turnover brand, growing 100 per cent per year and becoming the country's foremost innovative producer and supplier of excellent-quality, farm-produced artisan delicacies for the discerning customer. Chase saw his role as 'doing the thinking, moving the business forward, anticipating issues and responding to potential cracks before they appear'.

By visiting trade shows, talking to retailers and observing customers, he predicts international market trends, and has a growing export business: 'I'm learning all the time, gaining ideas from the United States and Spain.' Based on the successful first few years, Chase invested a further £2m to build a new factory on the farm, doubling the production area and potato planting acreage, whilst moving into muesli, oats, fruit and cereal bars, and other healthy and organic products. Chase credits much of the success to the staff: 'a successful business attracts people – you find and develop the best people, who come to work with passion.' The business success was recognised in 2005 when William Chase won National Business Awards for Entrepreneur of the Year and Small-Medium Sized Business of the Year.

www.tyrrellspotatochips.co.uk

entrepreneurship as being aligned only with starting and managing new or small enterprises, because Opportunity-Centred Entrepreneurship can be applied in a wide range of different contexts, including large, corporate organisations and the social and 'not-for-profit' sectors. Entrepreneurship is not limited to those people who start and run their own businesses: increasingly, managers, technologists and professionals from many backgrounds must learn to think and act as entrepreneurs.

Also, everyone working, teaching or researching in the field of entrepreneurship must take an international and multicultural perspective. Many of the 'classic' texts on entrepreneurship were written from the economic and cultural context of the United States of America, and were rooted in the assumptions of the US internal market. Today, the entrepreneurial person may be acting in any economy, worldwide. Nations which once had state-controlled economies, including China, Russia, Poland and the other East and Central European states, now have flourishing enterprise economies. Increasingly, these are interdependent, with the domestic markets of each country opening up to global trade and competition. The entrepreneurs of today and tomorrow are more likely to be Indian, Chinese, African or Arab than they are to be either white or American. They are increasingly likely to be female. They will come from any occupational background, including the rural economy, food production, tourism, creative arts, health care and many others. And they will come from a broad age spectrum: young people and students, early career entrepreneurs, and increasing numbers of mid-career and 'third-age' entrepreneurs.

Although, when considering any entrepreneurial opportunity, the obvious first place to look may be the immediate, accessible local market, the challenge should always be to think of the wider international markets, both the opportunities and competitors, and the international and multicultural networks and potential alliances and partnerships which are possible. The Global Entrepreneurship Monitor (GEM website www.gemconsortium.org) is an international research resource which is recommended because it allows international comparisons of entrepreneurial performance.

Entrepreneurship is not a 'pure' subject which can be studied in isolation. It is an area of applied knowledge and practice which connects with related subjects and draws on skills, expert knowledge and contextual application from them. You may already have studied some of these subjects, and if so you should be able to apply them in entrepreneurial working. Equally, you may need to develop your skills and knowledge further in some of these areas. Entrepreneurship is an evolving subject which is expanding to create new and related areas of knowledge. Figure 1.2 (overleaf) shows that entrepreneurship is an applied subject which connects other subject areas by applying them in practical ways.

activity

The purpose of this activity is to help you to identify goals for what you would like, and can expect, to learn from the book.

1. From what you have read so far and know about entrepreneurship, what questions do you have about the subject?
2. What aspects interest you? What aspects do you find less easy to understand?
3. What skills and knowledge do you think it would be useful to learn?
4. What would you like to be able to do as a result of reading the book?
5. Write these questions and goals down.
6. Then read through the rest of this chapter, including Tables 1.1 and 1.2, to understand the structure of the book and to see if you can find the chapters where your questions will be covered, and note these against your questions.

how to use this book

The book is structured in nine chapters, which are introduced below.

Chapter 1. Opportunity-Centred Entrepreneurship

This sets out the wider context for the book, introduces the key concepts and outlines the approach and structure.

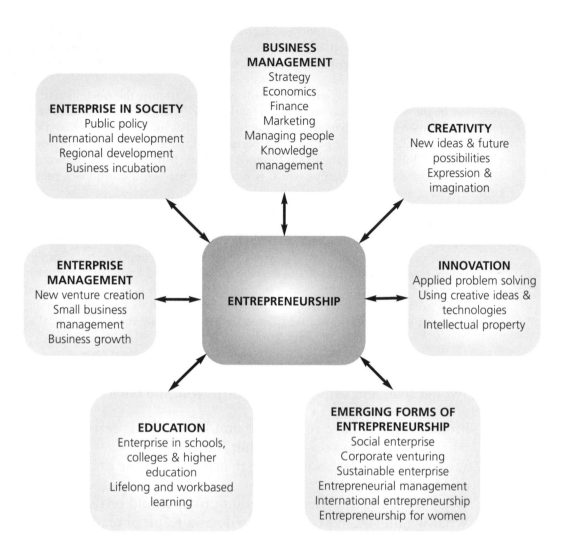

FIGURE 1.2 **Locating entrepreneurship as a subject**

Chapter 2. The context of Opportunity-Centred Entrepreneurship

This chapter is intended for the academic reader who needs to understand how Opportunity-Centred Entrepreneurship is located in relation to the wider academic literature and conceptual landscape of entrepreneurship and opportunity. Readers who simply require a practical understanding of entrepreneurial skills and tools can skip this chapter and go on to Chapter 3. Its purpose is to provide a critical assessment of related theories of entrepreneurship and opportunity recognition.

Four critical questions are posed, arising from entrepreneurship theory and practice. These are:

- Who or what is the entrepreneur?
- Are opportunities discovered or created?
- Is entrepreneurship based on personality or learning?
- What is the role of entrepreneurship in society?

The chapter outlines the limitations of an economics-based approach as the dominant paradigm in entrepreneurship studies in understanding human and social behaviour. It suggests that the development of an international entrepreneurial culture is taking place, and that this requires a learning process in which we recognise and value internationalism, cultural diversity and contextual awareness.

Chapter 3. Personal enterprise: connecting opportunities and personal goals

This chapter concentrates on the human aspects of the entrepreneurial process, especially in exploring how you can learn to work in entrepreneurial ways, why people select the opportunities they do, and the connections between learning and selecting opportunities. It covers the first quadrant of Opportunity-Centred Entrepreneurship.

It introduces a conceptual model of entrepreneurial learning which you can apply to help your own development. The role of values and self-confidence in entrepreneurial working are explained. Methods for assessing the 'fit' between ideas and personal goals are evaluated, together with personal orientation to risk and uncertainty. Personal skills and readiness for entrepreneurial working, including personality, learning and working style, expertise and capabilities, are explored. You can apply the skills of leadership in forming and leading entrepreneurial teams to your own preferred role and development. The skills required to seed opportunities through networking, influencing and selling are explored. Finally, a self-assessment of personal confidence, self-belief and essential capabilities for entrepreneurship is undertaken. The outcome of the chapter is a reflection on personal entrepreneurial learning, and an explicit understanding of the types of opportunity which you can best select, either individually or acting with others.

Chapter 4. Opportunity exploration

This chapter aims to provide an introduction to the subject of opportunity recognition and exploration. Together with Chapter 5, it demonstrates how entrepreneurial opportunities can be created, identified, assessed and evaluated. The two chapters together provide a detailed exposition of the second quadrant of Opportunity-Centred Entrepreneurship, creating and exploring opportunities. Chapter 4 takes a creative approach to opportunity generation whilst Chapter 5 takes an analytical approach in relation to opportunity selection, since the combination of these approaches is essential.

The chapter introduces the recognition and generation of opportunities in the external environment. It explains the importance of time perspectives in opportunity recognition, and especially the use of future scenarios, in which the roles of creativity and innovation in the entrepreneurial process are indicated. Creative thinking tools are used to generate ideas and build on them to form opportunities, through association. Opportunity mapping is introduced as a core technique, and methods of exploring opportunities by means of market and related investigation and research are covered in depth.

Chapter 5. Opportunity assessment

This chapter takes a practical approach to assessing and developing opportunities, and is based on the conceptual foundations of Chapter 4. It shows how gaps, needs and problems can be identified and matched with resources and capabilities. Skills and methods of screening, appraising, evaluating and making decisions on opportunities are introduced, with particular emphasis on discriminating between high-potential and low-potential value opportunities. Frameworks and tools for opportunity selection, assessment, evaluation and decision making are introduced.

Methods of connecting opportunities with organisational goals, strategy and culture, and idea-banking, together with the role of clusters and accessing resources through networks in facilitating opportunity development and innovation, are outlined, with particular reference to corporate organisations. The range of types of opportunity (knowledge, technology, product, service, trading, commodity) are outlined and the contribution of a supportive entrepreneurial culture, infrastructure and environment are explained. Finally the role of intellectual property rights and their importance in the entrepreneurial process are summarised.

Chapter 6. Planning to realise opportunities

The purpose of this chapter is to provide a practical and action-based guide to creating a venture plan, which may be applied to any opportunity, whether for a new business venture or within an existing organisation. It addresses the process of planning for new ventures and opportunity exploitation, connecting the decision to focus on a specific opportunity with the actions required to do so. Planning is considered as a future-oriented thinking and acting process of continuing dialogue between stakeholders, including investors, the venture team, suppliers and customers, in which the enterprise becomes a negotiated entity. The importance of creating and defining an identity for the venture is described. A storyboard approach is demonstrated to develop a venture plan from the initial opportunity map and as a means of individual or team-based planning. The need to create a robust business model is explained and the process of project planning, from idea to reality, is outlined. Essential aspects of the business plan are identified and a short section provides an overview of the key financial aspects of planning: investment, cash flow, break-even, risk and return.

The importance of setting goals, targets and success measures as integral parts of the plan, and of identifying key themes, strategies, activities and tasks, is explained and underpinned by a practical exercise which is centred on the development of a business model. Establishing resource requirements, to access different types of resource, potentially including knowledge, finance, human capital, plant, technology, land, permissions and licences, networks, access rights and distribution, is considered. The skills and approaches involved in presenting the business proposal to investors, supporters and partners, including selling, communication and influencing strategies, are considered and developed.

Chapter 7. Acting on opportunities

This chapter covers the final quadrant of the Opportunity-Centred Entrepreneurship map: acting on opportunities to make them happen. The limitations of entrepreneurship theory in this field are outlined and helpful approaches identified, including sensemaking, enaction and action learning. The chapter considers enacting the opportunity as a process of real-time dynamic learning by discovery, in which the models, tools and ideas from previous chapters are applied in making the venture happen. Factors in implementing the venture plan, going beyond planning, responding to new opportunities, and handling setbacks and failure are considered. Essential activities in an early-stage business and reasons for success and failure of businesses are considered. The practical theory approach is applied to establish both 'what works' in businesses and what happens when it doesn't work, and demonstrating how this can contribute to organisational sustainability.

The development of entrepreneurial management as a means of connecting entrepreneurial and managerial skills with a strategic focus is discussed. Strategic decision making, types of entrepreneurial strategy and methods of reviewing the effectiveness of strategy are explored. A final exercise prompts experiential learning from the enaction process, through problem solving, reflecting, using experience and moving forward both personally and organisationally.

Chapter 8. Opportunity-Centred Entrepreneurship in action

The purpose of this chapter is to provide illustrations and case studies of Opportunity-Centred Entrepreneurship in action. These demonstrate different facets of entrepreneurial working in three distinctive contexts, each of which has unique characteristics, and they also provide more generally applicable concepts which can be used outside the specific context. Each of the three sections can be used separately for teaching purposes, and suggested exercises are included for this purpose.

An example of a social enterprise is used to demonstrate venture planning for an international project to improve water supplies in developing countries. Entrepreneurship in the creative industries is explored through the concept of cultural diffusion and the case of Loudmouth music. The role of entrepreneurial management in the low-cost airline industry is compared by assessing the performance of the independent airlines easyJet and Ryanair with examples of corporate entrepreneurship in Go, Buzz and bmibaby

Chapter 9. Where do we go from here?

The final chapter proposes ways to continue the journey, personally, practically and academically, through developing ideas and strategies for personal career planning in the context of the future development of entrepreneurship. There is a section which explores entrepreneurial career options at different life stages, and activities intended to assist in personal career planning.

A number of emerging themes are proposed as being significant for the future development of entrepreneurial research, learning, policy and practice. These suggest possible topics for further study, including independent studies and dissertation projects. The themes include the role of science and technology entrepreneurship and innovation, and the implications for corporate and public sector organisations; the importance of an international and multicultural approach to entrepreneurship as a means of democratic, economic and social empowerment; the need for environmentally sustainable forms of entrepreneurship; the role of lifelong learning and education in entrepreneurial development; the vital importance of female entrepreneurship; and the role of the informal business sector and the relationship between criminality and entrepreneurship. The chapter closes with a challenge to the reader: what are you going to do to create your entrepreneurial future?

Appendices: toolbox

The toolbox contains a series of conceptual and practical tools for opportunity assessment, development and planning, and to support personal learning. They are referred to in the appropriate chapters by means of learning activities which use them.

Personal enterprise
● entrepreneurial skills and capabilities
● career planner

Exploring and assessing opportunities
● opportunity assessment questionnaire (pentagon model)
● opportunity recognition model (hexagon model)

Opportunity planning
● venture planning template
● finance planner

Acting on opportunities
● references, books, organisations and online resources

The book follows the two related themes of personal development and opportunity development. Personal development is concerned with the growth of your own entrepreneurial awareness, skills and confidence.

  Tables 1.1 and 1.2 enable you to identify and locate the practical activities in each chapter which will help you in developing your understanding and capabilities in these two themes. The personal development tools and exercises are listed in Table 1.1. Both tables also identify through 'routemaps' which activities are likely to be most helpful to the three main groups of readers:

● students with limited work experience, likely to be using the book on a first-degree course
● managers or people with work but limited entrepreneurial experience, likely to be using the book practically or on a postgraduate course
● entrepreneurs starting early-stage ventures or on a business start-up programme.

The parallel theme is developing opportunities, and the activities used to work on these are listed in Table 1.2.

  Finally, Figure 1.3 closes the chapter by providing a detailed map of the questions addressed in each of the four quadrants of the Opportunity-Centred Entrepreneurship approach.

TABLE 1.1 **Personal development tools and exercises**

Chapter	Activity	Student	Manager	Entrepreneur
Chapter 3 Personal enterprise	Entrepreneurial learning model:			
	• Personal & social emergence	√	√	√
	• Contextual learning		√	√
	• Negotiated enterprise		√	√
	Personal values, goals & motivations	√	√	√
	Drawing your learning map	√	√	√
	Assessing fit between ideas & personal goals	√	√	√
	Personal orientation to risk & uncertainty	√	√	√
	Entrepreneurial & management capabilities (toolkit)	√	√	√
	Leadership & entrepreneurial teamwork	√	√	√
	Mapping your personal networks	√	√	√
Chapter 9 Where do we go from here?	Developing your entrepreneurial career	√	√	√
	Career planner (toolkit)	√	√	

TABLE 1.2 **Opportunity development tools and exercises**

Chapter	Activity	Student	Manager	Entrepreneur
	Idea Space	√	√	√
Chapter 4 Opportunity exploration	Seeing needs as creative opportunities	√		
	Problem, opportunity & resource mapping	√	√	√
	Demand innovation feasibility & attractiveness	√	√	√
	Innovation function analysis	√	√	√
	Resource mapping	√	√	√
	Time perspectives	√	√	√
	Market focus funnel & market analysis questions	√	√	√
	Intellectual property	√	√	√

TABLE 1.2 continued

Chapter	Activity	Student	Manager	Entrepreneur
Chapter 5 Opportunity building	Opportunity evaluation report	√	√	√
	Seven types of opportunity analysis	√	√	√
	Environmental analysis for opportunity	√	√	√
	Opportunity assessment – five dimensions	√	√	√
	Business opportunity model	√		
	Cluster & network mapping	√	√	√
	Corporate entrepreneurship		√	√
Chapter 6 Planning to realise opportunities	Future thinking	√		
	Creating a storyboard for the opportunity	√	√	√
	Opportunity planning	√	√	√
	Creating an identity for the opportunity	√	√	√
	Evaluating a business model	√	√	√
	Creating a business model	√		
	Preparing a venture plan	√	√	√
	Contact identification	√	√	√
	Presenting the plan	√	√	√
Chapter 7 Acting on opportunities	Business success & failure	√	√	√
	Phoenix case study questions	√	√	√
	Newsline case: sensemaking questions	√		
	Learning to make it happen	√		
	What works? Practical theory framework	√	√	√
	Entrepreneurial management capabilities (toolkit)	√	√	√
	Resource, relational & opportunity strategy	√	√	√
Chapter 8 Opportunity Centred Entrepreneurship in action	Aquifer case: opportunity options	√		√
	Assessing opportunity, capabilities & venture plan	√	√	√
	Loudmouth case: creative enterprise	√		
	Cultural diffusion	√		
	Low cost airline case: entrepreneurial management	√	√	√
	Reasons for success & failure	√	√	√
	Questions on the case	√	√	

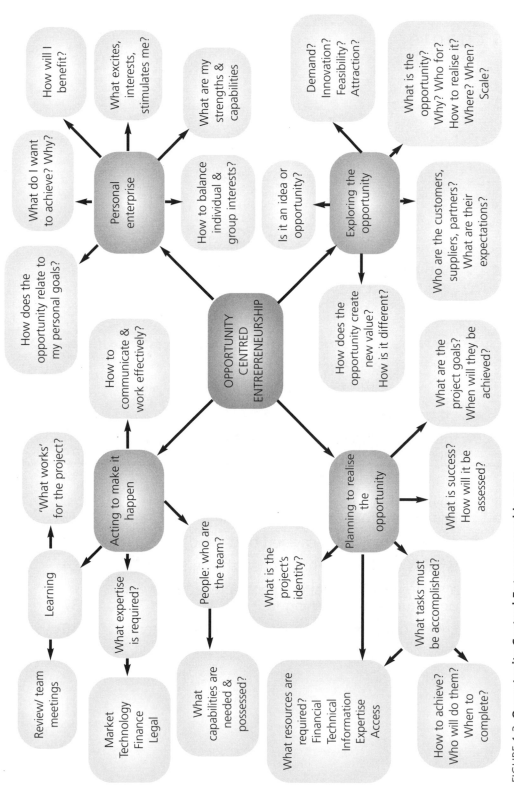

FIGURE 1.3 **Opportunity Centred Entrepreneurship map**

chapter 2

the context of opportunity-centred leadership

chapter contents

Introduction

The purpose of this chapter is to locate the concepts of entrepreneurship and opportunity in the context of the academic literature. It is intended for the student who needs an overview of the subject from an academic perspective. If your interest is entirely with the practical aspects, you may skim or even skip this chapter and move on to Chapter 3. The learning goals of this chapter are to enable you to:

- develop a critical awareness of the theoretical background of entrepreneurship
- consider the influence of different perspectives on entrepreneurship
- explain the role of entrepreneurship in societies and their economic development.

The chapter summarises the evolving nature of entrepreneurship theory, from a field dominated by economics to an intersubjective topic which draws on different areas of knowledge. Four critical questions are posed, as a means of exploring the relationships between the theory and practice of entrepreneurship, learning, opportunity and enterprise in society. These questions are:

- Who or what is an entrepreneur?
- How do people become entrepreneurs? What is the influence of personality and learning?
- Are opportunities discovered or created?
- What is the role of entrepreneurship in society?

The chapter provides a rationale for Opportunity-Centred Entrepreneurship as a learning-based approach which advances existing theories of entrepreneurship.

the changing perspectives in entrepreneurship theory

From its inception as a topic of study, entrepreneurship has been dominated by economic theories. There are moves towards a wider view of the subject, since approaches based on economics alone have limitations which are being recognised, and new interpretations are emerging to offer alternative perspectives. Economic thinking applies observable evidence, and assumes cause and effect relationships, such as supply and demand. As entrepreneurship is a phenomenon which occurs at the interface between different subject areas, as shown in Figure 1.2, relying on economics alone to understand it is not sufficient, and the contributions of human dynamics and social sciences are increasingly relevant.

Economists have a similar relationship to entrepreneurs to the one meteorologists have to farmers; it is very useful for the farmer to know what the weather trends, short and long term, are likely to be, but it is the farmer who takes the risk of deciding which crops to grow and reaps the reward if successful. Economists provide useful guidance of economic trends and theories, but it is entrepreneurs who must do the work of finding and exploiting opportunities.

Entrepreneurship analysis is primarily the study of people who act creatively in market situations to do new things. There is a tension in entrepreneurship theory between positivist thinking, which aims to define 'objective' generalisations and truths about entrepreneurship, and interpretive approaches, which seek to understand the human dynamics of entrepreneurship in their social context. It is important to be aware of the dangers of relying on a single approach to the subject, since new perspectives on entrepreneurship have emerged in recent years, characterised by the 'new movements in entrepreneurship' writing (Steyaert and Hjorth, 2003) which aim to move the study of entrepreneurship forward from being dominated by North American and economics-based theory.

The problem with seeing the entrepreneurial world only in a cause and effect way is that it limits the understanding which is conveyed to the learner and the future entrepreneur to a single perspective. This thinking is often unchallenged and accepted as 'correct' and 'scientific', since it enables 'things' to be 'proved'. This has great attractions for governments. If it can be 'shown', for example, that reducing taxation increases business start-ups and reduces unemployment, as argued in the 1980s in the United States and UK, this becomes an attractive policy option. There are dangers in such thinking; how do we know that a cause and effect relationship between fiscal policy and human behaviour actually exists? Could other trends be at work in society, and are specific factors being isolated from a broader range of phenomena? The situation is probably more complex and dynamic than a simple causal analysis can demonstrate.

This implies we should not take the entrepreneurial world as 'given', but rather accept that there are multiple interpretations of every situation, offering multiple possibilities. Spinosa et al (1997) argued that entrepreneurs are 'history maker[s]' who change the world around them through their actions. Entrepreneurs who create innovative new business models such as Google are examples of this. There are therefore many different aspects to the study of entrepreneurship and there has been extensive debate within the academic community over the theoretical base of the subject.

The 'people side of entrepreneurship' has been less effectively explored through entrepreneurship research until quite recently, with a gulf between the dynamic reality, experience and history of entrepreneurial life and the production and application of academic theory. The lived reality, the experiences and meanings which constitute entrepreneurial life, the shared understanding of events and their significance, have been captured and explored very imperfectly by research. We need to understand better the dynamic conditions of change and uncertainty in which entrepreneurs operate as 'change-makers', by exploring specific cases in their context, and developing insight and theory without losing the value and meaning of the human experience which is the essence of entrepreneurship. This will be explored through asking four questions on which there is a continuing debate rather than a consensus in the entrepreneurship literature.

who or what is an entrepreneur?

Is entrepreneurship a form of behaviour which is practised by people we can readily identify and label with a fixed identity as entrepreneurs, or is it instead a way of working which is flexible and contingent, depending on personal, social, economic and organisational factors?

Traditional sources support the view that 'the entrepreneur' is a fixed identity. For example, definitions include 'a person who creates organisations' (Gartner, 1989), 'the enterprising person' (Gibb, 1987), and 'the person who recognises and acts to exploit an opportunity' (Shane and Venkataraman, 2000; Stevenson and Jarillo, 1990).

This 'traditional' concept of the entrepreneur and their social identity has been formed largely through economic history (Hébert and Link, 1988; Chell et al, 1991). The entrepreneur was an agent of economic change and activity. From the time of Cantillon (1755) and Say, the entrepreneur was regarded as a person who would make buying and selling decisions in changing market conditions in the search for profit opportunities, buying in one place at a known present price and selling elsewhere at an unknown future value. Hébert and Link (1988) identified a taxonomy of entrepreneurial theories consisting of 12 distinct themes within the literature of economic history, as shown in Table 2.1. Significantly, they distinguished between static and dynamic; in static, traditional definitions, neither creativity, change nor uncertainty were involved and the entrepreneur is simply described as playing a fixed role in economic exchanges. Processual or dynamic theories, where uncertainty is assumed to exist, give the entrepreneur the chance to create or exploit innovations and profit opportunities.

Hébert and Link identified three mainstream theories of dynamic entrepreneurship that stemmed from Cantillon, characterised as the Chicago, German and Austrian traditions. The dominant ideas which emerged from these in the mid-twentieth century were founded on the writing of Schumpeter (the 'German School') and Kirzner (representing the 'Austrian school' although later resident in Chicago). Binks and Vale (1990) summarised three historical categories of entrepreneurial theory: the reactive entrepreneur as an agent of adjustment in the market economy (Kirzner); the innovative entrepreneur causing economic change (Schumpeter); and the entrepreneur causing incremental, gradual change through management of the enterprise (Leibenstein).

Schumpeter was one of the main originators of modern entrepreneurship theory, describing the entrepreneur as an innovator who engaged in a process of creative destruction by disrupting the circular flow of the market economics of production and consumption which tended towards price equilibrium, through initiating new products and processes which replaced existing offerings and firms which became marginal or uncompetitive. He characterised the entrepreneur as innovator rather than profit seeker, as an initiator and agent of change who would then become the manager of a business. However Schumpeter (1934) also described the entrepreneur as a leader characterised by qualities of intellect, will, initiative, foresight, and especially intuition: 'the capacity of seeing things in a way which afterwards proves to be true … learning in his natural and social world so that actions can be simply and reliably calculated'.

These notions of intuition and 'learning in the natural and social world' are important, connecting entrepreneurship with social learning. Kirzner (1973), conversely, characterised the entrepreneur as an 'alert opportunist', constantly watchful for short-run profit

TABLE 2.1 **Static and processual definitions of entrepreneur**

Static definitions of entrepreneur	Processual definitions of entrepreneur
The person who supplies financial capital A manager or superintendent The owner of an enterprise An employer of factors of production	Risk-taking Innovating Decision-making Leading an industry Organising economic resources Contracting Arbitrage (market-maker) Allocating resources

Source: Hébert and Link, 1988.

opportunities arising from market disequilibrium, in which speed of movement and shrewd decision-making ability were essential: 'entrepreneurs immediately notice profit opportunities that exist because of the initial ignorance of the original market participants and that have persisted because of their inability to learn from experience.'

Kirzner viewed the entrepreneur as being motivated by profit in a market environment, and needing to search unceasingly for new opportunities as buyers and sellers achieved market equilibrium and minimised price differentials. Entrepreneurial activity, in his view, involved creative acts of discovery learning, and he suggested that the entrepreneur outperforms others operating in the market because of a superior ability to perceive and act on opportunities, the difference centring on the ability to learn from experience faster and more effectively than competitors. Kirzner offered a tactical, short-term and street-wise understanding of entrepreneurial behaviour in which the entrepreneur discovers and exploits short-run price differentials as supply and demand move towards equilibrium. In contrast Schumpeter proposed a more strategic and innovative conceptualisation of 'what could be', in which the entrepreneur sees possibilities for new solutions unrecognised by others and innovates through making 'new combinations' which make existing products obsolete and change the economic context of the market.

Capitalist economic growth theory has been highly influential and often dominant in defining the principal theories of entrepreneurship and the related field of business growth (Low and Macmillan, 1988; Davidsson et al, 2002). The concepts of resource-based theory (Penrose, 1959; Garnsey, 1998), of opportunity recognition (Kirzner, 1973; Stevenson and Jarillo, 1990), the creation of new economic activity (Low and Macmillan, 1988), of necessity and opportunity entrepreneurship (Reynolds et al, 2002), and of predictive models of business growth (Greiner, 1972; Churchill and Lewis, 1983) all draw on such economic theory.

As discussed earlier in this chapter, there are limitations in basing entrepreneurship theory mainly upon economics, since economists provide theories which explain economic phenomena rather than entrepreneurial behaviour. So to understand the entrepreneurial experience, an approach based purely on economic theory has limitations, and different approaches are needed.

Rather than seeing the entrepreneur as having a fixed role of economic agency, it is more helpful to focus on the processes and behaviours of entrepreneurship as a way of working which is contingent and flexible, which people can learn to move into as well as out of, and which does not imply the possession of implicit 'qualities', 'traits' or a fixed identity. Instead, any person has the potential to learn and act in ways that are 'enterprising' and can engage in identifying, creating or taking advantage of opportunities, to a greater or lesser extent. Entrepreneurial behaviour is therefore a matter of degree rather than of 'being' or 'not being'. This is not only true in a business context but also encompasses social and other forms of entrepreneurship in the 'not-for-profit' sector (Leadbeater, 1997; Dees, 2001).

The introduction and application of innovation is a vital aspect of entrepreneurship (Drucker, 1985). Combining innovation with recognising and acting on opportunities is an important aspect of entrepreneurial behaviour, which involves 'going beyond' the boundaries of what is known and accepted, rather than simply replicating something which already exists, although the scale of innovation may be small. Also, there are gradu-ations of entrepreneurial behaviour, from the cautious and incremental level of 'building on what works' to the risk-taking and adventurous 'leaps into the unknown'. This is not confined to starting a business venture; it includes developing and building a business which, as we will see, opens up the related subject of entrepreneurial management.

So a dynamic conceptualisation of the entrepreneur's role views it as being the agent who creates, recognises and acts on opportunities. This includes using innovation to do new things, operating flexibly and adapting to the wider context, working in conditions of risk and uncertainty, achieving change and gaining reward through profit. If entrepreneurship is viewed as a process, it consists of the person, the search for market opportunities, innovative behaviour and bringing together the resources needed to exploit those opportunities.

activity

1. How significant do you think is the role of economics in understanding entrepreneurship?
2. What do you consider are the most important elements of the entrepreneurial process?

how do people become entrepreneurs? the influence of personality and learning

The question of whether entrepreneurs are born or made is an old but not particularly valid or helpful one because it suggests that there is fixed supply of entrepreneurial people. However there has been significant research on personality, and entrepreneurial learning has recently become a focus of research. This section explores the connections between entrepreneurship, personality and learning which enable us to understand how people can learn to become entrepreneurs.

The nature of entrepreneurial working is being explored increasingly as a human, social, behavioural and cultural phenomenon in order to understand the thinking, behaviour and interactional dimensions from which entrepreneurial activity in the social world origin-nates. There is increasing recognition in the entrepreneurship literature of the limitations of our understanding in this area. The quest for definitive 'theories' and 'models' to define entrepreneurial personality, based on identifying fixed characteristics and traits, paid little attention to exploring the human processes of how people actually learn and work in entrepreneurial ways.

Edith Penrose (1959) considered enterprise to be a psychological predisposition on the part of individuals to take a chance in the hope of gain, through risk-taking behaviour. This view – that enterprising behaviour and the related identity of 'the entrepreneur' are psychologically implicit – reflected considerable interest from the 1960s onwards in defining the innate or learned characteristics of entrepreneurs. This was based on the psychological notion that personality traits and factors could be identified and categorised, and that so doing would enable human behaviour to be explained and even predicted (Brockhaus, 1982; Timmons et al, 1985).

McClelland (1961) was influential in highlighting the 'need for achievement' or 'nAch', which he claimed as the key motivator for entrepreneurial performance which divided people into 'achievers' and 'non-achievers'. This assimilated the cultural values of post-1945 US society, which strongly encouraged achievement, so that people behaved in the 'achievement oriented' ways they felt were expected. Similarly, the 'locus of control' identified by Rotter (1966) – which claimed to identify whether people considered they were in control of the world around their lives, or whether their destinies were determined largely by external factors – has been associated with the need for achievement as a key attribute of entrepreneurs. Other writers also highlighted variable factors or traits of personality as 'the essence' or cause of entrepreneurial behaviour, including Carland et al (1995) on the need to create or grow a business venture, Bird (1988) on 'intentionality' as the defining factor in goal-directed behaviour, and Boyd and Vozikis (1994) on 'self-efficacy'. All of these probably have some element of validity but none provide a complete answer to the question of entrepreneurial formation.

There are many lists of entrepreneurial traits and constructs: for example, Timmons (1999) lists six 'desirable and acquirable attitudes and behaviours' exhibited by entrepreneurs as, 'commitment and determination; leadership; opportunity obsession; tolerance of risk, ambiguity and uncertainty; creativity, self-reliance and ability to adapt; motivation to excel'.

In a UK context, Gibb (1987) set out a list of entrepreneurial attributes which are typical of those evident in the literature:

TABLE 2.2 **Entrepreneurial attributes**

Initiative	Problem-solving ability
Strong persuasive powers	Need for achievement
Moderate rather than high risk-taking ability	Imagination
Flexibility	High belief in control of one's destiny
Creativity	Leadership
Independence/autonomy	Hard work

Source: Gibb, 1987.

Such personality and trait-based approaches to defining entrepreneurial behaviour and performance have been widely criticised for their lack of consistency and inability to connect assessment of traits with actual performance (Chell et al, 1991; Gray, 1998; Bridge et al, 2003). Gartner (1989) attacked both the lack of definitional clarity and the validity of trait-based research studies of 'the entrepreneur', and this helped draw to a close the inconclusive quest for definitive personality traits of entrepreneurs. He recommended that researchers should study what people do: the behaviours, skills and knowledge used in the entrepreneurial process of creating organisations. The focus in this book and other studies on learning as a means of acquiring these behaviours, skills and knowledge is one result of this.

However, although their validity has been criticised, there is an underlying consistency in a number of the studies of entrepreneurial personality. Gray (1998) suggests that the 'clue' to entrepreneurial behaviour lies in cultural, family and social class background. The connection between the notions of need for achievement, self-efficacy, intentionality, self-actualisation, and drive to achieve and grow emerges from this literature and suggests that they cannot be dismissed altogether, whether these 'motivations' are implicit in personality or whether they are learned.

Also, it is questionable how far the people called 'entrepreneurs' are necessarily different from others who were not 'entrepreneurs'. Many of the traits, competences and behaviours which were observed in 'entrepreneurs' might also be present in career managers of organisations, for example, or people who are successful and achievement oriented in other ways. If, rather than trying to isolate 'what makes entrepreneurs different', we say that enterprising behaviour is not exceptional but is an integral aspect of how people normally behave in society to survive and 'make ends meet', then we can reject the notion that a few individuals are innately 'naturally talented entrepreneurs' and act in ways that cannot be learned by others. Rather, we can suggest that enterprising activity can be learned, but that differences in ability are likely to lead to differing outcomes in achievement. If this is so, then the roles of both formal education and informal learning processes must be considered.

Education can play an important role in the creation of the 'enterprise culture' by encouraging enterprising skills and behaviours. It is increasingly assumed that education can stimulate entrepreneurial action within a supportive enterprising culture. There has been considerable study of enterprise education, which offers insights into how people learn about entrepreneurship and develop enterprising behaviours. However classroom education alone may be insufficient to enable entrepreneurial learning that can be applied in the external world. Reviews of enterprise education have found content-fixated approaches to teaching widely used, in which more activist approaches to learning are often needed, but concluded that 'entrepreneurship can be taught' (e.g. Garavan and O'Cinneide, 1994; Gorman et al, 1997; Centre for Education and Industry, 2001).

There is a consensus that enterprising learning should draw from the dynamic environment of the small firm and aim to incorporate 'enterprise essences into the classroom environment', using dynamic, action-based enterprise learning rather than traditional content-oriented academic methods (Gibb, 1996). This approach to learning should be active, holistic in developing the person, and applied in the real-world context. Gibb proposed seven challenges for entrepreneurial learning: creating the 'way of life' of the entrepreneur; sharing the culture and values; supporting the development of enterprising behaviours, attributes and skills; designing the entrepreneurial organisation; developing learning-to-learn capacity; sensitivity to different contexts; and adding value to existing ways of learning (Gibb, 2001).

Jack and Anderson (1999) suggest that entrepreneurial learning can be enriched through, for example, role models, personal networks and apprenticeship placements within small firms. The 'art' of entrepreneurship, in their view, is not amenable to teaching but is experiential and inductive, best learned through working with entrepreneurs in the social context of a business combined with practitioner-led learning. Whilst education can provide cultural and personal support, knowledge and skills, entrepreneurial practice is learned experientially in the business environment. The importance of tacit knowledge, of the unplanned and of acting knowingly rather than always knowing before acting, confirms Schumpeter's 1934 thesis that entrepreneurial learning is acquiring intuition through practical experience: 'The success of everything depends upon intuition.'

Writing from an experiential career development perspective, Gibb Dyer (1994) proposed a theory of entrepreneurial careers which suggested that the influence of changing family, partner and business relationships could have profound effects on entrepreneurial career choices. Entrepreneurial career development is explored further in Chapter 9. Mitton identified a group of eight entrepreneurial behaviours, including the fact that:

> They actively bank experience: they learn with a need to know. ... [T]hey come to know their core competencies and core values. As well as learning special personal abilities, they learn a special knowledge of technologies, processes, products, markets, systems and industries. This exploring approach becomes a life-long habit.'
> (Mitton, 1997)

This suggests that work experience in an entrepreneurial firm can provide rich learning opportunities and the chance to develop enterprising skills in a dynamic environment through deep immersion in a business.

Recent studies of entrepreneurial cognition have developed understanding of how entrepreneurial knowledge is gathered and applied, using a cognitivist paradigm of individual rather than social conceptualisation (Minniti and Bygrave, 2001). The cognitive paradigm concentrates on the individual acquisition and comprehension of knowledge. This has dominated the study of learning, but has limitations in understanding human behaviour and the ability to learn through social interaction (Bandura, 1986). The understanding of entrepreneurial learning has been limited by the divide between cognitivist methods which propose rational models of learning based on cognitive theory, and interpretive methods which offer dynamic approaches based on inductive inquiry into the entrepreneurial experience (Harrison and Leitch, 2005). Approaches based on cognitive science have emphasised the role of entrepreneurial knowledge and rational decision making rather than social or team-based learning and behaviour (Mitchell et al, 2002). Interpretive approaches have sought to understand the situated nature of the entrepreneurial experience in a 'lifeworld' perspective by using a range of qualitative research methods within social and behavioural learning (Deakins and Freel, 1998).

There is a need to progress beyond this divide between to create a fresh and useful understanding of what is learned as well as how this is learned through entrepreneurship as a human process. Experiential and social theories of learning have been developed which combine action, conceptualisation and social practice, whilst the study of language and discourse has also contributed to understanding learning through people's stories of their experiences. Wenger (1998) developed a comprehensive social and behavioural theory of learning as a transformational process of identity creation, including dimensions of meaning, practice, identity and community. This provides a conceptual foundation for understanding learning which accommodates social participation and human action as well as cognition, enabling advanced learning theory to be applied to entrepreneurship, as will be demonstrated in Chapter 3.

It can be concluded from the extensive writing on entrepreneurship education that, whilst such education can provide cultural and personal support, knowledge and skill development about and for entrepreneurship, the 'art' of entrepreneurial practice is learned mainly in the business environment through inductive, practical and social experience, rather than in the educational environment (Gibb, 1993; Gorman et al, 1997). This leads to the exploration of learning as a situated and active experience – rather than as a purely educational and theoretical process – in which the emergent social identity of 'becoming' an entrepreneur features as well as the social and contextual experiences which shape identity and learning (Jack and Anderson, 1999). Table 2.3 illustrates the development of theories concerning entrepreneurial learning.

Significant progress has been made recently in developing new theoretical perspectives on entrepreneurial learning, which can be summarised in the following six observations (Harrison and Leitch, 2005).

- Entrepreneurial learning is a dynamic process of awareness, reflection, association and application.
- This involves transforming experience and knowledge into functional learning outcomes.
- It comprises knowledge, behaviour and affective or emotional learning (Cope, 2005).

TABLE 2.3 **Conceptualisations of entrepreneurial learning**

Author(s) and year	Contribution
Schumpeter (1934)	Imagination and innovation resulting from natural and social learning
Kirzner (1973)	Creative discovery learning that generates alertness to opportunities
Reuber and Fischer (1993	Value of recent concrete experience related to context of use
Young and Sexton (1997)	Acquisition, storage and use of entrepreneurial knowledge as expert resource
Deakins and Freel (1998)	Five key learning abilities within the small firm
Minniti and Bygrave (2001)	Algorithmic model of entrepreneurial decision making based on experience
Rae and Carswell (2001)	Confidence and self-belief that connect learning resources with achievement
Gibb (2001); Hartshorn (2002)	'Lifeworld' of the small firm as a dynamic entrepreneurial learning environment
Mitchell et al; Shepherd and Krueger (2002)	Rational models of knowledge structures, cognition and decision making applied to stages of the entrepreneurial process
Cope (2005)	Dynamic learning process with phases, processes and characteristics
Politis (2005)	Dynamic framework of career, transformation and knowledge, distinguishing learning process and knowledge outcomes
Dutta and Crossan (2005); Lumpkin and Lichtenstein (2005); Corbett (2005)	Connections between organisational learning, opportunity recognition, creativity and entrepreneurial learning processes

- It is affected by the context in which learning occurs, and includes the content of what is learned as well as the processes through which learning takes place (Politis, 2005).
- It is individual, with personal differences in ability producing different learning outcomes, as well as social and organisational (Corbett, 2005).
- There are close connections between the processes of entrepreneurial learning with those of opportunity recognition, exploitation, creativity and innovation (Lumpkin and Lichtenstein, 2005). These conceptualisations provide a basis for the development of a framework through which entrepreneurial learning can be understood in Chapter 3.

We can conclude that entrepreneurial behaviour is acquired through social learning, but formal education is only part of this process. Although research on entrepreneurial personality has not defined a single or dominant personality type, that should not lead to our rejecting the notion of personality altogether. However it is clear that the focus on 'getting inside the mind of the entrepreneur' which has progressed from personality to cognition has yielded only limited understanding of entrepreneurial development that we can use. Therefore it is more helpful to regard entrepreneurial development as social learning, which is practised actively and behaviourally with others in cultural and organisational settings.

activity

1. Do you think entrepreneurship can be learned? If so, what might be the best ways of learning to be entrepreneurial?
2. What roles can formal education and informal, practical experience play in developing entrepreneurial skills?
3. What attributes or behaviours do you think people working in entrepreneurial ways are likely to display?

are opportunities discovered or created?

The discovery, exploration and exploitation of opportunities are fundamentally important processes in entrepreneurial activity (Stevenson and Jarillo, 1990). The question is whether people discover and recognise opportunities which are held to already exist, as Kirzner suggested, or create and enact new opportunities (Gartner et al, 2003)? Shane (2003) has proposed a general theory of entrepreneurship to fill this gap in understanding, based on the nexus, or connection, between individuals who discover opportunities and the entrepreneurial process of opportunity exploitation and execution.

There is both purely 'opportunistic' behaviour, which centres on the short-term exploitation of currently available opportunities, and the creation of future new opportunities which do not yet exist, through innovation, generally over a longer timescale. Studies of opportunity recognition in successful US entrepreneurs have suggested that they identified many opportunities and were highly alert and sensitive to opportunity (Hills,1995; Hills and Shrader,1998). The opportunities they selected were mainly problem and solution oriented, the identification of opportunity was a multi-step process rather than a single event, and opportunities were often interrelated and sequential. This suggests that opportunity recognition was often based on prior experience within an industry, with long-term exposure to markets and customers. The discovery of opportunities can be seen as a creative process, and Wallas' (1926) model of creative thinking was adapted by Lumpkin et al (2004) to propose the model of opportunity recognition based on creativity which is shown in Figure 2.1. This moves from the discovery to the formation of opportunities through five stages of preparation (unconscious awareness), incubation of ideas, insight (the moment of discovery), evaluation and elaboration.

A range of other theories and conceptual models of opportunity recognition have also been proposed, some based on sequential, step-by-step activity. Vesper (1980) suggested a systematic search effort, Long and McMullan (1984) proposed a four-stage process of opportunity

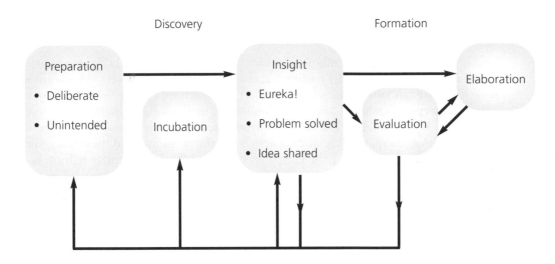

FIGURE 2.1 **Creativity-based model of entrepreneurial opportunity recognition**

Source: Lumpkin, Hills & Schrader (2004).

identification, and Kaplan (2003) suggested a five-step model of opportunity analysis. Bhidé (1999) proposed that the decision to create a new venture depends on assessment of its viability and attractiveness, with viability being based on low capital requirements, high margin for error, significant pay-offs, low exit costs, and multiple exit options, with success depending on creativity and capacity to execute, and attractiveness based on the fit between the entrepreneur's motivation and capability. Recent work has confirmed the conceptual links between opportunity recognition, individual learning modes within the context of an industry, and creativity (Lumpkin and Lichtenstein; Corbett, 2005).

The debate over opportunity recognition was summarised by Gartner et al (2003), who compared the economic perspective, in which opportunities are held to exist objectively and be discovered, with Weick's (1979) enaction theory in which individuals make sense of their world through scanning, interpretation and action. They termed this the enactment perspective: 'opportunities would be the result of what individuals do, rather than … of what they see.' This reinforces the importance of individual prior knowledge and experience, and the contribution this makes to the ability to recognise opportunities.

We can conclude that, as Kirzner argues, short-term opportunities do exist and await discovery by the alert entrepreneur. However the circumstances that can give rise to new opportunities may be recognised by people with the imagination, experience and judgement to do so, and that they can create and enact the opportunities which they assess as worthwhile. The vital skill lies in recognising the future opportunities with the greatest long-term potential which the entrepreneur can gather the resources to exploit.

activity

1. Do you think that entrepreneurs generally recognise opportunities which already exist?
2. Do you think that entrepreneurs generally create new opportunities which did not already exist?
3. What do you think are the main steps in opportunity recognition?

what is the role of entrepreneurship in society?

Enterprise and entrepreneurship have become significant issues in government policy in many countries, at regional, national and even international levels. Many governments seek to create 'an entrepreneurial society' or 'enterprising culture' because they value the role of entrepreneurship in creating economic growth and employment, as described in Chapter 1. Entrepreneurs find new opportunities, they innovate and connect resources in new ways, they increase value-adding activity in the economy, and their enterprises create growth and employment. In the global economy, a vibrant enterprise culture is essential for economic health because other forms of economic management have led to stagnation. However the relationship between government and entrepreneur is not a simple one, since they do not necessarily have the same ends in mind. We therefore need to explore how government policies on entrepreneurship affect the individual as a potential or actual entrepreneur, and what influence they might have on government policy.

The role of enterprise culture has become pervasive in British political and policy discourse, as explored by Carr (2000) and Carr and Beaver (2002). Carr noted that a 'discourse of entrepreneurial management' has been created to achieve economic, cultural and social change, at national as well as organisational and individual levels. Whilst governments aim to use enterprise as a liberalising force to achieve economic, policy and political outcomes, these are not generally perceived as relevant by entrepreneurs: 'What emerges strongly from conventional understandings of the enterprise culture is the notion that government and individuals in the context of small business and enterprise development are pitted against one another.' (Carr and Beaver, 2002).

The Entrepreneurial Society (Gavron et al, 1998) set out an enterprise policy blueprint for the new Labour government in the UK, which led to significant policy initiatives in support for new and small business, enterprise education, business incubation, and tax incentives for enterprise. These aimed to replicate the economic model of the MIT-Boston nexus in the UK, and officials of the Department of Trade and Industry conceded that UK policy on enterprise was to follow the US model. Supranational organisations such as the European Union (EU) and Organisation for Economic Co-operation and Development have incorporated rhetoric and policies very similar to those of the UK government into their work. The EU through its 2000 Lisbon Agenda aimed to establish itself as a centre of knowledge-based innovation and enterprise, but to a great extent failed, partly because the 'base culture' of most of the large and long-standing EU states remained broadly unsupportive of this North American cultural model of entrepreneurship.

At an international level, enterprise is widely seen as a means of reducing poverty and creating employment, and as a route towards economic empowerment at an individual, family and community level. In South Africa, President Thabo Mbeki spoke of enterprise as ' the spirit of creativity among ordinary people' and his government explicitly promoted Black Economic Empowerment, and entrepreneurship for women, young people and in rural areas to create economic and social development. The New Partnership for African Development (NEPAD) aimed to create the right environment for African entrepreneurs, including micro, small, medium and informal enterprises. This represented a major shift away from the high degree of state control experienced by a number of African countries, which have failed to deliver economic growth (ICSB, 2004). As Carr and Beaver argue, governments are seeking to create and use enterprise discourse and culture to engineer changes in society.

Enterprise education and the learning process are seen as fundamental to developing the entrepreneurial culture. International studies such as the Global Entrepreneurship Monitor (GEM) have highlighted the links between education and entrepreneurial performance as one of six factors in the development of an entrepreneurial economy. Yet the role and significance of education in constructing and popularising entrepreneurial culture have been little explored. There is a tendency in political discourse to assume that enterprise must be 'a good thing', exemplified by Gordon Brown in the UK declaring that every teacher should be 'fluent in the language of enterprise' and every pupil between 14 and 16 being expected to benefit from mandatory enterprise learning.

Do these policies and the accompanying rhetoric matter? Clearly, everyone is affected by them, and tax revenues are used to finance the policy initiatives. Political leaders must achieve results if they are to survive, and increasingly there is the question of what happens if 'the enterprise culture' fails to deliver expected results, as has happened in the case of the EU Lisbon Agenda. Scotland, through the Scottish Enterprise agency, had a long-standing business birth-rate strategy which absorbed considerable investment and expectations, but which ultimately failed to achieve acceptable outcomes and was ended. During the 'enterprise years' of the Thatcher government in the UK in the 1980s, there was significant encouragement for unemployed people to become self-employed through the 'enterprise allowance' but, other than temporary reductions in unemployment statistics, little long-term increase in the stock of small businesses (Storey, 1994).

Political leaders and their advisers tend to assume that by taking top-down policy initiatives, frequently copied from measures which have appeared to work in a different situation such as the United States, they can achieve comparable results in their own country. This assumes that individuals will choose to play the economic role determined by the state, for example in starting new businesses. If short-term financial incentives are offered these may well be taken up, but longer-term cultural and economic change is much more difficult to achieve. Government initiatives to increase entrepreneurial activity often do not seem to be informed or welcomed by entrepreneurs themselves, and there is an absence of dialogue in the top-down relationship between government and entrepreneurs, for example in the ways in which small business support programmes are constantly changed by governments.

Government and public sector policy advisors, especially those responsible for policy implementation, often appear to inhabit different worlds and use different language from those starting and running small businesses. This can be frustrating for enterprising individuals who hear encouraging messages from government leaders and agencies, but who encounter practical difficulties in gaining access to the resources, support and opportunities they need to start and run their businesses. So the relationship between government policy and rhetoric, which espouses the values of an enterprising society and culture, and the practice of entrepreneurship by individuals is not well understood.

Four factors need to be considered in relation to the role of enterprise in society. First, the policy objectives need to be clearly understood within the national context. Is the aim to alleviate poverty, to create employment, to reduce or replace state activity, to replace declining industries, or to increase innovation and value-added activity? All of these may be desirable but they require different strategies, policies and delivery mechanisms in different contexts. Entrepreneurship is understood and works differently in various cultures, so it is necessary to beware of over-simplifying the issues or ignoring the underlying reality in a national economy. There are many societies where enterprise, small business and trading activity has always been a way of life and does not require stimulation although the level and ambition of enterprises can be enhanced, India being an example.

Second, the nature of enterprise and entrepreneurship needs to be considered. The dominant ideology in the field is the US model of 'free-market' economic growth, but it is not the only one and it cannot be assumed to be appropriate to every situation. Given the level of state protection and subsidy provided to many US businesses, including corporates, it is questionable whether the term 'free-market' is appropriate in the cases of American subsidised agriculture, aerospace and defence industries. Other models of enterprise in different cultures, including the village economy, the family business, the social and community enterprise, rely on social interaction and meet market needs whilst also providing income and employment. There are serious economic questions over the policy of developed countries subsidising farmers to grow crops such as sugar and cotton which can be grown at lower cost by farmers in developing countries.

A third question is how inclusive or exclusive this approach to enterprise is. In the UK, government policy is that 'enterprise is truly open to all'. This democratic intent is laudable in principle but requires sustained change to achieve in practice. In most countries, the role of the illegal, informal or 'grey' economy is substantial and long-standing, often practised by people who consider themselves excluded from participating in the mainstream economy. In many Central and East European post-socialist economies, entrepreneurship was illegal before the fall of the Berlin wall, and in Russia there were serious concerns that entrepreneurship meant a transfer of assets from state to private ownership by an exclusive elite. Social structures such as apartheid in South Africa constrained Black entrepreneurship, and even today, governments act to stifle entrepreneurship by groups within their populations. The government of Israel promotes Israeli businesses, but has forced many Palestinian entrepreneurs out of business. So a challenge to governments and societies is whether enterprise is seen as a means of economic empowerment for the majority, or self-enrichment for a few.

The fourth question is to ask: what is the role of government in creating and implementing policies for enterprise in an entrepreneurial society? Policy rhetoric requires the will, resources and organisation to implement it, and interaction with other agencies and actors in society, such as education and business networks. Government and international organisations often have substantial resources, yet also have limited understanding and capability to stimulate and support entrepreneurship. Most officials and government ministers responsible for enterprise do not have first-hand experience of entrepreneurship or small business. The culture of government is to control, regulate, and standardise, which is inimical to the entrepreneurial culture of experimentation and informality. It can be argued that government organisations can possibly contribute most effectively to an entrepreneurial culture by not

activity

1. Why do governmental organisations favour the creation of an enterprising culture and society?
2. Do you know what the government policy objectives for enterprise are in your country, e.g. in relation to increasing the birth rate of new businesses?
3. Using the four questions set out in this section, how effectively do you think these are being implemented?

intervening. The European Commission is a case in point, whose bureaucratic (in the proper Weberian sense) nature is probably not capable of delivering the intentions of its policies on enterprise.

a summary of the issues in entrepreneurship, opportunity and learning

This chapter has summarised the arguments in four areas of entrepreneurship, from which it can be concluded that:

- Entrepreneurship is a dynamic and contingent process, rather than a fixed role or state, and operates flexibly in connecting people, their search for market opportunities, their innovative actions, and their efforts to find the resources needed to exploit those opportunities.
- Short-term opportunities may exist and await discovery by the alert entrepreneur. The circumstances giving rise to potential opportunities can be recognised by people with the experience and judgement to do so, and they can create and enact the future opportunities which they judge to be worthwhile.
- Innovation is a vital aspect of opportunity development, distinguishing higher-level from imitative 'me-too' entrepreneurship.
- Entrepreneurial working can be learned, but formal education is only part of this process, and there is little evidence of a single or dominant type of entrepreneurial personality. Therefore entrepreneurial development can be conceptualised as a social learning concept, practised actively and behaviourally with others in cultural and organisational settings.
- The development of entrepreneurial culture and society is perceived by governmental organisations as an important policy objective, but the relationship between this policy rhetoric and initiatives with the experience of entrepreneurship by individuals, is often problematic and not well understood.

This book proposes that Opportunity-Centred Entrepreneurship is a way in which people can respond and work effectively in relation to these issues. Given that entrepreneurship is a process, not a fixed role, that the highest-potential opportunities are created rather than discovered, that entrepreneurial working is learned, and that the policy environment may be well intentioned but still not create the 'right' conditions for enterprising activity, an approach is needed which helps the individual to adapt and to act flexibly and effectively in these circumstances.

There is no single theory or model of entrepreneurship which is universally applicable in all contexts and situations. However we can accept that the arena for entrepreneurship is international and multicultural, and that it covers all forms of economic activity from rural and agricultural enterprise in developing countries to high-technology entrepreneurship. Also, entrepreneurship can be practised in a range of organisations including new ventures, small and family businesses, social enterprises, corporate and public sector. As a result, it is ever-evolving, dynamic and innovative, so that a single theory or model is unlikely to be generally applicable. The purpose of this book is to propose an approach which can be used as a means of understanding, interpreting, making decisions, planning and acting for entrepreneurship in widely differing contexts. The central theme is the human learning process in the 'natural and social world' where opportunities can be found and created, and that is where we will start in Chapter 3.

critical questions to consider from this chapter

This section asks you to reflect on the four questions relating to major issues in entrepreneurship theory and practice which were discussed in this chapter.

● Consider the four questions explored in this chapter which relate to the entrepreneur, to how people become entrepreneurs, to opportunity recognition and to the role of enterprise in society.
● What do think are the most useful learning points which you can draw from each of these questions?
● What do you think are the implications of these points – for example, for academic study, for entrepreneurs in practice, and for government policy on enterprise?

1. Who or what is the entrepreneur?
    Useful learning points:

2. How do people become entrepreneurs?
    Useful learning points:

3. Are opportunities discovered or created?
    Useful learning points:

4. What is the role of entrepreneurship in society?
    Useful learning points:

What are the implications of these learning points?
Implications for academic study:

Implications for entrepreneurs in practice:

Implications for enterprise policy:

chapter 3

personal enterprise: connecting opportunities and personal goals

chapter contents

introduction

The purpose of this chapter is to explore personal enterprise: the human aspects of the entrepreneurial process. It explores how people learn to work in entrepreneurial ways and become entrepreneurs, why they select the opportunities they do, and the connections between learning and selecting opportunities. It asks you to relate these ideas to your own development.

The chapter explains the important concept of entrepreneurial learning and key elements which relate to this. A model of entrepreneurial learning is introduced to help you to reflect on your own personal experience and development. There is a series of exercises to help you map your personal learning to date and identify areas and needs for development. These involve reflection and self-assessment of your personal values, goals, motivations, self-confidence and capabilities.

The learning goals of this chapter are intended to enable you to:

- relate your own learning experiences to a framework for entrepreneurial learning
- identify and reflect on your values, goals and motivations to help develop your confidence to take entrepreneurial actions
- assess your entrepreneurial capabilities and skills
- develop a learning map to summarise and plan your entrepreneurial development.

The outcome of the chapter is to develop a map of your entrepreneurial learning at a personal and social level, and to show how this connects with the types of opportunity which you can select. This chapter covers the first quadrant of Opportunity-Centred Entrepreneurship, which focuses on personal enterprise and includes the questions shown in Figure 3.1. Activities in the chapter encourage you to reflect on the importance of self-confidence, motivation and achievement in entrepreneurial working. The chapter explores personal goals, motivations, and ways of assessing the 'fit' between these and ideas. Personal skills and capabilities are assessed in relation to changes in roles and skills at different stages of the entrepreneurial venture. You will be asked to consider your preferred role in forming and leading entrepreneurial teams. The social skills required in entrepreneurial working to seed opportunities through networking, influencing and selling are explored.

key ideas on entrepreneurial learning

If we accept that people can learn to work in entrepreneurial ways, the question is: how? This chapter is based on research which explored how people learn to work in entrepreneurial ways and identified the significant processes and experiences in their learning (Rae, 2005b). This is used to develop the entrepreneurial learning model included in the chapter.

We know that entrepreneurship consists of the interrelated processes of creating, recognising and acting on opportunities, by combining innovating, decision making and enaction. Learning is an emergent, sensemaking process in which people develop the ability to act differently. Learning comprises knowing, doing, and understanding why (Mumford, 1995). Through learning, people construct meaning through experience in a context of social interaction, and create new reality, or sensemaking as Weick (1995) termed this process. Both entrepreneurship and learning are behavioural and social processes, so they are not just about 'knowing' but also acting, and they are not simply

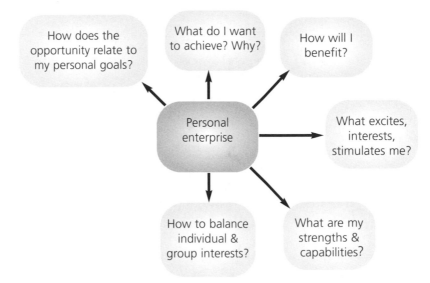

FIGURE 3.1 **Relating opportunity to personal goals**

individual, but constantly involve interaction with other people as an inescapable part of the learning process. The term 'entrepreneurial learning' means learning to recognise and act on opportunities, for example by working socially and by initiating, organising and managing ventures in social and behavioural ways.

If entrepreneurship can be learned, can it be taught? If you are reading this book as part of an entrepreneurship course, then either you or your tutor probably assumes that it can. However the extensive research into entrepreneurship education suggests that while education can provide cultural and personal support, knowledge and skill development about and for entrepreneurship, the 'art' of entrepreneurial practice is learned from experience rather than the educational environment alone. So learning must take place through action in the 'real world', rather than being a purely educational and theoretical process. Gaining practical experiences and 'learning by doing' is a key part of the entrepreneurial learning process.

Increasingly entrepreneurship is viewed as 'plural not singular' – that is to say, entrepreneurial effectiveness depends on several people working effectively together rather than just on the 'lone entrepreneur'. So a business is often the product of an entrepreneurial team, in which people must learn to work effectively together. Therefore it is essential to develop skills of leadership and teamworking for a venture to grow, and for individuals to appreciate the distinctive contribution they can make.

a model of entrepreneurial learning

Figure 3.2 introduces a model of entrepreneurial learning. This is a social learning model, which connects individuals with their social context (Wenger, 1998). It centres on people's *lifeworlds* as they develop their entrepreneurial identity and capability through social learning (Berger and Luckman, 1967). The model includes the three major themes of:

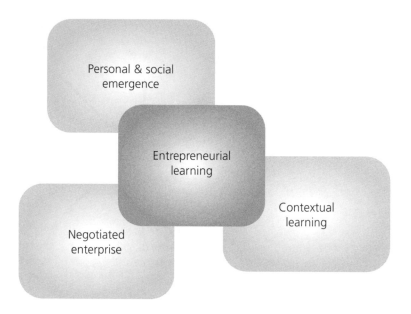

FIGURE 3.2 **Three major themes in entrepreneurial learning**

- *Personal and social emergence*: becoming an entrepreneur.
- *Contextual learning*: how people use their experience to find and work on opportunities.
- *The negotiated enterprise*: how entrepreneurs interact with others to create ventures.

Opposite is a short example which illustrates all three major themes.

Each of the three themes is developed at a detailed level by specific sub-themes. There are 11 sub-themes added, and these are shown in Figure 3.3 (overleaf). A set of reflective questions is integrated into the model to help you to develop your personal awareness of entrepreneurial and business practice.

Personal and social emergence: becoming an entrepreneur

Creating an entrepreneurial identity, or 'becoming an entrepreneur', is an outcome of personal and social emergence, including:

- narrative construction of identity – our changing story of who we are
- identity as practice – how what we do shapes our identity
- the role of the family – how family relationships influence us
- tension between current and future identity – how dissatisfaction can lead to entrepreneurship.

Opportunity recognition arising from contextual learning.

Recognising and acting on opportunities is an outcome of contextual learning, which includes:

- learning through immersion within an environment such as career or work experience within an industry or community

example

Mike: Shires FM

Mike, the founder of Shires FM, an independent radio broadcaster, describes his personal emergence from employee to entrepreneur, and the development of his own commercial radio station as a negotiated enterprise that began after he recognised the opportunity through his contextual learning within the industry.

Personal and social emergence

'I grew up around here, there was no commercial radio station. I went to work for another radio station where I was successful in building audiences and advertising, but became increasingly fed up with the way it was being managed.'

'I decided I couldn't stand the contradiction with what I knew worked any longer, so I agreed to end my contract with them. I took a huge risk, it was a really dangerous thing to do because any sensible person would have stuck in there until they'd got another job.'

Negotiated enterprise

'I applied for the licence for this station when the Radio Authority offered it, along with one of the directors from my old station as a backer. There were five applicants for it and we were the outsiders, but we won and that's how I got to be running it. I found the shareholders and I persuaded them to invest £500,000 in the operation.'

'In radio you have to start big time, because you spend a huge amount of money winning an audience before you get a single penny in revenue. You're winning customers who don't pay you a penny to listen, and it only comes when you can turn round to advertisers to say 'Hey, all these people can listen to you if you advertise with us.'

Contextual learning

'This station, down to the last dot of the 'i' in the prospectus, was mine. It was my opportunity to run the station from scratch in the way I knew it would work. I hadn't enjoyed having to do things in a radically different way from what I believed was right, I had been successful and I believed the way I wanted to set up the organisation would work.'

'You couldn't start it like a small business. Even when we started we weren't the smallest radio station, we were employing 22 or 23 people, so it's not a small start-up situation, it's straight in there.'

- opportunity recognition and innovation through participation – developing ideas from experience
- practical theories of entrepreneurial action – finding out 'what works for me'.

Negotiated enterprise

Starting and growing a business venture over time is an outcome of processes of negotiated enterprise, which include:

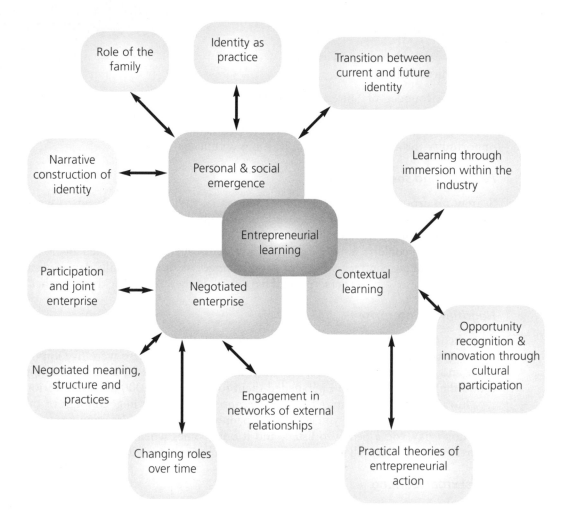

FIGURE 3.3 **The entrepreneurial learning model showing sub-themes**

● participation and joint enterprise – working with others on the venture
● negotiating meaning, structures and practices – developing shared beliefs about the venture
● engaging in networks of external relationships – building and managing relationships with people around the venture
● changing roles over time – roles growing with the venture.

Personal learning and entrepreneurial working

We will use each of the three themes of the entrepreneurial learning model in turn to explore personal understanding of entrepreneurial working. Figure 3.3 is a diagram of the full entrepreneurial learning model, showing the three major themes and 11 sub-themes.

How to use the entrepreneurial learning model

The purpose of the entrepreneurial learning model is to stimulate deeper personal awareness and reflection on your journey of entrepreneurial learning. It is not a simplistic 'Am I an entrepreneur?' questionnaire. This section explains the model and provides a set of questions on each of the sub-themes. It aims to help you to reflect on your entrepreneurial development, either individually or in a small group discussion with other people.

Read through each of the three themes and clusters of sub-themes to gain an overall understanding, then return to the first theme, personal and social emergence.

Not every sub-theme will be relevant to your experience at present, unless you have been involved in a venture of some kind. Focus first on those which make sense to you. Those where you may not yet have had experience, for example in the 'negotiated enterprise' theme, may be where you can aim to gain experience through the practical activities included in the following chapters by working on an opportunity as part of your development.

Start to take notes as you go through it, which will help make sense of your own learning. You can do this by using the opportunity mapping approach to map your learning so far and ideas for your development, taking each sub-theme as a branch and making notes of your thoughts on each of the questions as you go along. An example is shown in Figure 3.4 to help you to get started. In this way, you can build up your personal map of your entrepreneurial learning.

Allow several periods of time for this, to reflect on each theme in turn.

Personal and social emergence

Personal and social emergence is the development of *entrepreneurial identity* expressed through a person's narrative or life story. We all tell stories to explain our biography. Emergence is the story of the person you are becoming, as you move through transitional life experiences, being influenced by early life and family experiences, education and career formation, and social relationships. Forming an entrepreneurial identity means becoming and behaving as an entrepreneurial person.

Through personal and social emergence, people develop an identity which expresses their sense of who they are, their self and future aspirations. Becoming an entrepreneurial person often involves people renegotiating and changing personal and social identity which expresses who they are, who they want to be, and how they prefer to be recognised within their social world.

Questions in each of the four sub-themes aim to help you reflect on your personal and social emergence:

- Narrative construction of identity.
- Role of the family.
- Identity as practice.
- Tension between current and future identity.

Narrative construction of identity

We relate our lives and identities to other people through the stories we tell about ourselves. Personal and social identity develops over time, shaped by life experiences of change and learning. This identity is negotiated with others through self and social perceptions, and as we renegotiate or 're-invent' ourselves, we can develop an entrepreneurial identity through

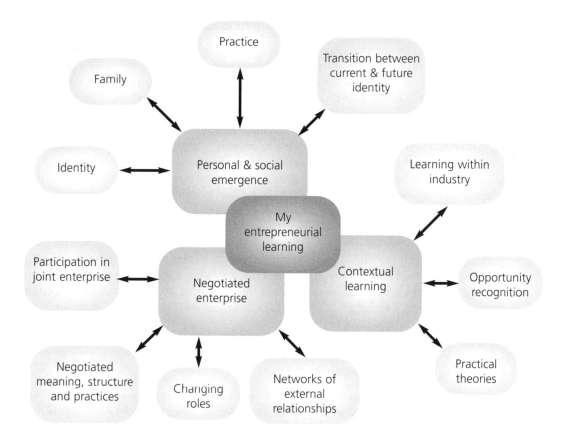

FIGURE 3.4 **Entrepreneurial learning map**

our life story, as if we are the lead actor within a self-narrated entrepreneurial drama. Think of when you meet someone new at a business networking event: how would you describe being an entrepreneur?

- How would you tell the story of your life? Reflect on your past, your present, and how you expect your future to be.
- How do you feature in your story? Think of examples of when you have acted as an enterprising person who seeks out and takes advantage of opportunities, or as an innovator who experiments with new ideas.
- How do you want your identity to change as your life story unfolds?

Role of the family

Families are often significant in shaping people's identities and actions. Families in which parents have started or run businesses often encourage their children's entrepreneurial behaviour as role models. Entrepreneurial stories are constructed with reference to personal relationships with spouses, parents and children. In turn, relationships with family members and expectations are renegotiated through entrepreneurship. This is especially the case within the 'family business', where traditional gender and cultural

> ## example
>
> ### Kal: Sawari Culture
>
> Kal explains why she wanted to start her business, called Sawari Culture, and demonstrates the creation of entrepreneurial identity through personal and social emergence. See if you can recognise in her story the four sub-themes of narrative construction of identity, the role of the family, identity as practice, and tension between current and future identity.
>
> > I was working in my husband's print business, doing the accounts and I realised I wanted something more than that. The industry is male dominated, most of our clients were men who thought that 'she just does the book-keeping'. At the time I accepted that. I'm not like that any more, I do challenge it.
> >
> > It was a major thing for my husband to realise that I wanted to start my own business because we'd come from a very orthodox upbringing. I started to do computer design work which I enjoyed, and found my talent for creative design. But there came a point when I didn't want to be seen as only a wife and a mother. I wanted recognition as a person in my own right. Something inside me said, 'I can do a lot more than this.'
> >
> > That made me realise that I wanted my own business: you have an idea for something you want to do and you develop it. I want to achieve something for myself. It's not that I want to say 'I've done all this myself, created a business of my own', because you need to have support from other people. But I've always had this energy and belief that I want to achieve something.

roles such as husband and wife, father and mother, can play an important part in the construction of identity, as Kal described. These can constrain people's development through an assumption that they will conform to stereotyped roles, for example the role of women in certain communities, unless they are able to renegotiate their roles by changing social perceptions.

- What are your roles in your family? What does your family expect of you?
- Has the experience of family members in business influenced your aspirations?
- How do your family's expectations affect your life, career and entrepreneurial aspirations?
- How do you feel about these family expectations?
- How would you wish to change your family's expectations of you?
- What consequences for your own relationships and future family could result from your becoming an entrepreneur?

Identity as practice

People also develop their identity from their activities, practices and roles in social interactions. They discover from experience what they are good at, through education, hobbies or interests, through finding and gaining confidence in natural talents and abilities, and learning how these can be applied and be of value within networks of social relationships and situations. Identity and capabilities developed in education and early employment are often applied in the core activity of a new enterprise.

- What are you good at doing and what do you enjoy doing?
- How can you best apply your skills, talents and abilities?
- How can you find the situations, opportunities and people where you can make best use of your capabilities?

Tension between current and future identity

There is often a significant point at which an enterprising person becomes dissatisfied with his or her existing reality and identity, and seeks to change this by starting a new venture. For example, employees may feel increasingly at odds with work roles and practices that are defined by others and just 'don't feel right' for them. Some of these people may seek to change their reality through a new business venture, enabling them to work in harmony with their personal values and practices. This may lead to a change in identity by becoming an entrepreneur.

- What do you want to achieve from your life at work or in education?
- Does your existing work or educational environment give you the space and opportunity you need to achieve this?
- What might cause you to move on from your current role? Would you start your own business?
- Is there a 'future reality' you want to create which is different from the present? What could this be?
- Do you believe you can make this happen? How can you start to do this?

The entrepreneurial act is imagining the possibility of 'what could be' and acting to make it happen. Entrepreneurial people create their new reality, taking responsibility for shaping future events. They move from assuming an identity defined by others, through work and family roles, into creating, changing and renegotiating a new identity as the author of an entrepreneurial drama. They will experience emotional uncertainties, and need to draw on resources of personal confidence and self-belief that it 'feels right' and they are able to make it happen.

Self-belief and motivation in entrepreneurial working

Self-belief and self-efficacy, our confidence in our ability to accomplish a task, are fundamental in entrepreneurial behaviour and performance, as described in Chapter 2. Self-confidence is a way of thinking and behaving in which individuals see the interrelationships between themselves, the world and other people around them as being one that they can change if they wish to do so. Self-efficacy is the belief that they can accomplish what is important to them. People can demonstrate the ability to change the world around them through the way they think, speak and act. Self-confidence grows and develops through successful experience, social learning from others, positive feedback and reinforcement, and personal maturity. People who work in entrepreneurial ways are less likely to accept 'given' conditions, and to act to change things around them in order to get things done. If they decide to do something, they will often set out to accomplish it, 'no matter what'.

Look at the following list of behavioural characteristics which often mark out entrepreneurial people:

- ambition to be successful
- motivation to achieve and accomplish difficult tasks
- pursuit of opportunities
- creative, unconventional thinking
- innovating, experimenting, causing change and pioneering new activities
- resilience in learning from failure and setbacks
- desire to be independent and in control of their lives and businesses
- desire to make a difference, for themselves and frequently for others.

What would you say are your dominant behavioural characteristics? Which ones are similar and which ones are different from those listed above? What could be the disadvantages or limitations of each of these behaviours?

These are questions to reflect on, which may help your personal emergence into an entrepreneurial way of living and working, if that is what you want.

Not all entrepreneurs display all of these characteristics, and most of them are displayed by many 'high achieving' people we would not categorise as entrepreneurs. Athletes, performers and scientists, for example, might well display similar characteristics. So these characteristics might be seen as behaviours practised by achieving people who wish to be successful in their given field. They may be inherent aspects of personality, but equally they may be developed through experience.

Personal and social emergence: review

Creating personal goals involves learning through self-discovery and social emergence. Forming and agreeing goals, and deciding how to assess their success are important processes in considering the wider impact and outcomes we aim to achieve. This exercise on personal and social emergence encourages you to reflect on your intentions. What do you seek to achieve in your life and career, and why do you feel this is important? What are your emotional, social, material and achievement needs? The development of self-belief and social confidence is essential for entrepreneurial attainment.

What do I want and why? Personal values, goals and motivations

- What personal values are most important to you? Values are the enduring beliefs which always guide our direction and decision making.
- What factors motivate you? What would you say you want out of life?
- What excites, interests and stimulates you?
- What does 'success' mean for you? Think of what success means in each of these life dimensions:
  - business
  - career or employment
  - financial and material terms
  - social success as judged by you and others
  - self-fulfilment
  - emotional success.
- What are your goals? What do you want to achieve, and why?

- What gives you confidence in your ability to achieve these goals? Would you describe yourself as a naturally confident person, or is your self-belief affected by what other people say?

Contextual learning

Our learning is shaped by the context, the environment or situation within which it takes place. In entrepreneurship, this often happens in the workplace and through social participation in social, cultural, industry and other networks. This learning is interpersonal and shared, occurring through people relating and comparing their individual experiences, at work and in other arenas. Through these social relationships and contextual experiences, people create shared meaning, learn intuitively and can develop the ability to recognise opportunities and generate the ideas for innovation.

Contextual learning connects people's personal emergence with the negotiated enterprise, as they learn in their social world 'who they can become' and 'how to work with others to achieve their goals' as well as the realism of 'what can and cannot be'. But contextual learning can be limiting and discouraging, for if the social context does not encourage innovative or entrepreneurial activity, or is poor in opportunities, people may learn that they have to change their context by leaving it and moving to a different environment.

Questions to help you reflect on your contextual learning are given in each of the three sub-themes:

- learning through immersion within the industry or community
- opportunity recognition and innovation through participation
- practical theories of entrepreneurial action.

Learning through immersion within the industry

People develop skills, expert knowledge and social contacts from their work, often as employees gaining experience, understanding and know-how in an industry. This learning is gained from discovery and experience, and socially by interpersonal participation. It is often functional, technical and problem solving in nature, finding out how things are done, developing intuitive practices and skills which work in given situations and which people can go on to use in creating their own businesses.

- What are the most useful skills and expertise you have developed? In what situations could you apply these?
- What intuitive, tacit abilities and skills have you developed, which you use without needing to think about them?
- What social, industry and professional relationships, contacts and networks have you formed? Who do you know within these networks?
- How might you use these contacts to your advantage in creating a new venture?

Opportunity recognition and innovation through participation

Opportunities are apparent to those who are alert and learn to recognise them, using knowledge, experience and behaviour. By being active within social and industry networks, paying attention to what people say, noticing what goes on, you can recognise and imagine future

---

example

Opportunity recognition: Cryosolve

'I'd worked in the engineering industry for many years, I'd started and run a business and like so many we found it was always a struggle to make a profit. Then a couple of years ago I was in the States and noticed the way that cryogenics – using very low temperature treatment of materials and components – was expanding. I thought there must be an opportunity to make that work in the UK – there are lots of applications in engineering and no-one here was offering a good service, so we decided to do it.'

Derek, Cryosolve UK

---

possibilities in that environment. If you identify an opportunity to create a new venture within a familiar context, you can find out how things are done and who to talk to.

Contextual learning also aids innovation: you can use your knowledge of what exists now, and combine this with imagination to create future reality. Thinking prospectively is envisaging the future and imagining how an opportunity can be created, before all the necessary knowledge or circumstances exist. This creative and associative learning brings together ideas, opportunities, technologies and resources in innovative ways. Such resources may include people and their expertise, finance, technology, information and physical resources, and acting ahead of others.

- What needs and problems do you recognise in your everyday life or career?
- Which of these could provide possible opportunities for you?
- How can your experience and contacts help you to create new opportunities?
- What ideas can you think of for future creative and business possibilities?
- How could you combine existing knowledge, technology and ideas to create new possibilities or innovations?

Practical theories of entrepreneurial action

People develop rules, routines and ways of working which work for them in getting things done successfully. This is knowledge of 'what works', why, how and with whom, gained from contextual experience, intuition and sensemaking. These are practical theories which enable people to reduce risk through experience because they 'know what they are doing'. The concept of practical theory in business is developed further in Chapter 7.

- What 'works' for you, in developing new ideas and making them happen?
- How do you make this work, and why? Which people does it work with?
- What are your 'practical theories' and how could you apply these in a business venture?

Contextual learning: review

Contextual learning connects personal goals and opportunities. The reasons why people select particular opportunities are various, and not necessarily or exclusively rational.

Self-learning about the relationships between personal goals and motivations, shared interests between people, and the decision to focus on a specific opportunity is important. Our interests and experiences are likely to be significant in the commitment and ability to act on an opportunity successfully.

● What experiences and interests do you have which could be useful to you in finding and selecting entrepreneurial opportunities?
● How would you relate these opportunities to your personal goals?
● How could you use your contextual learning and life experiences from work and community to select and develop opportunities?
● How do you assess 'risk' and uncertainty? How could you use previous learning and experience to manage or reduce risk in acting on opportunities?

The negotiated enterprise

The concept of the negotiated enterprise is that a business venture is dependent on negotiated relationships between people, and is not enacted by one person alone. As Wenger (1998) noted, 'the enterprise is joint … in that it is communally negotiated'. The ideas and aspirations of individuals are realised through interactive processes of negotiation and exchange with others in and around the enterprise, including customers, investors and co-actors such as employees or partners. The negotiated enterprise includes four sub-themes:

● participation and joint enterprise
● negotiated meaning, structures and practices
● engagement in networks of external relationships
● changing roles over time.

The negotiated enterprise is a process which doesn't happen until you start developing a venture with other people. So some of the questions related to the sub-themes below can only be answered from experience of working with others, for example in a business or organisation. If you are a student, you may not yet have gained this experience. If you work on a business idea as a project with one or more other people as a venture team, this

example

Negotiated enterprise: Blue Fish, a creative marketing business

'Three of us started Blue Fish. After a few years we took time out for each of us to write down what we wanted for this business, when we wanted to sell it, and what tone of voice we wanted to present to the market. We wrote down four words between us: creative, effective, fun, and integrity. Those words summarised the business and became our values.'

Tony, Blue Fish

will give you experience of negotiated enterprise. 'Young enterprise' company projects at school or college can also provide useful experience of team venturing.

Participation and joint enterprise

People act together to create enterprises which they could not achieve individually. Entrepreneurship is often plural, not singular. Even the sole founder of an enterprise is dependent on successful interactions with others to become an entrepreneur. A vital aspect of the entrepreneurial learning process is the ability to engage and work constructively with others towards the goal of venture creation. It is necessary for the entrepreneur to create shared belief in the potential of the venture to exist and succeed. Participative action is required to create this new reality, and to realise personal dreams and aspirations. Co-participants must put the collective identity of the enterprise as a project of shared significance before their individual identity. This is accompanied by social learning in which people learn to work together. Shared interests or goals, such as wealth creation, economic survival or the desire to enact a particular activity, are necessary for joint enterprise.

- How effectively do you work with others in agreeing shared goals and working towards them?
- Do you know what your preferred role and strengths would be in a team venture? What are you best at?
- Are you more of an individualist or a team player? How well are you able to put a team's shared interests ahead of your own?
- How do you recognise and employ the abilities of others – even when you disagree with their methods?
- Can you trust people you work closely with, and do they trust you?

Negotiated meaning, structures and practices

In an enterprise, people develop practical theories of 'what works' as individuals and these become a shared repertoire of practices and routines within the business, often described as 'the way we do things round here – what works for us'. This produces a distinctive culture within a business, where what is known and done does not belong to any single person, but rather is shared amongst the members.

An enterprise depends on these negotiated ways of working, which often reflect the founders' style, language, values, ambitions and ways of working, and those of the employees. Tom Kirby, CEO of Games Workshop, asserts that organisations have a 'spiritual life' with which people engage – or not. The lives, interests and aspirations of people within the business must be recognised by the founders who hold formal power and ownership of the business, which is of limited value without the employees' participation. Conflict and disagreement are inevitable from time to time and form an integral aspect of this negotiation.

In many enterprises, there is a strong emotional engagement between the people and the business, in which the culture is expressed through the style, language, behaviours, and feeling between people. For many people, this is why they enjoy coming to work. The 'buzz', the emotional and spiritual life and energy of the enterprise, comes from people expressing themselves, their identities and their abilities in their work, and in sharing this with their customers.

- What works for you and others within a shared project? How do you share goals, values, ways of working?
- How do you stimulate and sustain the emotional life of the venture: the passion, buzz, excitement and fun?
- How do you turn individual learning into shared learning?
- How can you manage conflict and disagreement to positive effect?

Engagement in networks of external relationships

The enterprise depends on relationships being developed and maintained with key individuals and networks. These may include customers, suppliers, investors, lenders, and others such as technology experts, resource holders and opinion formers. This starts as soon as you start to talk to people about a possible venture. Social capital ('who you know') is vital in affording access to resources and expertise. Entrepreneurs are selective in developing social networks, seeking to influence certain groups whilst choosing not to participate in others.

Similarly, customers need to be engaged as active participants who identify culturally with the enterprise, not simply as passive consumers; more than economic value is then generated in the interchange. Relationships and 'rapport' with some customers and suppliers may be more productive than with others.

The cultural identity of the enterprise is formed and enacted through the interactions between it and these external groups. The skills of listening, understanding the other party's position, negotiating and storytelling are essential in maintaining effective relationships. The enterprise depends on its identity, practices and the credibility of its message – its story – being accepted and understood within its chosen networks.

- What are the most important external relationships for an enterprise? With whom, and why?
- What would your expectations be of them, and theirs of the business? Are these realistic and can they be met or, if not, renegotiated?
- How can the customer be engaged in the life of the business?
- Are there gaps in the external relationships with key groups and individuals, and what actions are needed to fill these?

Changing roles over time

A business evolves through a process of ongoing learning and negotiation. If this is successful, the business tends to grow, becoming larger and more complex in operation and structure, and employs more people. This clearly applies to existing businesses, though you may not yet have experienced it. It is a series of transitions from informal to formal roles, relationships and structures. Significant changes in the roles of founders and others are inevitable as the business develops. Growth occurs through changes in human and social behaviour and relationships, and productive interpersonal negotiations around the enterprise. Different capabilities are required to manage the enterprise at different stages of its development, and people who do not grow with the business may be best advised to leave it.

This negotiated change in roles means that self-sustaining capability can be developed gradually, through people other than the founders taking responsibility for managing the business. Developing entrepreneurial and work teams, competent managers and functional experts is integral to the growth process and depends on managing relationships effectively, changing past expectations, sharing practices, and resolving interpersonal tension and conflict effectively. As new people are employed by the business, a mark of its cultural effectiveness is how well they learn to integrate and identify with it, adopting its cultural values of participation, behaviour and language.

- Can you accept that your role and others roles will change as an enterprise grows?
- How easily can you 'learn to let go' and entrust important roles to others?
- How well can you integrate new people into a team or business?
- How would you deal with people whom you have worked with from the start but who have not grown with the business, and whose skills no longer fit?

Negotiated enterprise – review

These questions focus on an opportunity and potential new venture you may be considering:

- What skills, capabilities and expertise do you think your opportunity will require, which you do not possess yourself?
- How could you identify people with those characteristics through using networks of contacts?
- How could you engage compatible people with the venture?
- What would be the basis for negotiation? What are the prospective benefits for them, and what input would be required?
- How can your individual interests be balanced with bringing other people into the business?

assessing the fit between ideas and personal goals

Why do people choose the opportunities that they do? The relationship between entrepreneurs and the opportunities that they choose to work on is not well understood. People perceive different opportunities, even when the same information is available to them, because of their differing past experiences, learning and individual perspectives. Here are some of the factors which are often significant in connecting ideas, opportunities and personal goals:

- family background
- personal interest or hobby
- previous career experience
- education, training and professional development
- social and community network and connection.

Family background may be significant where there is a family history of starting and running businesses in a particular trade, industry or profession. There are many examples; the Forte family ran hotels and restaurants, and Rocco Forte launched his own hotel chain; Stelmar tankers was the first business started by Stelios Haji-Ioannou, whose father also ran a shipping business. Experience within the family may be influential, but there are also many cases of sons and daughters deciding not to follow in the 'family footsteps', for example rural people moving away from family farming businesses, or second-generation Indian and Chinese young people in the UK deciding not to join the retail or food businesses started by their parents. Gender can also be a factor: for example, women entrepreneurs often recognise opportunities and start businesses in ways which are qualitatively different from men.

Personal interests or hobbies can provide a means of learning about a particular activity and starting a business, either early in working life or, as is increasingly common, after a career in employment. The numbers of mid-career and 'third-age' entrepreneurs is growing, as people leave corporate careers and seek self-fulfilment and additional income rather than retirement. Often these businesses can be termed 'lifestyle', turning a leisure interest into a source of income; if the numbers of hobby-based businesses were counted they would be very large indeed. At one extreme is someone like Mike, who in his teenage years is fascinated by independent radio, and persistently works his way into hospital radio, progressing to running a radio station as his first job and then founding the business that he builds into a chain of commercial radio stations. At the other is a lady such as Rosa, who participated in a business start-up programme and after a career in financial services started a niche business selling bird-seed to garden birdwatchers, having spotted an unmet need in her own hobby. It is of course vital for the market opportunity to be thoroughly understood and for such a business to be run on strictly commercial principles, not as an extension of the hobby.

Previous career experience often provides the starting point for a business. Employment in an industry enables 'niche' opportunities to be identified, networks of contacts to be built up and skills developed, as demonstrated in the contextual learning theme of the entrepreneurial learning model. People develop distinctive expertise which they can use in their own business. The commercial and technical or professional skills and insights or 'practical theories' provide a knowledge base and reduce risk. However the move from employment to self-employment or entrepreneurship is not always simple, and many who have done this have found that they needed to learn the additional skills of running a business, for which their previous career had not prepared them. These are covered in the section on 'personal skills and readiness' later in this chapter.

Education, training and professional development often provide the knowledge, the realisation that entrepreneurship is possible and some of the contacts necessary to start a business. There are more graduates in certain subject areas, such as art, design, fashion and computer gaming, than there are career opportunities, and self-employment is a necessity for an increasing number of them. Unfortunately this can produce too many small creative businesses struggling to make a living, and business skills may not have been developed at college to the same extent as creative skills. Practice and experience in the industry provides a major advantage over education alone, and whilst graduate enterprise is to be commended, it may not be an ideal initial career choice.

Social and community networks and connections provide many experienced entrepreneurs with subsequent business opportunities; through their networks, they become aware of opportunities and are able to use these to develop business ventures. The community can also be a resource and stimulus for social enterprise. Social and economic problems in communities, such as unemployment, lack of amenities such as leisure facilities, a shop or childcare, have been the spur for many social entrepreneurs to get started. One advantage of social enterprise is that there is an almost inexhaustible supply of needs which can be translated into opportunities, as social problems and needs change with demographics. So needs such as community dentistry, teenage literacy, and English language learning for asylum-seekers constantly present themselves, together with the considerable challenges of how to create a viable and sustainable business model which avoids grant-dependency, and developing the skills and confidence people need to make the business happen.

These are the main reasons why people select the type of opportunities they do. As suggested in the section on contextual learning, the prior experience, knowledge and social connections which people develop play a significant part in forming their choices and enabling them to recognise opportunities which others would not. Sometimes, this prior learning may blinker people and prevent them from seeing better, more rewarding opportunities. However, prior experience and learning reduce risk, and the track record of people pursuing business opportunity completely outside their previous experience shows it is considerably more risky. An example is the chairman of a successful furniture retailing business who, after achieving a merger and flotation of the business, was invited to chair an engineering business. Having spent his career in furniture retailing, and despite very highly developed managerial skills, he did not have the experience to understand the very different context of the engineering business, which came close to failure as a result. Contextual learning is therefore extremely important in entrepreneurial learning and opportunity selection.

activity

Consider these factors in the selection of entrepreneurial opportunities:

● family background
● personal interest or hobby
● previous career experience
● education, training and professional development
● social and community network and connections.

Are there any other factors you would add to these from your own experience?

Which factors are most influential in the types of opportunities you look for?

personal orientation to risk and uncertainty

Risk is the uncertainty of a given outcome and will be explored further in Chapter 5 in relation to opportunity assessment. People have markedly different orientations to risk-taking in business. We should not accept the popular stereotype of 'entrepreneur as risk-taker' without exploring the issue of risk in opportunity selection more carefully. Contextual learning can be seen as a means of reducing risk. Mike, for example, took what others saw as a big risk in leaving his job to start a radio station but his career experience had provided him with the confidence to know 'what worked' in building a successful commercial radio business. The negotiated enterprise also plays a role in risk reduction, as in many ventures the entrepreneur or entrepreneurial team do not carry the entire risk, as other investors or partners share the exposure to the business success or failure. However that still leaves the issue of personal exposure to risk.

These are some of the factors involved in considering risk

- *Self-confidence* and the personal belief in the ability to make a new venture or innovation work is an important factor. Personal dynamism, and intense and sustained effort to achieve change are required, but are not sufficient on their own.
- The ability to *manage emotional tension* and arousal connected with risk is significant, in that people who are prone to become anxious and fearful are better off not taking such risks.
- *Negotiated risk sharing*, by engaging investors, partners and others in the venture to share risk is a sensible strategy, and is necessary in any venture where the entrepreneur does not wish or is not able to fully self-finance a venture which is an attractive investment.
- *Iterative*, step-by-step working, can break apparently big risks down into smaller, limited ones where the exposure at each stage to failure is reduced. An example is checking that each stage of an innovation works before going on to the next, and that each decision has been evaluated to determine its impact before the next is made. However, time pressure can reduce the scope for this form of risk management.

example

Entrepreneurs often calculate the percentage chances of success in their decision making as one form of reducing risk. Here Tony, in the marketing business Blue Fish, describes how they learned to evaluate their prospects for success in competing for new clients:

> A lot hangs on whether we think we have a chance of getting a job. With one client, we had lots of background in the business, so we had a good chance of winning it. We're up against four other agencies. We managed to find out a little about the others: one we dismissed straight away, it was down to three others, so 25 per cent chance. It was worth a quarter of a million, and it was a bigger job to go for with lots of ongoing work. We've drawn up a set of criteria now on which we act. It has to be the start of an ongoing relationship; if it's a one-off job it's not worth it. If the next job after that is going to be a pitch, then we don't even go for the first one.

This demonstrates the use of 'practical theory' in decision making and in this case evaluating the chances of success against the risk of wasting time on an unproductive business development. Entrepreneurs also assess the 'downside', the worst possible outcome from the decision, and their ability to accept this.

entrepreneurial personality, roles, skills and capabilities

This section summarises the skills which are needed to develop entrepreneurial ventures. The focus is on skills and capabilities to complete given tasks, because skills are behavioural and can be learned, although each individual has differing degrees of innate ability and readiness to learn them. They are not dependent on personality, which is individually variable, although personality does influence the readiness and personal style we bring to learning and practising the skill. This emphasis on skills also helps in understanding the issue of roles in the entrepreneurial venture.

Personality

There is little firm evidence of a correlation between one's personality type and entrepreneurial success, as outlined in Chapter 2. However, by being self-aware, you can behave in ways which are more effective. An understanding of personality is important to entrepreneurship because it facilitates self-knowledge and of course the interrelationships between ourselves and others. If we know and are comfortable with 'who we are', our self-confidence, rapport and relationships with others in their roles as customers, investors and employees are more likely to be productive and profitable.

Roles

In developing an opportunity and creating and subsequently managing a business venture, a number of roles may be assumed by an individual. A role can be seen as a socially defined identity which comprises certain functions, attributes and types of behaviours used in accomplishing the tasks which normally accompany the role. Here are some of the roles which the creator of an entrepreneurial business may play, or be expected by others to play:

Inventor: creates a new product.
Innovator: applies a new technology.
Entrepreneur: starts a business to exploit a future opportunity.
Manager: builds and runs a business organisation.
Marketeer: creates a market for a new product or service.
Leader: leads and inspires people to achieve business goals.

The difficulty with viewing entrepreneurial work as a series of roles is that they are static, whereas entrepreneurship is a dynamic process which will involve some or all of these roles being played during the first few years of a business. It should not be assumed that the founder of the business can or will play all of them, or that he or she has the personality preferences or capabilities to excel in a particular role. A venture often requires multiple contributions, and roles will be taken on by others within a team in which flexibility is important.

If we consider Trevor Bayliss as an example, he is best known for developing the clockwork radio, and has a long history of inventing new products which tend to use existing technologies and materials in new ways. Trevor describes himself as an inventor. The business which he founded, Freeplay, has required all of the other roles to be played at various stages, but this has been accomplished by other people and the business has its own professional management team. It is more helpful to identify the skills and capabilities which may be required by a business at particular points and periods in its development, than to be over-concerned with individual roles, which often overlap and change. The concept of entrepreneurial teams has become influential, and in the development of an enterprise the range of capabilities needed in the team should be considered (Shepherd and Krueger, 2002).

Capability

We can identify a number of capabilities, or clusters of skills and behaviours which are required in entrepreneurial activity, and these do change at different points and stages of

FIGURE 3.5 **Entrepreneurial management capabilities**

the development of a business. These clusters are shown in Figure 3.5 and grouped in Table 3.1 under the broad headings of entrepreneurial capabilities and management capabilities. Entrepreneurship is concerned with the creation and exploitation of the opportunity, connecting innovation with market need, whereas management is concerned with the organisation of the business venture. Both are needed to establish and then to grow and develop a successful and sustainable enterprise.

Individuals operating in both areas need skills of personal organisation and interpersonal interaction, as well as technical capabilities relevant to the business activities. The combination of the entrepreneurial and management skill-sets can be defined as entrepreneurial management, or an entrepreneurial way of running an organisation. Entrepreneurial management is a capability-based approach which identifies and develops or finds the skills needed for an organisation at that stage in its development. A range of skills are required, contributed by different people, which change and evolve over time. This takes the emphasis off one particular role – and the person who is seen to be in that role, such as innovator, entrepreneur or leader – which may be emphasised at one stage in the life of a business. Entrepreneurial management is explored in greater depth in Chapter 7.

being a leader: forming and leading entrepreneurial teams

An important application of your entrepreneurial capabilities is in considering what contribution you can make to an entrepreneurial team. An entrepreneurial team is a group

TABLE 3.1 **Entrepreneurial and management capabilities**

Entrepreneurial capabilities	Management capabilities
Personal organisation* Interpersonal interaction* Investigating opportunity Applying innovation Strategic venture planning Market development	Leading and managing people Managing organisation and operations Managing finance and resources Responsible management – social, legal, environmental and ethical responsibility

* These are both entrepreneurial and managerial capabilities

activity

The toolkit includes a section which enables you to assess yourself in terms of the personal, entrepreneurial and managerial capabilities which are generally required for the development of a new business venture. Work through this now to help you to assess your own preferred approach to entrepreneurial work. Include the capability of leading and managing people.

who have come together to exploit an opportunity, usually by setting up a new venture. The ideal entrepreneurial team is likely to have:

- complementary skills and expertise
- compatible goals and motivation – people want to achieve the same things
- compatible personalities and working styles
- trust, honesty with each other and mutual respect
- effective leadership.

The map of entrepreneurial management capabilities in Figure 3.5 includes 'leading and managing people', and effective leadership capability is needed in any business. There are many different approaches to defining leadership, and these have some parallels with the development of an understanding of entrepreneurship discussed in Chapter 2, for there has been considerable reliance on defining personality traits and what might be classified as 'the *great man* school of leadership'. However, more helpful approaches have started to emerge, including distributed leadership, where the cultural norm is that everyone in an organisation can demonstrate leadership, an approach that is of value in the flat, non-hierarchical entrepreneurial organisation. One such approach originates from the Sloan School of Management at Massachusetts Institute of Technology, where entrepreneurial leadership is taught. The model of leadership developed at Sloan includes five core leadership capabilities (Ancona, 2005):

- *Visioning*: fostering individual and collective aspiration towards a shared vision.
- *Analysing*: sensemaking and strategic planning in complex and conflictual settings.

● *Relating*: building relationships and negotiating change across multiple stakeholders.
● *Inventing*: inventing new ways of working together – social and technical systems.
● *Enabling*: ensuring the tools and resources to implement and sustain the shared visions.

These capabilities can be compared to the model of entrepreneurial and managerial capabilities shown in Figure 3.5 to identify points of connection. The model includes leading and managing people. Additionally, visioning and analysing connect with strategic venture planning; relating connects with interpersonal interaction; and inventing connects with applying innovation.

activity

Leadership and entrepreneurial teamwork

From your self-assessment of entrepreneurial and management capabilities in the toolbox:

● What are the top two or three capabilities you bring to an entrepreneurial team?
● Looking at the Sloan leadership capabilities, do you think you can demonstrate leadership, or would you prefer to support someone else in a leadership role by being a team member?
● What aspects of personality, roles, capabilities and expertise would you look for in others to complement your own?

networking, influencing and selling: vital skills in seeding opportunities

As discussed in the negotiated enterprise theme, the interpersonal skills of networking are highly important in finding, exploring and resourcing opportunities. You may find it helpful to look back at your answers to the questions in the sub-theme of 'Engagement in networks of external relationships' and your self-assessment in the capability cluster of 'Interpersonal interaction'.

Entrepreneurial effectiveness does depend to a significant extent on being able to develop and utilise networks of contacts. This is not about simply having a world-class collection of business cards or e-mail addresses, or sending hundreds of Christmas cards, or even being a compulsive attender of business breakfast meetings, networking events or parties, although some of these may be useful in generating and maintaining contacts. Effective networking is constructing and participating in a world of social connections to create new opportunities and enable existing opportunities to be taken forward. Even reserved people, who may not feel comfortable in social gatherings, can do this.

Effective entrepreneurial networking depends on a number of behaviours which are outlined below.

- Create a distinctive and confident identity. People need to now who you are, what you are about, and what is interesting and memorable about you (personal and social emergence).
- Be strategic, purposive and focused in your choice of networks and investment of time in them. Which ones are useful and which are not?
- Work towards getting to know the decision makers, resource holders, experts, influencers and most useful people in your chosen networks.
- Practise conversational skills of listening and asking questions, finding out about people's needs, interests and their networks (interpersonal interaction).
- Manage contacts. Keep a contact file, database or business card folder up to date, and categorise groups of contacts, e.g. all the news media people you know, as they will be useful when you want to get media coverage.

Remember that human relationships depend on trust and reciprocity, so be prepared to do favours for people and to keep your promises. This builds up 'favours in the goodwill bank'. Successful entrepreneurs often 'give without the expectation of receiving in return' and find that goodwill consistently repays them. Renew and keep warm the contacts you value and want to maintain, but be selective. By participating in separate networks, covering a range of industries, and expert-professional, interest, cultural, even international domains, you will be the point of convergence and be able to introduce people from one network to contacts in another. When you need information, advice or access to a resource, then use your network – once you have developed it.

Networking activity

This is an action-learning approach which can help you to develop further your skills and confidence in entrepreneurial networking.

- Identify a need, opportunity or question you want to explore.
- Use your contacts or other research (e.g. Internet search, Chamber of Commerce) to identify a network where you can find out more about the opportunity. This should not be a network in which you have previously participated. It may be an expert, professional, trade, industry or interest group. Internet groups can be used to locate networks, but face-to-face contact is vital.
- Negotiate your way into the group and attend the next possible meeting.
- Talk to at least ten people you have not met before to find out about their areas of interest, points of connection with your own interests, and who they know who could help you further.
- Review your success in starting a new network and exploring your opportunity.
- Keep your promises to your new contacts.

One important reason for participating in networks in this way is to represent your business, and to make sure both that people are aware of you and that you can find opportunities for influencing, finding prospective new clients, and other forms of relationship development. It is not about selling, because social contacts generally find it embarrassing to receive unsolicited sales pitches at parties, and few people are good at delivering them. The aim is to identify prospective clients who may be interested in what your business can do, to create a relationship of rapport and trust with them, and to obtain their details, promising to contact them later. The next day, you can contact them and suggest a meeting or, if this is not possible, ask questions to find out about their needs, listen attentively, and only open a selling conversation if that is appropriate. The effective entrepreneur is always alert to the possible sales opportunity!

review

Look back over your work in this chapter, including your learning map following the entrepreneurial learning model, your self-assessment of entrepreneurial capabilities, the leadership and entrepreneurial team exercise, and your development of networking skills.

Use the following questions to update your entrepreneurial learning map, to reflect on your learning so far, and to plan your continuing development.

- What are your personal values, goals and motivations?
- How would you select the best opportunities for you, and how would you make use of your contextual learning in doing this?
- What are your most developed entrepreneurial capabilities, and how could you apply these to your best advantage?
- Which capabilities do you most need to develop, and how could you achieve this?
- Do you see yourself as an entrepreneurial leader, and if so how can you develop in this role?
- What complementary expertise, personality and capabilities would you look for in other people as team members?
- How will you develop the networks you need for your opportunities and business?

opportunity exploration

introduction

This chapter focuses on how to create and explore opportunities. The purpose is to demonstrate how entrepreneurial opportunities can be created, identified and developed through a process of opportunity exploration. This chapter takes a creative approach to finding opportunities, which is then developed in Chapter 5 by an analytical approach to show how opportunities can be assessed and evaluated. The two chapters provide a detailed exposition of the questions in the second theme of Opportunity-Centred Entrepreneurship, creating and exploring opportunities, which is shown in Figure 4.1.

The learning goals for this chapter will enable you to:

● identify and define problems as potential opportunities
● generate ideas and solutions to problems using creative thinking techniques
● use mapping techniques to explore problems, opportunities and resources
● define and follow a structured process of creativity from idea to innovation.

The chapter explores the roles of creative thinking and innovation in generating ideas and building on them to form opportunities through associative thinking. Gaps, needs and problems can be identified and analysed as a starting point for creative problem solving and opportunity recognition in the external environment. Opportunity, problem and resource mapping are introduced as core techniques. The use of future scenarios and time perspectives in opportunity recognition and innovation is explored. Models and methods for exploring opportunities through market and related investigation and research are covered in detail. Finally, idea-banking of opportunities as a knowledge resource, and protecting intellectual property rights in the entrepreneurial process are summarised. Use is made of practical business examples and 'cameo' mini-cases to illustrate the concepts. The chapter is activity based, and you will be asked to identify potential opportunities to explore and work on.

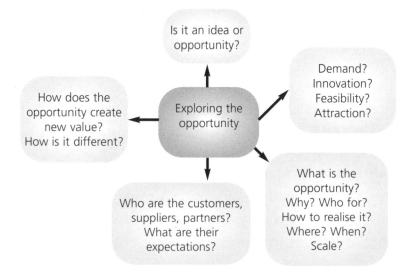

FIGURE 4.1 **Exploring the opportunity**

The outcome of the chapter is for you to develop an idea into an opportunity by using mapping techniques, and then to plan how to undertake detailed market investigation of the opportunity. As a result you will be able to use this information to assess and evaluate the potential of the opportunity by using the techniques to be covered in Chapter 5.

creativity and innovation in entrepreneurship

Entrepreneurial opportunities require both creativity and innovation to progress from idea to solution. Creativity and innovation are often associated, but the terms are not synonymous and their respective meanings are important. The creative act can be defined as 'bisociation', or combining two unrelated pieces of information to form a new third idea (Koestler, 1964). Creativity is the association of ideas, information or materials to form new concepts – or as Schumpeter described, 'new combinations'. Creativity sees the world in new ways, through free expression, by developing new and original ideas and concepts. This involves divergent, associative and non-linear thinking which may appear illogical to others. Creative art, for example, is judged by aesthetic criteria and subjective perception, so creative activity does not require practical or financial value.

Creativity has several important roles in the entrepreneurial process. It enables people to develop completely new ideas and to envision possibilities of 'new reality'. Imagining a business or a product which does not yet exist is a creative act. Creativity enables people to imagine the future and to construct future scenarios for business ventures. This is strategic creativity, by imagining and then enacting a new reality. However there are at least two other significant roles for creativity. One can be described as tactical creativity; it involves thinking and acting in creative ways to exploit opportunities or to manage and develop the business, often dealing with problems of limited time, expertise or resource. Entrepreneurial working is applied creativity, and entrepreneurial people are frequently creative in practical ways, in devising new product ideas, routes to market and solutions to problems, and it is certainly worth developing and using skills of creative thinking and working.

The other aspect is the application of creative skill within the business, for example in designing or producing creative media, products or experiences. Chapter 8 introduces the concept of cultural diffusion and outlines ways in which the growing number of enterprises in the creative economy are developing.

activity

Creative thinking using the 'Idea Space'

The purpose of this activity is to introduce a method for stimulating creative thinking by associating ideas, to show how this can assist innovation.

The Idea Space has four boxes (see Figure 4.2), headed 'resource', 'information', 'attributes' and 'environment', which feed into the Idea Space. All the factors listed in these boxes can be changed, depending on the specific details of the idea you are working on.

1. Select a 'resource'; this may be a product, technology, material or process which is easily available to you.

2. Select from the list of 'attributes' those which apply to this resource, e.g. purpose, shape, colour, structure, texture.
3. Select the 'information' which is available from the list about the resource, e.g. knowledge of a problem, opportunity, demand, 'what works' or does not work, 'what-if' idea for improvement.
4. Select the 'environment' factors which affect the conditions in which the resource is used, e.g. people, place, posture, language, close or remote.
5. How can the resource, attributes, information and environment factors be combined in new ways? Experiment with making different connections.
6. Think of how each of the attributes can be changed in turn to see what ideas this produces.
7. List the new combinations from stages 5 and 6 in the Idea Space in the centre.
8. Harvest the best, most feasible or interesting ideas from the list.

The Idea Space is based on a simple concept of making information explicit and then connecting this information in new ways to create new ideas. Associating or combining information in new ways can help us to imagine new possibilities by shifting our perceptions of reality, even if no practical use or innovation results from the creative insights. If we 'flip-flop' by looking at different perspectives, such as seeing a problem through the customer's eyes rather than the organisation's, or starting from the end of a process rather than the beginning, and working back, creative insights begin to emerge.

The relationship between creativity and innovation is shown simply in Figure 4.4. Creative thinking is divergent, often intuitive and unstructured, opening up new ideas, connections and possibilities. Innovative working is convergent, focusing on combining a limited number of ideas on a workable application or solution to a problem. Think of pouring water into a funnel: the mouth is broad and contains splashes and turbulence, but the spout is narrow and produces an easily directed and consistent flow of water.

Divergent thinking is valuable in generating ideas for an opportunity or project. It includes these activities:

● identifying and defining the opportunity, need or problem
● researching – gathering and analysing information
● exploring – open-ended quest for new information
● investigating – focused search for specific information.

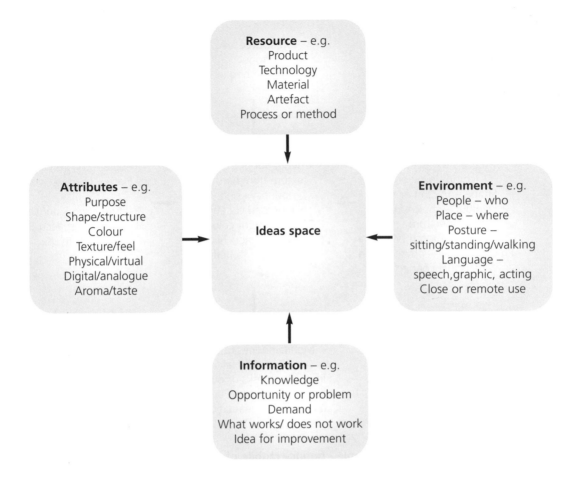

FIGURE 4.2 **Idea Space**

Convergent thinking focuses on moving from many ideas and rich data to concluding, developing and implementing an opportunity or project. Convergent activities are structured and focused on completion – making decisions and choices, taking action, getting results, and 'making things happen':

- deciding the possible solutions
- planning what to do
- developing and implementing the innovation (e.g. a product or service)
- communicating the idea to stimulate demand
- monitoring progress, measuring and reviewing the results.

Creativity involves imagining a new reality, and innovation is required to make it work. Innovation is developing ideas into applications and solutions. Innovation introduces new products, methods or technologies through convergent thinking, by moving from opening-up many options to selecting between alternatives. Innovation integrates knowledge to solve problems and meet needs in new ways, by applying ideas, technology and resources to create

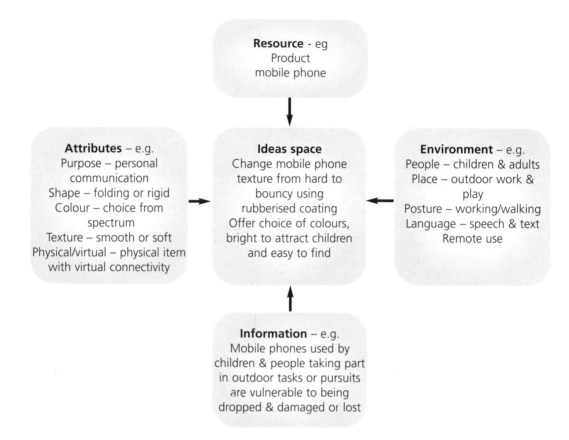

FIGURE 4.3 **Idea Space example - bouncy mobile phone**

Divergent thinking generates new associations and possibilities

   Creativity: generating ideas

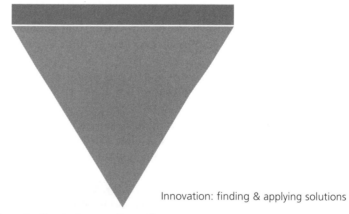

Innovation: finding & applying solutions

Convergent thinking enables selection between alternatives

FIGURE 4.4 **Divergent and convergent thinking**

new solutions. Innovation is an iterative process, driven by the search for 'what works'. It is assessed by the utilitarian criteria of meeting a need successfully, and producing applications which work and are economically viable.

Innovation is integral to the entrepreneurial process. New ideas are of little value without the ability to apply and harness them as value-creating products, services or processes. It includes research and new product development, and applying science, knowledge or technology in new ways to create new methods, processes, and applications. It can take many forms, from technology, science or engineering-based activities to simple forms of 'doing something new'. However it is best considered as a logical process, often iterative, going back repeatedly, by trial and error, to find the best approach.

The ability to innovate can provide vital advantages for an entrepreneurial organisation. Being able to think creatively and identify new applications and markets for ideas, products and technologies, working quickly and flexibly, is essential. Innovative companies have higher rates of new or improved product introduction, and are faster or first to market compared with competitors. They are more flexible, better able to attract external finance, and experience more positive impact on company performance, turnover, profitability and return on investment than the norm. However innovation is inherently uncertain because it involves risk and is resource-hungry, so effective project management is vital for successful innovation. Moving effectively between divergent and convergent activity is one means of achieving this.

Innovation vanguard firms show the way to beating the downturn

Robert Tucker (2002) suggested five points as strategies for creating new value through innovation-led growth in corporate organisations, including BMW, Herman Miller and Whirlpool. Innovation must:

- be approached as a discipline
- be approached comprehensively
- include an organised, systematic and continual search for new opportunities
- involve everyone in the organisation
- be customer-centred.
  (Source: www.innovationresource.com)

the innovation journey

During this chapter and Chapter 5 we will go through a journey from generating ideas to establishing innovative solutions as business opportunities. The process of developing and implementing innovation is described as a journey rather than a conceptual model because, as on a journey, you can have different starting and finishing points, you may well go backwards as well as forwards, and diverge to explore interesting avenues, possibly becoming lost or side-tracked at times. That is what the innovation experience is like in practice, because it often involves trial and error, experimentation and even luck.

The journey is shown as a diagram in Figure 4.5. The steps along the journey are the main stages to work through, showing the techniques and activities included in the book which can be used at each step. So whilst there is no one 'correct way' of innovating, it

---

example

Kelly was an art and design student, skilled in designing fashion accessories. One night, whilst ironing clothes on the floor of her flat, she accidentally welded an item to the carpet. Investigating the damage, she found that the unintentional heat-treatment had turned the carpet into a different material. She decided to experiment further, and found that this new material could be easily shaped and formed in three dimensions.

Being environmentally aware, she found out that huge quantities of both new carpet offcuts and old carpets were dumped as landfill each year, and this presented two opportunities: a limitless source of recyclable material, and a way of reducing waste.

Kelly experimented for months with different methods of heating and forming carpet, finally perfecting a simple process which resulted in a malleable material. Raising money from the Prince's Trust, she applied for and eventually secured a patent to protect her rights to this process and started her business, Carpet-burns.

Kelly progressed from being a design student into becoming a designer-maker of fashion accessories, and then into an innovator and young entrepreneur. She had to overcome disadvantages of being young, having little money and no business skills or experience to persuade people to take her seriously. Initially, she designed and made small batches of products such as mobile phone cases and handbags, which gained attention and won awards and sponsorship.

However she realised that these products alone would not provide a viable base from which to grow her business. Being involved in business networks and working with others, she identified that by producing sheets of heat-treated carpet, this material could be made available for a range of industrial uses such as packaging and re-manufacturing into shaped products. Five years on, she repositioned the business to focus on this opportunity.

The Carpet-burns story demonstrates that opportunities and innovations can occur through serendipity or by chance, but that major investment of focused time, energy and resources is then required to develop, protect and exploit the innovation. Also, the individual's initial view of the market and application for the innovation may not be the most promising. To be successful, people have to develop their personal skills, especially in finance, marketing and team-working to engage others with complementary skills to help to grow the business.

---

does need to be seen as a process in which knowledge is generated and used, and different skill-sets and methods are required to develop and manage innovation at each stage of the journey.

recognising opportunities in the external environment

An opportunity was defined in Chapter 1 as: 'the potential for change, improvement or advantage arising from our action'. The opportunity may be an existing one which we can

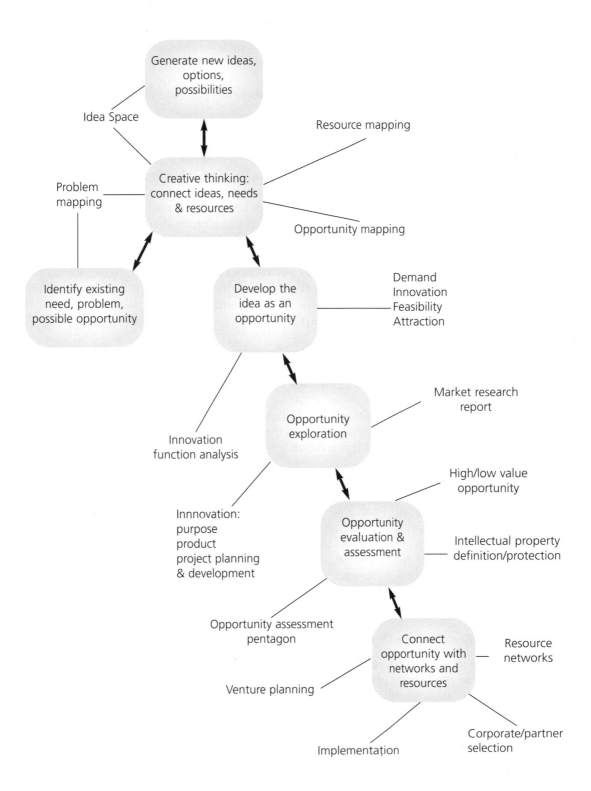

FIGURE 4.5 **The innovation journey**

identify now, or it may be a future one for which we recognise the potential. This chapter deals with the following types of opportunity:

- 'gaps in the market' or a mismatch between supply and demand
- current and future opportunities
- the solving of a problem, e.g. developing and applying a solution
- a new product, service or experience people would find useful.

Is an idea the same as an opportunity? This is a simple but important question. An idea is a creative connection between two or more pieces of information. An opportunity can exist where there is a need, problem, and either actual or potential demand for a product, service or experience. It may be that an idea includes the demand – but again it may not. There have been many ideas for new products where the demand did not exist and could not be created.

It is also possible to identify needs and to think creatively about them without being able to solve the problem or to fulfil the demand. If the idea is not technically or otherwise feasible it is not a real opportunity. These considerations help to define three of the four essential features of an opportunity:

> *Demand*: there is a need, problem or potential demand to be satisfied.
> *Innovation*: there is an idea for the product, service or experience to be provided.
> *Feasibility*: the idea is technologically feasible.

These can be investigated objectively, but we need to add a fourth, based on more subjective judgement, which in practice often makes the vital difference between opportunities which are exploited and those which are not:

> *Attractiveness*: the potential reward and the level of interest to the entrepreneur.

Together these produce the DIFA (Demand, Innovation, Feasibility, Attractiveness) method of defining whether an opportunity actually exists.

The factors which give rise to opportunities can be divided between, on the one hand, 'supply-side' or 'push' factors, which arise from the availability of technology, resources, economic and policy changes which provide the ability to create new opportunities, and on the other, 'demand-side' or 'pull' factors which arise from market need. In both cases, changes in these factors over time can create the space for new opportunities.

Supply-side or push factors

- technological advance, new possibilities and innovations
- new products or processes becoming available
- legislation, compliance and standardisation
- increase or decrease in cost and availability of resources
- increase or decrease in transaction and process costs
- supplier and distributor capabilities
- availability of skilled people.

Demand-side market and customer needs, or 'pull' factors

- demand for innovation or novelty
- social and consumer trends, e.g. rising expectations, increasing disposable income, less free time
- demand for value for money
- the effects of competition, e.g. rising or falling prices
- potential advantages, e.g. saving of time or cost, convenience,
- demand from supplier and distributor chains
- reduction in risk, uncertainty or variability.

These lists are not exhaustive, but they indicate the range of factors which affect and give rise to opportunities, and provide an initial framework for opportunity analysis. As shown in Figure 4.6, the entrepreneur operates in the space where supply and demand converge, connecting supply-side resources with market opportunities to create new value.

example

easyJet and the low-cost airline industry in the UK

Supply side

The EU 'open skies' legislation provided the deregulation which gave rise to the possibility of timetabled cheap flights from the UK to continental Europe. The Southwest Airlines business model in the United States demonstrated that a low-cost model based on minimising transaction costs and service levels combined with maximising aircraft and staff utilisation was viable and more profitable than the industry norm. Aircraft and air crews could be hired, ground services provided by sub-contractors, and take-off and landing slots provided at less congested secondary airports.

Demand side

Air travel had been maintained at high fare levels through an industry cartel. Rising income levels, growing demand for European travel, and congested roads and expensive rail travel created the potential demand. Offering low fares would stimulate people to travel and gain value for money, for short breaks or on business, especially if it was made easy to book. There was an opportunity to create a completely new market for air travel.

   The demand (the potential market) could be created; the innovation (the business model) was based on the Southwest Airlines pioneer; and the feasibility came about through deregulation and the ability to lease or sub-contract the services and assets required. For easyJet founder Stelios Haji-Ioannou, the attraction was to be the disruptive innovator, breaking into an established industry with a new business model and using limited assets to build a business with potentially high profits and asset value. The case study in Chapter 8 provides a fuller account of this industry.

creative problem solving

Business opportunities can be based on devising a solution to a problem which affects enough people to make the solution viable, following the old maxim of 'find a need and fill it'. This activity leads you through a systematic approach to defining the problem before starting to look for solutions.

opportunity and problem mapping

We will apply a technique called 'opportunity mapping' in several different ways. This is a variation of mind-mapping, developed by Tony Buzan (2003), and is used as a means of defining problems, exploring opportunities, establishing resources, planning and developing an opportunity. The next activity could easily be done using a problem map.

Opportunity mapping, like mind mapping, is a creative way of connecting ideas together by association rather than by step-by-step logical thinking. It can be used with pictures as well as words, and gives great flexibility in the way information is expressed and processed. Opportunity mapping works by enabling us to generate thoughts quickly, creatively and intuitively, by 'free association' rather than sticking to a logical process. It can be used by one person, or more productively by a small group – for example to sort the results from a brainstorming session where a group of people 'freewheel' to come up with as many ideas as possible.

Opportunity mapping has a range of applications in entrepreneurial working, including:

- reviewing and making connections between ideas, experiences and resources
- creating and developing new concepts
- developing ideas, strategies and plans for projects and business ventures.

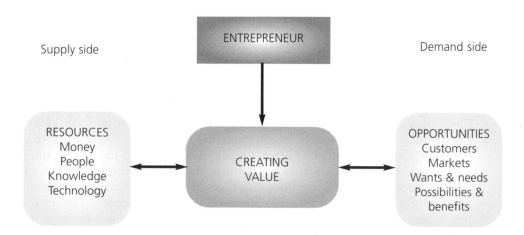

FIGURE 4.6 **The entrepreneur: creating new value by connecting supply and demand**

Seeing existing needs as creative opportunities

Think of a problem which continually recurs, or a repetitive unmet need. It could be something you have noticed, which affects or annoys you.

   If you cannot think of anything, choose one of these real problem-based opportunities:

- how to find part-time jobs in term-time for students
- how to use resources such as old CDs, personal computers, text-books or supermarket food which has reached its use-by date
- how to reduce the number of solo-occupied cars in city rush hours.

Now go through the following stages to define the problem by answering as many of the questions as you can; guess or estimate to fill in the gaps.

- What is the problem you have identified?
- What are its results or effects? What is the scale or measure (e.g. numbers of people affected)?
- Why is it a problem? Why does it happen? What factors cause it?
- Who is causing, and who is affected by, the problem? How do those causing the problem benefit from it?
- Where, when, and how does it happen?
- What are the costs – financial, time, resources – that are incurred?
- What are the potential gains from solving it?

At this point you can review the problem and consider:

- Is the problem capable of being solved? Is a solution feasible?
- Does solving it offer a big opportunity? What benefits or value could be created?
- Is the problem interesting and useful to solve?
- Is this an isolated, individual problem or a recurring one which affects many people?
- Could resources potentially be found to solve the problem? Asking questions like these can screen out problems on which it may not be worth investing further time.

Here is how to draw a problem or opportunity map. The starting point is shown in Figure 4.7.

1. Write or draw the topic, such as the problem or opportunity, in a bubble in the centre of a piece of paper, flipchart or whiteboard.
2. Draw branches out from the centre, label each of these 'who, what, why, when, where, how', or use other labels if they are more relevant.
3. Print the ideas/pieces of information on lines going outwards from each branch.
4. Use different colours or simple pictures if this helps.
5. Make connections between associated ideas on different branches.
6. Review the map to remove any irrelevant ideas.

The result is a map which connects the key ideas and information associated with each branch or sub-topic. This can then be used to develop the opportunity further. The important stage is in moving from 'implicit' understanding (information in people's heads) to explicit information on paper where different pieces of information become connected, leading to fresh ideas, insights and possibilities.

FIGURE 4.7 **Starting point for a problem or opportunity map**

creative thinking to generate innovation

Creativity generates new ideas by bringing existing knowledge together in new ways, opening the door to innovation. Opportunity mapping can be a useful way of associating information visually to produce new ideas, as we will see in the next section. A new concept only needs two or three elements, which may already exist separately. So a customer need and a technology can be combined to create a new product innovation. If we think of creative resources that we can use, these can include knowledge, technology, materials, skills, production and distribution capacity and many others. There are numerous examples; think of the increasing applications being found for Broadband technology, for radio frequency identification devices (RFID), and so on.

Creativity can result from 'breakthrough' thinking: taking something out of its existing context and applying it in a new situation. Most innovations are adaptive – small-scale incremental improvements on existing products, such as the latest model of the VW Golf for example. Radical or 'disruptive' innovations, which create entirely new concepts and which can transform their industry, are much rarer, and generally higher risk. However any successful innovation requires other ingredients, which include a clear focus on the customers: how will the innovation benefit the customers' life or business, what will it do for them and what will they value? It makes sense to involve customers in the creative process, to find out about their needs, problems and desires, and what innovation they would value. Another ingredient, good design, can make the difference between an ordinary and outstanding innovation. The principles of design can be applied to any innovation, from a physical product such as a digital camera, an Internet or computer gaming virtual application, or a service such as a travel tour organiser. Good design makes the customer's experience 'natural' and enjoyable, whilst also being functional, robust and economical and conveying the distinctive identity of the product. Finally, the innovation must function effectively and provide the benefits the customer expects. This means that all aspects from design, production, delivery, customer information and support must be provided and managed effectively. All these aspects can form part of the creative process of originating the innovation.

example

time wasted by missed appointments

Every year, many working hours are wasted by people failing to turn up for appointments with professionals whose time is at a premium and costed by the hour. This especially affects doctors in the UK National Health Service, where it is estimated to cost £162m a year, but it is also experienced in other professions such as law, accounting, and consultancy. The map in Figure 4.8 (overleaf) defines the problem by presenting information on the causes, effects, costs and other factors.

innovation function analysis

The purpose of this technique is to assess the detailed requirement for an innovation by establishing the design and performance parameters which it needs to achieve. It can be used for a more detailed investigation once the existence or potential of an opportunity has been identified, and helps the innovation journey to move from 'idea' to 'opportunity'.

The method is to identify, analyse and specify systematically the job, task or function which has to be performed. This can be applied to any situation, from a personal service

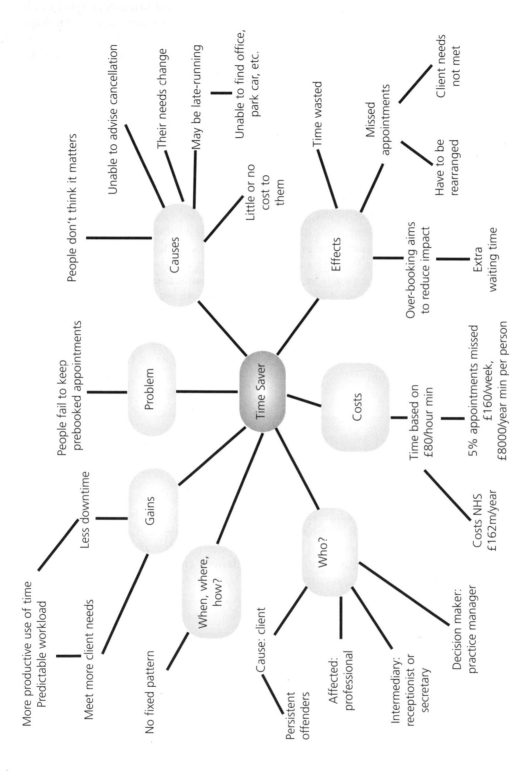

FIGURE 4.8 **Mapping 'time saver' problem as opportunity**

or product, such as a digital entertainment device, to new business models and industrial and public service applications. The technique is to identify customers, users or 'performers' of the function, and gather information by interviewing and observing them in order to analyse the function. The aim is to specify the job the innovation must perform by collecting as much of the following information as is applicable:

- What is the job, task or function which has to be completed?
- What is the value produced as an outcome or result of this function?
- What are the success criteria of this function for the user? And for the customer of the end result (if different)? These success criteria should include:
  - value-added
  - cost/value for money
  - speed
  - consistency of performance
  - how the quality of the outcome is assessed.
- What inputs are used to complete the task (materials, information, human effort, energy, money)?
- What is the cost of these each time the function is performed?
- How is this task or function performed at present? What is the process?
- What problems, deficiencies or frustrations arise at present (e.g. what costs, time, effort, inconsistent performance or quality occur?)
- What desire or scope for improvement can the user or customer suggest?

As well as the function being specified in this way, the scale of adoption of the task also needs to be assessed or estimated as far as is feasible:

- How many users of this function can be identified? Are they increasing or decreasing in number?
- What is the cost of this activity (number of users x frequency of use x cost per use)?
- Which products and organisations benefit from the function being performed at present?
- What would be the costs to the user of changing to a new system?

Once the function and its scale has been specified in this way, it can be assessed whether this is a 'problem worth solving'. If it is a widespread task in which users experience variable performance and frustration, and if there may be scope for enhancing quality of outcome and performance, or reducing cost, then further investigation is worthwhile. If so, the specification which has resulted from the function analysis is the starting point for creative thinking and problem solving to develop an innovation which is capable of meeting it.

Figure 4.9 (overleaf) shows the innovation function analysis as a diagram. This format can be used as a problem map to gather the information.

innovation and solution development

We can now move from defining the problem to thinking creatively and developing ideas about potential solutions. Just defining the problem may have started to trigger ideas. Start to write these down, either on Post-it notes or on a piece of paper. Rather than using

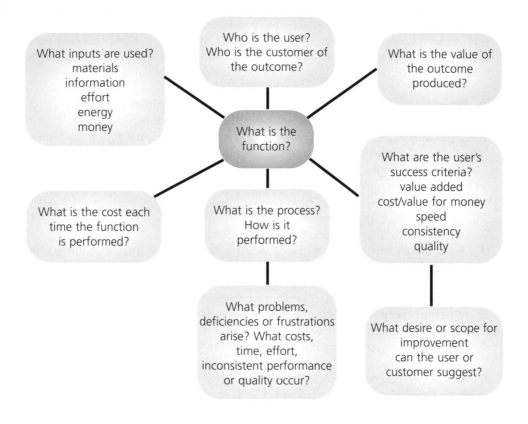

FIGURE 4.9 **Innovation function analysis**

a checklist, which may not be helpful to creative thinking, some of the following questions can be used to stimulate analysis of the problem, and result in generating ideas of how to work on the opportunity:

- Consider each of the branches and how it relates to the problem.
- What are the causes, and how could these be prevented or minimised?
- What would people affected by the problem see as the ideal solution?
- What factors need to change for the problem to be solved? These may include:
  - changing people's *behaviour* (e.g. that of people who cause the problem)
  - changing or introducing a *system* as a formal way of doing things

- changing or introducing *technology*
- changing *awareness* by educating or making information available
- changing or influencing *environmental* factors.
- What resources are available? How can you combine these resources in new ways to solve the problem?
- Resources could include:
  - information
  - skills and know-how
  - technology
  - social, supplier and distributor networks
  - capacity, land, finance.
- How have similar problems been solved by others? What can be learned from them?

Once you have identified one or two possible ideas to work on, start to draw an opportunity map of how these might work.

For the 'time saver' problem introduced earlier, the result is shown in the opportunity map in Figure 4.10. The underlying cause and the 'change' to be worked on was the behaviour of the people making the appointment. Various options to achieve this change were identified, including:

- introducing or raising charges for missed appointments
- confirming appointments by e-mail or text message
- downgrading or dropping clients who missed more than two appointments
- informing clients about the negative effects of their missed appointments.

A way to change clients' behaviour was identified; this used an automated system to remind them of appointments by sending e-mail or text messages which they had to respond to in order to confirm the appointment. This could become a commercial software product which could be sold to medical practices, consultancies and other professional businesses. This is shown in the opportunity map in Figure 4.10, which now represents the 'flip-side' of the problem. It starts to show how a technology-based product could be developed to solve the problem and to provide a more widely applicable opportunity from this solution.

opportunity building: matching needs and resources

activity

Use the approaches shown so far in this chapter – of analysing the problem, thinking creatively, and opportunity mapping – to develop a potential solution to the problem you identified earlier.

Review whether it includes the four key features of an opportunity in the DIFA model:

- *Demand*: what is the need, problem or demand to be satisfied?
- *Innovation*: what is the product, service, process or experience?
- *Feasibility*: is it technologically feasible?
- *Attraction*: is it worth doing? Why?

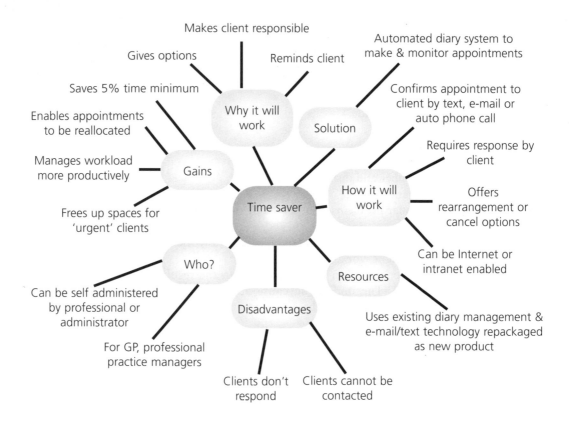

FIGURE 4.10 **Opportunity map for 'time saver'**

There are three important points here, each connected with how we recognise opportunities.

We perceive, recognise or create opportunities in our subjective consciousness. This is part of our learning process. Ideas are not the same as opportunities, since an idea is simply a creative thought, which may not be practical or viable in any sense. However an opportunity is something which can be acted on and made to happen. So turning a business idea into a business opportunity involves demonstrating that it is feasible, viable and worthwhile. The same opportunities are not apparent to everyone, and some people will perceive the same opportunity more quickly than others through imagination and foresight. Opportunities start off as individual, unique perceptions, even if different people who are quite unconnected coincidentally recognise the same opportunity at around the same time.

The second point is that time is an important dimension in recognising and working on opportunities. Opportunities are transient and temporary, occurring through combinations of such forces as technological change, social and market trends, or even the weather. The 'opportunist' trader at the seaside will sell ice-cream on sunny days but switch to waterproofs and umbrellas when it rains. So opportunities are time-limited, and if we recognise one then the decision to work on it or not should be made quickly, since others may already have noticed it or will become aware of it. Inevitably this leads to competition where the first or best comes to dominate. Future-based rather than current opportunities give greater scope for strategic innovation and developing something new in a 'white space', unoccupied future market niche, rather than an intensively competitive existing market.

Third, just because we recognise an opportunity that does not mean it is a 'good' opportunity for us. We live in an opportunity-rich society. Being opportunistic and pursuing every opportunity will quickly exhaust personal resources of money and energy. 'Good' opportunities, those which we should select and develop, are likely to be ones where we already have some relevant skills, knowledge, experience and understanding, where we have an interest or fascination which excites us, and where the opportunity is in harmony with, or at least compatible with, our personal and business or career goals. And it is only an opportunity we can exploit if we can gain access to and harness the necessary resources – of finance, information, technology and people – to do so.

So here are some basic questions to use in assessing and filtering an opportunity you have identified:

- Is it an idea or an opportunity?
- Is it a current or future opportunity?
- Has anyone else already noticed or seized the opportunity?
- Is the opportunity distinctive and different from existing approaches?
- Is the opportunity compatible with my goals, interests, and experience?
- Where are the resources which would be needed?

One important process in developing an opportunity is to match the need, problem or demand with the resources needed to make it happen. That does not mean the entrepreneur needs to own or control the resources, but is rather able to find them and connect them with the project in a negotiated way, for example by offering the resource owners the opportunity to participate as investors or partners in the venture. The resources which may be required to exploit an opportunity could include:

- knowledge – skills, expertise, specialist know-how and information
- technology – existing technical capability or capacity
- physical equipment and plant or materials and components
- finance – investment capital and start-up capital
- human – skills, expertise and capability which is required in the venture
- access – permission, licences, distribution networks
- intellectual property – patents, brands, trademarks, design rights, copyright
- capacity – facilities which need to be bought-in or sub-contracted.

Opportunity mapping can be used to create a resource map of the resources and capabilities needed to develop the opportunity. An example of a resource map for the 'time saver' product is shown in Figure 4.11.

This leads to the conclusion that because of the type of knowledge-based resources required in this case, the opportunity could best be developed through seeking a partnership with an existing IT services provider which possessed some of the technology-based expertise and distribution and marketing capability, but which would be unlikely to develop this niche-market product independently.

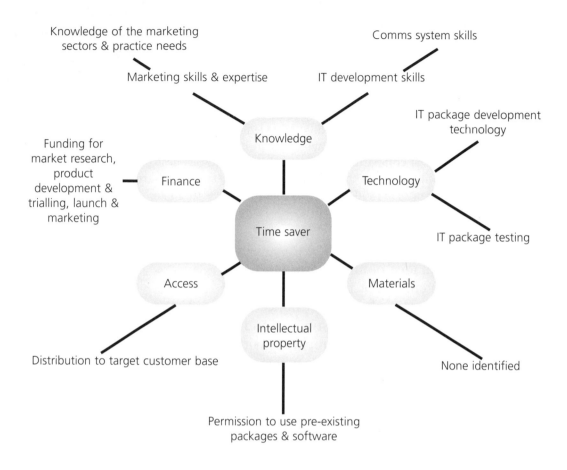

FIGURE 4.11 **Resource map of the opportunity**

- Draw a resource map for the opportunity you have identified, using the categories of knowledge, finance, technology, materials, access, intellectual property and any others which apply.
- Review it to identify where these resources currently exist and could be located.

current and future scenarios for opportunity creation

Acting at the right time is a critical factor in opportunity recognition.

Current opportunities are those where customer demand already exists and the innovation is feasible now; the idea may be a new one, an adaptation of an existing one, or a simple replication. Generally, current opportunities are less innovative than future opportunities, or may not be innovative at all. The opportunity may result from the market growth being greater than existing businesses can fully exploit, making competition possible, or exploitation of a defined market niche feasible. A new market does not have to be created. Current market opportunities involve less uncertainty, but it is certain that increased competition with possible price-cutting will result. The technology already exists and is known, and the risks and costs can be defined with greater certainty.

However if one new firm is able to enter the market, then it is likely that others will also do so, potentially leading to price-cutting and over-supply. Competition is almost inevitable with existing opportunities, although introducing an innovation which gives a clear cost or customer advantage into an existing market, especially one which is growing, can be a viable strategy.

Opportunities have an optimum period in time at which they can be exploited, when the need can be created or is self-generating, the resources and technology can be brought together, and the potential return is greatest. We can use creative thinking about the future to imagine opportunities which do not yet exist, but which are possible or emergent, because the resources required to make them happen are or will become available. Future thinking is inherently innovative, yet risky, demanding confidence and the availability of significant resources into the future.

Potential market opportunities arise where the demand may not yet exist but can be stimulated, where the technology either already exists or will become available in the foreseeable future, and where the innovation, or idea, has not yet been applied. Future

example

Fascia Mania Ltd – 'rooflines Britain looks up to'

Fascia Mania Ltd was started by two brothers in the UK East Midlands during the early 1990s. The family business was in building and carpentry, and they identified the replacement of uPVC fascia and soffit boards to domestic property rooflines as an emerging market with strong prospects for growth. There were no specialist firms, whilst poor installation, product and service standards were being offered by double-glazing and general building firms. The brothers set out to offer a well-operated, reliable and professional roofline replacement service.

The firm showed early promise and the brothers learned important lessons about marketing, developing and training installation teams, planning business finance and managing the business effectively. They became established as the market leaders in the regional market and were able to attract investment capital which funded a market-ing-led growth strategy, including showrooms, local radio advertising, additional installation teams and movement into the housing refurbishment contracting market. They expanded to cover the Midlands region, aiming to become the UK's most trusted name in the industry.

However, their early success was noticed by people who started 'copycat' busi-nesses based on the same business idea; names such as Familiar Fascias, Fascia World, and numerous small imitators sprang up, aiming to undercut Fascia Mania on price. In this type of business there is little intellectual property to protect other than the brand name, and Fascia Mania's strategy was to use their reputation for quality and superior buying power to defend their market presence, reinforced by their effective sales capability.

opportunities require prediction of future market, customer and other trends. The further into the future, the higher the degree of uncertainty or risk in implementing the opportunity. Significant investment may well be needed and it may be difficult to quantify how much is required. However the entrepreneur may also have the potential to gain a much higher return from being first to exploit the opportunity, to gain a market lead, and possibly to secure intellectual property rights on the innovation.

Amazon.com in Internet-based book and cultural media retailing, and Sky in satellite pay-TV are two examples of future opportunities which were exploited successfully. In both cases the potential was identified by the founders significantly in advance of their competitors. Substantial investment was made in establishing the technological, market and product bases for the businesses. Establishing a controlling position in a new industry which they created was the goal, rather than short-term return or profitability. When the businesses were launched they provided a unique service which was impossible for rivals to copy quickly. The founders continued to invest substantially in the businesses to build up market dominance over a period of several years, this being considered more important than short-term prof-itability. Both businesses developed a market, product and technological dominance which competitors who entered the market later with similar offers have not been able to rival.

These, like easyJet, are examples of successful future opportunity exploitation. However, future opportunities can have significant disadvantages, in particular the uncertainties giving rise to risk, the uncertain time period before implementation and break-even or profitabil-ity, and the uncertainty over the investment needed to support this. There are many cases of unsuccessful attempts to create and exploit future opportunities, and the reasons for failure are important to learn from.

example

ITV Digital TV

This satellite service was launched in the UK in 1998 and failed in 2002. The reasons for its failure provide an interesting comparison with the success of Sky TV:

● The technology did not work effectively or consistently in all areas.
● The service was not sufficiently differentiated from those already available, with too few new benefits for customers.
● The service did not meet a clear market need and was not adopted widely enough.
● The investment required to fully develop the service was too high and could not be financed.
● The pricing was too high to be competitive.
● It depended on an alliance between two terrestrial TV companies which both had to provide short-term returns to investors.

exploring opportunities: market and related investigation and research

This section explores the market-related aspects of the opportunity in increasing depth. This will provide information for the opportunity assessment and evaluation in the next

Future thinking

Assess the opportunity you have identified in relation to time perspectives.

- Is the opportunity current, or one which will exist in the future?
- If it is in the future, how many years ahead will this be?
- Is it currently being explored or exploited by others?
- Do all the conditions exist for it to be exploited? Which do not?
- Are you bringing a significant innovation or advantage to exploit the opportunity?
- What assumptions about future conditions are you making? (e.g. demand, innovation, technology, resource availability, social trends etc)
- What factors could change to affect these assumptions?
- What are the most significant risk factors in the opportunity? How could these be reduced?

chapter. Exploring the market is a key learning process for any opportunity, especially if it is in a sector which is new or unfamiliar to the entrepreneur. The market focus funnel in Figure 4.12 visualises the market exploration as a progression where we move from an overview to detailed and specific probing. You may recognise this as an example of moving from divergent to convergent thinking.

- Identify potential markets.
- Market characteristics:
  - total value, growth, accessibility.
- Decide on target market.
- Identify customer segments within market.
- Identify segment characteristics:
  - total value, growth, accessibility.
- Decide on target segment(s).
- Identify customer needs, preferences.
- Decision-making factors, pricing.
- Identify media, promotional and sales channels.
- Develop marketing plan.

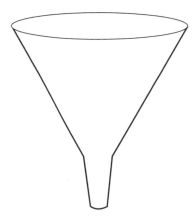

FIGURE 4.12 **The market focus funnel**

To use this model we need information at several different levels: the overall markets available, the target market, the customer segments available, and the target segment. We may already have assumed that there is a given market and target group of customers. However in developing an opportunity, it may become apparent that the initial target market is not the most attractive or rewarding. Therefore even if a single potential market has been identified, it is worth moving back up the funnel to ask 'What are all the markets available for the product?' or, as one entrepreneur challenged his team, 'What is the *sales universe* for this product?'

If you are unfamiliar with marketing theory, the definition we are using of a market is the demand for a product or service within a given geographical, social or industry boundary. Segments are defined as the discrete customer groups within the market, using a number of characteristics that enable different segments to be identified at increasing levels of precision.

Questions to use in conducting market research

The following questions are intended for use within the market focus funnel, in order to gauge the size and value of the market and to move from the 'big picture' of the potential markets to the characteristics of the target customer segment in the chosen market.

---

example

Recorded music

The market for recorded music in the UK is one of a number of major world markets for the product. This market can be segmented by using the following characteristics:

- Type of music: classic, jazz, pop, rock, punk, R'n'B, urban, dance, easy listening etc.
- Format: Internet download, I-tune, CD, DVD, audio tape, MP3, LP.
- Preferred mode of purchase: online MP3 or iPod, mail order, multiple store, independent store, club, file-swapping, other.
- Average monthly spend: less than £5, £5–£10, £10–20, £20–30, £30–40, £40+.
- Age group: under 10, 10–15, 15–20, 20–30, 30–40, 40–55, 55+.
- Media channels most used – terrestrial TV; satellite or digital TV; BBC radio; independent radio; magazines, newspapers, Internet sites.
- Gender: male or female.
- Ethnic group: white, Afro-Caribbean, Indian, Chinese, Arab, other.

From these characteristics the target segment for a new online music magazine and catalogue business could be defined as:

> Male/female aged 15–30, listening to R'n'B, urban and dance in CD and MP3 format, currently buying increasingly by online download, spending £30+ per month, listening to independent radio, in any ethnic group.

Detailed consumer research could then take place with this group to identify their likes, dislikes, dissatisfaction with existing channels and their buying criteria for the new product.

Potential markets

- What are all the potential markets for the opportunity?
- What is the size of each market: global, national, regional, local?
- What is the total value of each market in sales per year?
- Is each market growing, static or declining?
- What is the intensity of the competition in each market?
- What percentage share of each market could be achieved within (say) two years?
- Which is the most attractive market to enter?

Target market

- How many customers are in the target market?
- What is the anticipated lifetime of the market in years?
- What are the key factors which drive demand and price in the market?
- Who are the dominant sellers in the market?
- What are their market shares by per cent, their competitive strengths and weaknesses?

Customer segments

- How can the market be segmented, for example by geography, industry sector (business/institutional), socio-economic group, age range, occupation, interests (consumers), average spend and media consumption?
- What are the customer segments?
- Which of these are most attractive in terms of under-met needs or aspirations, growth in size/spend and affinity with product?

Target segment

- Who are the target customers?
- What is the average spend per customer per transaction and per year on this product?
- What percentage of the annual spend by this segment can the business secure?
- What is known about these customers?
- What do they want or need? What do they like and dislike?
- Why do they want or need the product? What benefits do they gain from it?
- How far are these wants and needs met at present? How well are they met?
- What problems or dissatisfaction do the customers experience?
- What are their buying criteria: what, how and from whom to buy?
- What factors do they see as 'value for money' and 'quality'?
- What are their 'affinity habits' – what related purchases do they make, what are their listening, viewing, Internet-browsing, reading, visiting habits?

Gathering this information is a process of market research. At the top three levels of the funnel this is mainly secondary research. This can be done through the Internet and by using information normally held in university and business libraries. The Small Business Service, official publications and statistics, Mintel and other reports can be used. The references section in the appendices lists useful sources. At the bottom level of the funnel, secondary information will only provide limited intelligence, so primary, direct research will be needed to generate the very specific information needed to really build up detailed understanding about the segment characteristics, to get to know the customer, and to be able to make informed decisions. A market research project that targets individuals or groups of people in the segment will be required. Corporate and well-resourced entrepreneurs may commission market research specialists to undertake this, whilst students, start-up entrepreneurs and smaller firms can normally do it themselves, which takes time but facilitates direct learning from the customer.

The methods available for direct market research can include:

- direct one-to-one interviews
- focus group meetings
- informal conversations at trade shows, network events etc.
- telephone interviews
- e-mail survey questionnaires
- postal survey questionnaires.

Direct, personal contact requires the greatest investment of time, but also yields a higher level of qualitative knowledge about the customers and the opportunity than is achieved through remote questionnaires. Also, an initial list of prospective customers can be developed by retaining customer details.

From the research process, a detailed picture of the market, the segment and the customers can be built up. This can be used to start developing the opportunity as a business model and provide vital information for the venture plan. This will be expanded in Chapter 6. Here are some of the important questions to be considered in analysing the market research information and developing the business opportunity. Not all questions are applicable to every opportunity, and even if they were, not all the information will be available. However the important point is for the entrepreneur to be posing the important questions for the business, trying to find the best information, and deciding at what point there is enough information on which to make decisions.

Analysing the industry

- What is the structure of the industry at present: globally, nationally, regionally, locally? What is the chain from supplier to end user?
- Who are the dominant firms which supply the market? How do they exercise control over the market?
- What is the strength of competition in the market? Who are the existing suppliers which the new venture will be competing with?
- What are their strengths and weaknesses?
- How will the new venture be differentiated from existing suppliers?
- How are competitors likely to respond to a new entrant to the market?
- Who else is known or likely to be working on a comparable opportunity? How far advanced are they? What advantages and disadvantages do they have? How fast can others replicate it?

The customer and the new venture

- What percentage of the annual spend by this segment can the business aim to secure?
- What advantages over competitors can the business offer customers?
- How will customers be persuaded of this?
- What is the added value to customers?

- How much is this worth to them?
- How will the product be priced?
- What selling and distribution channels will be used to reach the target customer segment?
- What are the costs of gaining and selling to a new customer?
- Is the customer relationship loyalty-based or (one–off) transaction-based?
- Is the product unique, desirable, essential or a discretionary commodity?
- What factors will affect customer retention, repeat and added-value purchases?

activity

This activity asks you to consider how you would use the market focus funnel as a research tool, and to apply it to a specific opportunity as described in this section. The objective is to gather as much relevant data as you can, which can be used to evaluate the opportunity in the next chapter and to reduce uncertainty. You may have limited time and access to information, so you will need to be selective and focused in your research.

- How would you go about applying the market focus funnel to a real market opportunity?
- How would you gather the primary market research information?
- If you are working on a specific opportunity, then decide on the most relevant questions to investigate that opportunity. There are 44 questions of which you should aim to answer at least 30.
- Then conduct initial research using the funnel approach, and go down the funnel gathering data on as many of these questions as you are able. If you cannot find the information go on to the next question. Some of the questions in the final section on 'the customer and the new venture' ask you to start making initial decisions on the business in relation to customers.
- Keep the information you gather in the headings of the potential and target market, customer segment, industry analysis. This information will be used in Chapter 5 to assess the opportunity.

idea-banking: opportunities as a knowledge resource

The purpose of idea-banking is to build up a resource bank of ideas which have not yet been used and are potentially applicable at the right time, combined with a market opportunity and other resources. An idea-bank is an information resource or library for organisations or groups to use. Some idea-banks are maintained by companies, universities and research institutes and have restricted access, with a 'stock' of creative and technology ideas and innovations on which they hold intellectual property. Unexploited patents which are held by companies, research institutes or universities can be a source of opportunities. It is possible to conduct patent searches to determine what has been patented in a particular field and by whom, and to explore the potential of these. However it would then be necessary to contact and open discussions with the patent holder to find out if they are prepared to negotiate a licence for another party to exploit it. Other idea-banks offer open access to subscribing groups, researchers or even to everyone. An example is in the social enterprise arena, where some groups openly share ideas developed in one context so that they can be copied, adapted and put to work in other situations. References to idea-bank and social enterprise websites can be found in the resources section.

To work, an idea-bank needs ideas to be held in a common format for cataloguing and access. So for example, each idea can be submitted and held as an opportunity map with defined branches. Alternatively, the same information categories can be used to hold the idea on a database. The information required to idea-bank an opportunity normally includes:

- what the idea is, what it does
- why – the purpose and rationale
- how it works
- any actual and potential applications
- innovation and unique features
- drawings, design or technical information and 'prior art'
- research or development work carried out, such as trials or proof
- limitations and disadvantages
- resources and conditions needed for use
- who could benefit from and use the idea
- originator and ownership with details of intellectual property ownership
- keywords to enable database searching.

intellectual property: protecting ideas

A vital area to consider in exploring opportunities is whether the ownership of the idea can be protected. The area of idea ownership is termed intellectual property (IP), and relates to the following forms of intellectual property rights (IPR):

- patents
- trademarks
- design protection, including registered design and design right
- copyright
- trade secrets.

Full details of intellectual property in the UK can be found on the Patent Office website (see the list of websites at the end of the book) and this organisation also publishes excellent guidance booklets. In summary:

- *Patents* protect original discoveries and inventions, such as processes and products, which must be new, inventive and capable of industrial application. An application is filed and a full patent may be granted after a search and examination has been carried out by the Patent Office. Once published, the patent gives the holder exclusive rights to use or licence the innovation for up to 20 years. It is vital not to disclose the invention to a third party, or to use it, before the patent is applied for, and the application must include full disclosure of all details since nothing can be added subsequently. The patent process is complex, and the use of an expert such as a Patent Agent or lawyer on a confidential basis is likely to be necessary. UK patents only provide protection in the UK or, by extension, within 23 European states, and beyond these areas other national patents have to be taken out. If a patent is infringed the holder needs to defend it, although insurance cover may be taken out against the costs of this. The process of securing, renewing and defending patents is complex and costly, especially for the solo inventor, but it is vital if the rights to a valuable invention are to be protected. Imagine how you would feel if you invented something and another organisation patented it, preventing you from using it; this has happened.

- *Trademarks* are signs, such as words, logos and pictures, which distinguish the products and services of one organisation from another. They include product and organisation brands such as Virgin, McDonald's and Orange. Registering a trademark prevents others from using the same mark in relation to the types of products and services for which it is registered. International registration can also be applied for.

- *Design protection* includes *Registered Design*, which is the total right of ownership to use the design. It covers the appearance of a product or part of a product, which must be novel, individual and not generic. It can be granted on submission of photos or drawings of the design with an application and fee, and lasts for five years with extensions to 25 years. *Design right* also exists as intellectual property when the design is unregistered, but provides less cover. It provides an exclusive cover against copying for up to five years, but only within the UK.

- *Copyright* is similar to *design right*, giving creators of all creative works the right to control use and publication for between 25 and 70 years, depending on the type of work. In both copyright and design right, it is up to the creators to record and retain proof of their origination of the work and the date this took place, so that they can subsequently defend their right to the work.

All these categories of IPR can be sold, licensed or given by the owner to another party; needless to say, the future potential value of the rights should be considered carefully before taking such a step, and professional advice obtained from a legally qualified IP expert in cases where there is substantive potential value. Just think that J.R.R. Tolkein, author of *The Lord of the Rings*, sold the film rights for a tiny proportion of the eventual value of his creative work, and many songwriters, authors and designers have never received more than a nominal payment from the exploitation of their work.

Trade secrets are unregistered intellectual property, which include confidential processes, techniques and recipes – for example, the secret ingredients of Coca-Cola. They can be protected by confidentiality agreements or by being handed down verbally from one family generation to another, effectively depending on trust. But once the secret is disclosed it is impossible to assert ownership, protect the product or prevent copying.

It is important for innovators to assess what unique intellectual property they are creating, and how their rights to its ownership can be protected most effectively. The future value of the opportunity and the ability to exploit it nationally or internationally may well depend on the strength of intellectual property. Also, it is not enough simply to register the patent, design or trademark. If it is infringed it is necessary to defend ownership, which is inevitably costly, especially on an international basis. However in a number of countries, intellectual property rights are almost impossible to assert or defend, since international trade agreements are not enforced, and copying and counterfeiting of products are widespread. China, India and a number of other developing countries are territories in which it is very difficult to enforce intellectual property rights.

activity

- What intellectual property could your idea potentially produce?
- In which category or categories of IPR would this fall?
- How would you go about securing your IPR?

critical questions to consider from this chapter

- What are the four essential features which distinguish an opportunity from an idea?
- What factors are most important in creating an opportunity?
- What methods would you use to investigate an opportunity to explore its potential? What use would you make of opportunity mapping and innovation function analysis? Develop your skills by using these techniques on the problems or opportunities you identify from working through this chapter.
- How can you translate a need or problem into an opportunity through creative thinking and the application of innovation?
- How are creativity and innovation different? In what ways do they relate to the entrepreneurial process?
- What have you learned from applying the market focus funnel to researching the market for an opportunity?

chapter 5

opportunity assessment

chapter contents

introduction

The purpose of this chapter is to demonstrate how to evaluate and assess entrepreneurial opportunities. It uses a series of frameworks and tools for opportunity selection, assessment, evaluation and decision making, using criteria to distinguish 'high potential' and 'lower-value' opportunities. These enable the higher potential opportunities to be identified and progressed, whilst less promising opportunities can either be adapted and reconsidered or abandoned. The approach, in comparison with the creative stance in Chapter 4, is rational and analytical, based on the need to gather and appraise firm evidence of an opportunity which can be used to present a convincing business case to investors or partners.

The chapter progresses through the 'innovation journey' presented in Chapter 4, including the stages of opportunity evaluation and connecting the opportunity with networks and resources. The range of types of opportunity and the importance of a supportive culture, infrastructure and environment are outlined. The roles of clusters and resource networks in facilitating opportunity development and innovation are explored. Finally, the section on corporate entrepreneurship outlines the potential for connecting the opportunity with corporate organisational goals and strategy.

The learning goals for this chapter will enable you to:

● assess and evaluate potential opportunities in relation to decision-making criteria
● prepare a report which evaluates the opportunity
● identify the extent of a supporting environment, clusters and networks which offer the potential to provide resources for opportunities
● assess the 'fit' between an opportunity and corporate strategy for entrepreneurship.

During the chapter you should continue to work on the example of an opportunity which you selected in Chapter 4. The outcome of this chapter is an assessment of the potential of this opportunity, a consideration of the strategic options, and identification of the networks and resources which are likely to be most useful in acting on it. This information will be brought together in the form of an opportunity evaluation report or portfolio, which will provide an essential contribution to the venture planning process in Chapter 6.

evaluating the opportunity

The purpose of opportunity evaluation is to assemble the known information about the opportunity, and use it to investigate essential, strategic questions. The answers will inform your decision making on whether to go ahead with a venture to act on the opportunity, and on planning how to do so. Opportunity evaluation aims to reduce the risk of project failure by researching thoroughly all the relevant information on the factors which affect the project. It also aims to ensure that the opportunity identified offers attractive rewards. The opportunity assessment (pentagon) and business opportunity recognition (hexagon) tools included later in the chapter are designed to help you to make informed judgements about the potential value of opportunities.

The market focus funnel in Chapter 4 and accompanying questions can be used to gather detailed market information on the opportunity. Through bringing this information together, critical factors such as these can be identified:

- the reasons for a perceived opportunity; what and where it is
- the market opportunity for the business; its size, value and duration
- key market segments and customer groups, preferences and distribution channels
- the industry structure, driving forces and competition
- the dynamic effects of change on the industry
- who may support or invest in the business
- the options, resources and key factors for the business project.

This can be presented as a report which sets out the key information showing what the opportunity is, and what is known about it. Potential venture team members, sponsors, investors and partners can consider this and decide whether to go ahead with further development and planning of the project. This information can then be used as the knowledge base for the business proposal, which will be explained in Chapter 6.

The opportunity evaluation report can take the form of a portfolio of information, structured under the following headings:

- *The opportunity*: from opportunity map and opportunity recognition model.
- *The market and customer information*: from market focus funnel.
- *The industry and competition*: from market focus funnel.
- *Impact of change*: from pentagon model.
- *Investment and return*: from pentagon model.

This covers the critical factors required to assess the viability and future prospects for the venture. A balanced decision on each opportunity can be taken, based on the relevant factors from these studies and other information. The evaluation reduces uncertainty through research and exploration, and can help to ensure that only higher potential opportunities that offer an acceptable degree of risk are progressed.

activity

- Refer back to the market focus funnel and the activity in Chapter 4.
- If you were able to complete the activity, use the information to start to put together an evaluation report for your opportunity, under the headings 'opportunity' and 'market and customer information'.
- If you did not complete the activity, do it now:
  - use the funnel approach to identify the target markets, available customer segments and target segment for your chosen opportunity
  - work through the questions
  - gather as much market information as you can about the target segment(s)
  - identify what information is missing, and how would you collect this, for example by primary market research.

You will return to and add further material to the opportunity evaluation report as you work through the activities in the chapter.

seven types of opportunity

There are many different types of opportunity, and it is essential for the entrepreneur to be aware of the nature of the opportunity and its characteristics. Each type of opportunity involves actual or potential market demand, as explored in the market research process you have completed. This section presents the seven general types of opportunity and summarises the advantages, disadvantages and critical points for exploration of each one. None of these types are intrinsically 'better' or 'worse' but they do have distinctive characteristics which need to be considered early in the evaluation process. Some opportunities will be combinations of two or possibly more types. However one type will normally be dominant, and the combination may make them more complex to manage and potentially more innovative and rewarding. The types are:

- knowledge
- technology
- product
- service or experience
- lifestyle
- physical resource
- trading and commodity.

Knowledge opportunities

Knowledge opportunities exist where specialist information, know-how or expertise can be applied to create value. The 'knowledge economy' arises from knowledge opportunity, and can be based on scientific, medical, market or other research, specialised skill or ability. Experienced professional and technical people often set up niche consultancy practices to use their specialist expertise, and these can be considered as knowledge opportunities. Knowledge resources can have major new markets, and knowledge opportunities are continually expanding. Universities, research institutes, consultancy practices, publishers and many others are players in the knowledge economy.

There are tensions between the drive for freely available information on the Internet and the business need to create commercial value by selling knowledge, and the related issues of ownership and protection of knowledge. These are unlikely to be resolved easily. For these reasons, successful exploitation of knowledge opportunity requires clear identification of the application of the knowledge, the target customers, and the value of the knowledge to the customer, and a business model which enables income to be generated and captured.

An example of knowledge opportunity is Experian, which started as the credit-checking department of the mail order retailer Great Universal Stores (GUS). GUS used the credit records of its customer base to develop Experian as a major business providing credit references and both personal and business financial information to a wide range of organisations. Experian has consistently innovated, extending its knowledge base and range of information services to become a market leader in financial, market and demographic information services.

Technology-based opportunities

Technology-based opportunities apply a technology to solve a problem, meet a need or create a new product or process. The technology may be physical, such as an engineering or manufacturing process or product, or a chemical, biological or information-based technology. Biotechnology, physical, material and earth science, organic and inorganic chemistry and computer programming are all examples of technology-based opportunity.

Whilst there are links and overlaps between the technology and the knowledge associated with it, in this case it is the application of technology through innovation which provides the opportunity. The development of the science and technology base continues to provide growing opportunities for technology-based innovation. The issues associated with technology-based opportunity again include the importance of securing intellectual property, for example through patenting, and of identifying both applications and potential customers.

Technology-based opportunity is usually highly skill and resource intensive, requiring significant research and development support and budgets. However the large organisations which have these resources often do not have the entrepreneurial approach required to exploit the opportunities and there is significant potential for innovation by entrepreneurs who can aim to develop opportunities and to gain partnership or support from corporate organisations. Recent years have seen significant growth in spin-off and spin-out companies from universities and research institutions to enable technology applications to be commercialised.

example

Wilson Turbopower

Many examples of technology-based opportunity have emerged from Massachusetts Institute of Technology (MIT). One interesting case is Wilson Turbopower, which started in 2001 as a spin-out company from MIT. This applies research on gas heat exchange technology using rotating discs carried out by Professor David Wilson, on which patents were taken out by MIT. The indexed-rotation regenerator heat exchanger called CEROTEX™ was the first major innovation in this field for 80 years and presents a disruptive, enabling technology with the potential to significantly improve the efficiency of heat exchange systems in industrial, power generating and military applications. To achieve this, major research and development was required to progress from the patented technology to actual working systems. A porous ceramic honeycomb rotating disc was developed, and a previous technical constraint, the durability of the circular seal of the disc, was overcome to eliminate friction between the disc and surrounding seal.

The unique attributes of Wilson Turbopower's technology include high temperature operation, high effectiveness, low pressure drop, relatively low cost, high tolerance to thermal cycling, long life, small regenerator size, light weight, and corrosion resistance. Wilson Turbopower identified energy, military and industrial sector applications as target markets for the heat exchange system, for example to increase the thermal efficiency of power-generating turbines, industrial refrigeration, and steel blast stoves.

www.wilsonturbopower.com

Product opportunities

Product opportunities are where existing products can be used to meet market demand as they are, or can be adapted by incremental innovation where new markets can be found. This means that significant product innovation may not be required, but market development is needed to research, prepare the market and promote the product. It is also necessary to be able to source the product, either by manufacturing or by buying-in. It is advantageous if the product is exclusive and sought-after, and the source of supply can be restricted or is intellectual property that can be protected through patents or design rights. Otherwise, if successful, it will quickly become a commodity product and be copied by other firms at lower cost; trading and commodity opportunities are covered below. Product opportunities of his kind are often best exploited by alert traders who are able to spot product/market opportunities, respond quickly, and move on as competition increases and prices fall.

An example from the fashion world is the Pashmina or cashmere scarf, sourced from Nepal as a rare and hand-crafted item spun from the wool of the chyanghra goat. These were introduced to the British fashion market as highly priced and exclusive fashion apparel during the 1990s, and this resulted in them being sought after and in great demand. Unfortunately the original importer was unable to protect her source of supply, and competitors were able to source, copy and import their own Pashminas, resulting in the item becoming a commodity within three years.

Service opportunities

Service opportunities exist where there is actual or potential demand for a service by business or public organisations, individuals or groups. The 'service economy' has grown steadily in the UK since the 1980s, when it overtook the manufacturing economy, and it covers a very wide range of activities. Services can include, for example, health, child and social care; office services; personal and social, telecommunications and computing, education and training; and financial, legal and property services. A service is intangible; there is no physical product, and whilst knowledge and technology are likely to be used in providing the service, they are generally not significant outputs from it. A service opportunity can include a 'new business model' which provides a service more effectively or at less cost than competitors.

There are a myriad of small and large service providers, from the freelance secretary/ personal administrator who runs a support service for self-employed consultants, to firms such as Regis who provide serviced office accommodation for small firms. There are clear advantages to service opportunities. Barriers to entry are often low, as is the level of investment required. By being innovative, spotting a gap in the market and working hard to build up a customer base through providing a personal, consistent level of service, a level of success can be achieved so long as there is scope to develop the market niche and the business is well managed.

Service businesses have much to commend them, and they are the backbone of the small business economy in developed countries such as the United States and United Kingdom. However most are destined to stay small (which may be all that the founders aimed for). There is a continuous flow of both start-ups and closures in this sector. Most service ideas are hard to protect and can be copied if the model is successful. The most important aspect of a service business is providing a high-quality experience which meets customers' needs. Service firms have to work hard to provide distinctive, memorable experiences and build up a repeat customer base. Many attempt to build recognisable brands and grow through such strategies as franchising, but few break through to become large businesses. It is often hard for a service business to grow significantly. Many exist because of the founder's ability to provide or supervise the work directly, but they may be unable to make the transition into managing others to provide the service or run the business day-to-day.

The economics of the service firm depend on the net profit margin between the sales revenue and the fixed and variable costs, in which staff costs are one of the largest elements. Competition tends to force margins down and it is difficult to build up retained profits to grow organically or by acquiring other businesses without external investment. Service businesses which grow significantly tend to be those in an industry sector which is growing rapidly, or those with entrepreneurial management who are able to gain external investment to fund a growth strategy. The Fascia Mania case in Chapter 4 is a good example of this.

Lifestyle opportunities

Lifestyle opportunity is a sub-set of the service sector, but has grown so rapidly that it merits its own category. Lifestyle opportunity is where customers are provided with an experience which makes their life easier or pleasanter. The fields where such opportunities arise include leisure, tourism, hospitality, culture and entertainment. These are all areas of discretionary expenditure, where people wish to consume or experience sports, food and drink, films, music, drama, dance and other pleasures. It should not be confused with what is sometimes described as a 'lifestyle business', which an owner-manager runs to finance his or her lifestyle rather than to grow.

Advantages of lifestyle opportunities are that in a growing economy demand increases as people have additional money to spend, although a downturn will reduce consumer spending. Consumer fashion and taste play a major part and can be fickle, with people becoming bored with an experience and moving on. Businesses such as restaurants are especially prone to this, but others such as personal fitness gyms and dance studios can have a more durable appeal if they meet their customers' expectations for service and innovate in ways they appreciate. The concept of 'cultural diffusion' applies to the appeal which creative and lifestyle businesses need to offer their customers, and this is developed in Chapter 8. Repeat business, referral and word of mouth promotion is vital for most lifestyle opportunities.

There are many examples of lifestyle opportunity businesses, one is the 'Blockbuster' home video rental chain. This has grown on the proposition of offering the widest range of visual media products (video, DVD and computer games) for rental in urban/suburban outlets, and of being able to meet the demand for a wide selection of recent and older film releases of all genres. They have made many independent video rental stores irrelevant, but in turn may be threatened by the growth of the postal DVD rental service and online movies.

Physical resource opportunities

Physical resource opportunities include the exploitation of land, water or naturally occurring resources. This includes extracting basic resources, such as oil, gas and minerals. It also includes land use such as agricultural production, and land, property and real estate development. Although this is a wide range of types of opportunity, in all cases the source is the ability to create value based on a natural or physical resource, either renewable (such as wind power and agriculture) or finite (such as minerals).

Advantages of physical resource opportunities include the increasing demand and pressure for access to and consumption of resources as the world population, energy needs and economic development increase. Greater innovation in the exploitation of resources enhances opportunity and the value created, as in the controversial area of genetically modified crop production. However, advances in the technology of food production have led to declining incomes for many farmers worldwide, and a challenge for many rural economies is how to add value and diversify to reduce their dependence on economically marginal food production, as shown in the Tyrrell's case in Chapter 1. Physical resource opportunities tend to involve long-term investment, with significant capital employed for long periods in land ownership, resource extraction or renewable power generation. Risk management is always a major factor in physical resource businesses, whether caused by natural factors such as weather or geology, or economic and social factors such as falling demand, changes in taste, or opposition to a particular policy or practice, such as mineral extraction.

The rapid growth in the production and consumption of bottled drinking water is an example of physical resource-based opportunity. In most developed countries, tap water meets acceptable standards for drinking, yet sales of much more profitable bottled water continue to grow rapidly for reasons of fashion, taste, convenience and perceived health benefits.

Trading and commodity opportunities

Trading and commodity opportunities are based on buying and selling in relation to market conditions of supply and demand. They encompass a wide range of trading opportunities, including wholesale and retail, energy (gas, oil, electricity), chemicals, raw materials, semi-manufactured items, food and agricultural produce, and any commodity which can be bought, traded, or sold, including securities, currency, stocks and purchase options. Trading requires the ability to predict and act on market trends, with exposure to risks of changing market demand and pricing. The potential for profit can be very high, but excellent information and significant reserves are required to support trading activity and to cover potential losses.

Online trading has revolutionised and expanded trading opportunities. eBay shows the way in which individuals can trade, creating a market and online business in the most specialised commodities. One example of trading opportunity was Enron, which owned a national gas pipeline network in the United States. The CEO, Kenneth Lay, recognised the pipeline network was an opportunity to buy gas where it was cheap and sell where it was needed. He created spot markets for energy, financial models for trading in energy futures and promoted deregulation which changed the industry. For a period it paid off. Enron was named one of the "most admired" companies by *Fortune* magazine and ranked No. 1 in innovation. It collapsed through over-expansion, lack of financial control, corporate mismanagement and fraud on a grand scale.

This section has discussed the different types of opportunity in general terms. Specific opportunities may overlap between two categories, or possibly more. Use Table 5.1 to consider the opportunity you are exploring and write your responses to the following points:

● Which of these type(s) of opportunity do you think it is?
● If it falls into more than one category, which is the dominant type?
● What do you think are the advantages, disadvantages and specific points for exploration of your opportunity in relation to this type?

TABLE 5.1 **Types of opportunity grid**

Type of opportunity	Advantages	Disadvantages	Points to explore
Knowledge			
Technology			
Product			
Service			
Lifestyle			
Physical resource			
Trading/ commodity			

assessing the environment for your opportunity

The developed world is an opportunity-rich environment. In economically less developed countries, there are also many opportunities but access to the resources, technology and other means of exploiting them can be much more limited and challenging. This section summarises the main factors which affect the context, or 'bigger picture' within which specific opportunities are explored and which are likely to be outside the entrepreneur's control. It is necessary to assess the relationships between economic, environmental, political, social, technological forces and entrepreneurial activity. You may have done a STEEP or PESTEC analysis on a Business Studies course; this approach is similar, but is focused on analysis of the environment for the opportunity. These factors may in themselves create opportunities and will either positively or adversely affect the ability to exploit the opportunity.

Economic factors

These include the economic stability of the country or market, the conditions of economic growth or recession, predictability or volatility in demand, pricing, level of inflation, exchange rates of the currency to be used, and availability and cost of investment or loan finance. These factors can differ markedly between neighbouring countries, such as South Africa, which has a stable and growing economy, and Zimbabwe which has experienced volatile economic factors and has a virtually untradeable currency, which makes business management very challenging.

Environmental factors

The natural and physical environment includes factors such as climate change (increasing unpredictability of weather patterns), lack of rain and water shortage or excessive rainfall, and availability of natural and physical resources. Geographical factors, including the concentration of population in urban areas or distribution in rural districts, transport and communications such as road networks, airports, fast rail links, telephone and data networks, and levels of congestion may all be significant factors. The cost of transport, either through delays caused by congestion or charges such as tolls for road use, is increasingly important but may present new opportunities for alternative logistics, communication and distribution businesses.

Political factors

Political factors include the level of political stability, and the extent of support for enterprise development at the local, regional, national and supranational levels. The level of legislation and regulation and the ways in which this is administered, the transparency of government processes and the presence or absence of corruption in government are all relevant and have a major bearing on the ease and attractiveness of operating a business venture. The time taken to start a new business in different countries varies considerably, from less than a day in the UK to several weeks even in other EU states. Certain countries are much more conducive to enterprise than others; registering and starting a new business in France or Germany, for example, is relatively bureaucratic and time-consuming when compared with the United States or UK, caused by regulation and procedures which were not designed with free enterprise in mind and have the effect of reducing opportunity entrepreneurship. Factors such as political influence and even official corruption can be significant in some post-Soviet and developing-world states.

Social factors

The cultural acceptability of entrepreneurship is changing markedly in many societies, but this is only one factor. Others include demographics; many developed societies have ageing populations, in contrast to the 'youth' of many developing countries. Health and diseases such as HIV/AIDS are having a major effect on many African and Asian countries. Levels of education, including literacy, numeracy and language, are important factors. Generational change brings changes in taste, fashion, media awareness and use of communications technologies in all countries, providing new market opportunities for such products and services.

For example, when the ten accession states joined the European Union in 2004, the levels of education, linguistic fluency and enterprising culture in some of the new states such as Estonia and Lithuania, especially among young people who had grown up in the post-Soviet era, were appreciably greater than in some of the existing EU members. The potential for entrepreneurial development either within those countries or by their citizens in other EU states is very significant. The development of Finland's economy in recent years illustrates the potential for relatively small states with high levels of education and entrepreneurial culture as they emerge from state control. It is increasingly clear that the high social costs, employment protection, legislation and taxation levels in some older European states, make them relatively less competitive and attractive for entrepreneurship, and reform is needed. The EU 'Lisbon Agenda' set out an intention to create a much more open and enterprising climate within the EU in which entrepreneurship and innovation would drive economic growth, yet in the period between 2000 and 2006, little progress was made in achieving the desired economic changes.

Technological factors

These factors include the level of technological development in the market. They include: access to communication media such as Internet, broadband and mobile phones; the support for technological development and innovation such as research institutes and universities with relevant expertise; enablers and constraints to the implementation of technology. Industry clusters and networks are major factors in technological development, and the role of these is considered later in this chapter.

The interaction between time and technology is important. There is a 'product lifecycle' between innovation and obsolescence, and in certain economies and industries this can be very short; for example fashion drives rapid innovation in Japanese mobile phone technology. Other markets have different rates of obsolescence for different products, so that product lifecycles may be longer in less developed markets such as Africa where utility rather than fashion is important.

Summary of contextual and environmental factors

Economic

- How could economic changes affect the opportunity – e.g.:
  - currency/exchange rate fluctuations
  - economic growth or decline in demand; boom or recession
  - strength of demand for key resources, e.g. people, land, materials, fuel
  - taxation.

Environmental

- Restriction and cost of resources, e.g. fuel, waste disposal.
- Transport, planning, environmental compliance.

Political

- Stability or volatility.
- Political support for entrepreneurship.
- Legal framework, impact of future legislation, and its effect on business.
- Harmonisation of laws or standards.

Social and cultural

- What are the relevant demographic trends?
- What cultural influences affect it? e.g. fashion; lifestyle; media?
- Acceptability of entrepreneurial activity

Technological

- How is new technology affecting the industry?
- What are the key innovations now and in the near future?
- How is the Internet affecting the market?

activity

The impacts of these factors will differ according to the type of opportunity. A physical-resource-based opportunity will be especially affected by environmental factors, for example. These factors may enable or constrain the opportunity. Some factors may not apply in a significant way to a given opportunity.

Assess the impact of economic, environmental, political, social and technological factors on the opportunity you have identified, using Table 5.2 to log your responses.

TABLE 5.2 **Environmental analysis of the opportunity**

Factor	Advantages	Disadvantages	Points to explore
Economy			
Environment			
Political			
Social			
Technology			

opportunity assessment and decision making

Clearly some opportunities are 'better' than others, and it is necessary to have methods for comparing, assessing and evaluating opportunities to enable the most attractive ones to be selected. This means that we can screen and select opportunities to identify those with higher or lower potential and use this information to decide which to invest effort and resources in, and which to avoid unless we can find ways of increasing their attractiveness as an investment of financial and entrepreneurial resources. This section introduces a framework for opportunity assessment and evaluation called the pentagon model, because it includes five dimensions. The assessment questionnaire and further information on its use is included in the toolbox.

The pentagon model: five key dimensions of opportunity potential

These five key dimensions show how the potential of any opportunity can be assessed. By using these, ventures can be evaluated as investment propositions and decisions reached on their attractiveness – initially by the entrepreneur, and by other investors. The five decision-making dimensions, which are called the pentagon model of opportunity assessment, are shown in Table 5.3 and described below. The information necessary to complete the questionnaire in the toolkit should be available from the activities already completed.

TABLE 5.3 **Five dimensions of opportunity**

The five dimensions of opportunity	
Investment of resource	from none to high
Risk and uncertainty	from certainty to unpredictability
Return and value created	from none to high
Impact of innovation and change	from none to great
Timescale	from now into the future

Investment

Resources must be invested to realise any type of opportunity. The nature of the investment is likely to be a combination of the following:

- Financial: capital belonging to the entrepreneur; venture capital from an investor; equity or loan finance. This may be used for start-up capital, to fund working capital, or for business expansion, and may be invested in fixed assets, product or market development, or working expenses prior to break-even.
- Non-financial resources such as productive capacity, staff time, and capability. These represent an 'opportunity cost' since the resources could be used alternatively for a different reward.
- Intangible resources such as knowledge, information, expertise, intellectual property rights.
- Reputation, such as branding, partnering, social capital and credibility.

The size of the investment as well as its nature is significant, and needs to be calculated: how much is required, over what period? What proportion of the entrepreneur's own resources does this represent, and what additional resources are required? If so, who will contribute them, and on what terms? Finally, what does the investment actually buy? Is it tangible assets which have a disposal value or simply an opportunity? This leads on to the concept of risk. Intangible factors such as branding can have considerable value: for example, a Walt Disney-endorsed cartoon toy product will have much greater market attraction than one without such endorsement.

Risk and uncertainty

It is essential to evaluate the degree of risk involved in exploiting an opportunity. Risk arises from uncertainty, so if complete certainty should exist, there is no risk; conversely, complete unpredictability of outcome produces very high risk. In a financial market, a UK or US government bond has a guaranteed rate of return and offers much greater certainty and hence less risk than, for example, a 'junk bond' or newly floated biotechnology stock where the outcome is highly uncertain and there is a high risk. Entrepreneurs are often stereotyped as risk-takers, but this has little bearing in fact; successful entrepreneurs seek to minimise and avoid risk as far as possible, preferring other investors to carry the financial exposure. However entrepreneurs frequently operate in conditions of rapid change and uncertainty which give rise to unpredictable outcomes. Also, where the venture innovates and introduces change into the marketplace, it introduces new risk factors because the outcome is to some extent unpredictable. The aim is to identify what factors lead to uncertainty, and how far these can be reduced.

Identifying the risk factors

The variable factors which cause risk need to be identified. They may include:

- *Knowledge*: lack of information about market factors and likely demand.
- *The economy*: fluctuations in macro-economic factors such as market stability, currency exchange and interest rates.
- *Technology*: will the technology work as planned?
- *Financial factors*: are the financial costings and plans realistic and achievable?
- *Competition*: how will competitors respond?
- *Customers*: will they buy and pay as expected?
- *Supply chain*: will suppliers and distributors deliver as expected?
- *Human elements*: does the venture team have the management skills, experience, credibility and expertise to manage the venture, based on their track records?

The potential risks to the venture should be identified and then be divided into *controllable* and *uncontrollable*. The former are those that can be reduced or eliminated. Examples include lack of market or product information, where focused research can take place to fill gaps; technology which can be demonstrated and tested; customer, supplier or distributor dependability, where research, credit rating and negotiation can take place; and skills gaps where staff recruitment can reduce risk. *Uncontrollable* risks are a function of factors in the economic and market environment together with the completely unpredictable. For each of these there is a need to establish:

- How serious is the risk – could it destroy the business?
- How likely is it?
- What are likely to be the earliest warning signs of the risk arising?
- What contingency plans can be drawn up to respond to the event?
- How can the effects of the risk on the business be minimised or insured against?

In these ways the risks to the venture can be established and either they can be prevented or their effects can be assessed and plans to deal with them made. But risk can never be predicted or eliminated entirely and managing risk is an integral aspect of entrepreneurial management, which will be addressed in Chapter 7.

Return and value created

The return on the investment, or reward, may vary from nothing – a total loss of the investment – to high, which may be a return of several hundred per cent. An assessment of the acceptability of the return should take into account the following factors:

- The amount invested; it may be acceptable to lose a small investment completely.
- Return in relation to risk: the higher the risk, the higher the return which will normally be expected.
- The timescale over which the return will come. Risk tends to increase further ahead in time.
- The form of the return, e.g. as capital growth of the investment or as a flow of income. An asset such as property or equity in a company might be expected to show both capital growth through a rise in its value and an income flow from dividends or rentals.
- The exit strategy from the opportunity, e.g. as liquidation of assets, sale as a going concern, flotation, value anticipated and timescale for exit.

The matrix in Table 5.4 shows the basic dimensions of risk and reward. In this simple model, clearly position 1 is the optimum, offering a high return at low risk. Positions 2 and 3 are both less attractive, 2 offering low risk but at low return and 3 offering high return but at high risk. Position 4 is clearly to be avoided since the prospects are of high risk and low return. Such a two-dimensional model may be used for personal investment decisions, but it is of limited application in appraising complex business opportunities, where many other factors, such as the characteristics of the industry sector, apply.

TABLE 5.4 **Risk and reward**

	Seek to increase ⟶	
High risk	4	3
		Seek to decrease
Low risk	2	1
	Low return	High return

Impact of innovation and change

Exploiting an opportunity both creates change and is affected by other changes in the market environment. Innovating and introducing a completely new concept or product, such as the pioneering online retailer Amazon, or the digital pocket camera, introduce fundamental changes into the market. Disruptive innovations such as these change the value creation process of the industry, making existing products or businesses obsolete, creating new markets and altering the power dynamics of the industry. An enhancement to a current product is a moderate, incremental change, and a replication of something that already exists represents little or no change.

It is necessary to assess the impact of change caused by the opportunity. Will exploiting it drive and lead a change process, or is it passive, causing little change but being affected by external change? Strategic and disruptive innovation can reduce competitors' power and create new markets. A process innovation which enables a new business to offer lower prices than existing suppliers will attract existing and probably new customers, thus changing customer expectations and behaviour; the introduction of low-cost air carriers has expanded the air travel market, polarising customer expectations between low-cost, no-frills service and high-cost standard service. A disruptive innovation may make previous standard products obsolete, as with the impact of e-mail on the fax machine. The impact of such changes can be felt throughout the supply chain, affecting suppliers, resellers, customers and sources of finance, as well as competitors. A new venture which offers something different also invites copying and retaliation from competitors.

The impact of introducing innovation and change into the market is to some extent unpredictable, because they increase risk rather than reducing it. Any business is also subject to external changes such as macro-economic factors and market trends that influence customer behaviour; supply and demand changes leading to price fluctuations; technological advance; and changes in the legislation, regulation and so on, which can be assessed under the heading of risk.

Timescale

The timescale for the venture needs to be assessed. Achieving the right timing is often a critical factor in entrepreneurial decision making, and points to consider here include:

● Is the timing of entry leading 'the rest' of the market, which may give an advantage but also require greater investment? Is it entering the market at the same time as competitors, or is it trailing others into a mature or declining market?
● What is the duration of the opportunity – from short to long term?
● What is the lead time needed to enter the market?
● When will the investment achieve a return?

Return and timescale are connected, because the essential distinction is between rapid profit opportunities which may be quite short term, and longer-term businesses which will take longer to establish and to achieve a return. Someone considering a soft drinks business could simply aim to buy and sell cold drinks to people in the summer as a profit opportunity, or might see a longer-term opportunity to offer new flavours and types of drinks with an innovative, appealing brand.

The return on the investment together with the expected timescale needs to be established as realistically as possible. 'Best case', 'most likely' and 'worst case' scenarios can be built into these forecasts to forecast:

● the investment required over the timescale

- the sales revenue to be generated as a cash stream and when this starts
- the gross and net profit margins on sales
- the break-even point
- the return on capital employed
- growth in the asset value of the investment.

The time period is highly significant. It may be that in establishing a new venture that a loss is made in year one, requiring further working capital, break-even is achieved in year two, and a profit is made from year three. The longer the investment period, the higher the rate of return needs to be. The nature of the gain to the investor needs to be clear, in terms of returns from trading profits and growth in the value of the investment, which can be realised through an exit strategy and sale of the equity at some point. Most businesses take longer to launch and consume more start-up capital than projected, as will be shown in Chapter 6 on venture planning. Computer spreadsheets make forecasting straightforward so long as accurate and realistic data can be obtained. The five dimensions of the pentagon model are shown in Figure 5.1, and can be used to evaluate the prospects for successfully exploiting an opportunity and therefore to decide whether the opportunity is an attractive one. The decision-making process is complex and it is likely that almost every entrepreneur would weigh up a venture in a different way. The process cannot be simplified to a bivariate '2 x 2' matrix such as 'risk related to return'

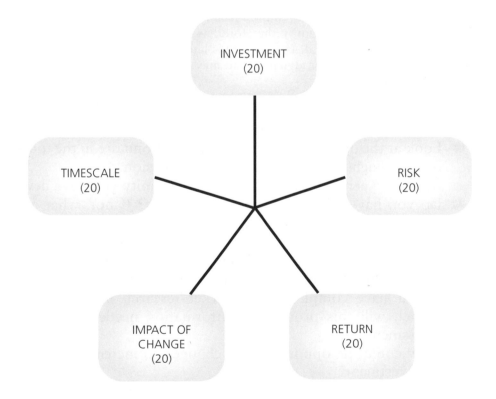

FIGURE 5.1 **The pentagon model of opportunity assessment**

alone. Therefore, having a standard method has advantages because it enables opportunities to be compared, and different approaches or business models applied to the same opportunity. The dimensions can be changed, so for example a social enterprise using this approach might well modify the 'impact of change' dimension to 'impact on community'. The questionnaire in the toolkit enables each dimension to be scored on a 20-point scale.

Using the questionnaire, a profile can be drawn on the pentagon model. Each dimension is given a scale from 0–20. Zero is 'none' and 20 is 'high'. Any given opportunity can then be given a series of values along the score. These in themselves will involve a series of objective (factual) and subjective, interpretative judgements being made, involving available information, past experience, prospective judgement, and so on. They may be relatively unscientific, but they do form judgements which would be made, often on the basis of 'gut feel', intuition or experience, by an entrepreneur. The scores along each dimension then represent a distinctive pentagon.

Opportunities that have characteristics of greater risk, higher reward, bigger investment, larger scale change and medium/longer-term timescales can be described as more 'aggressive' or ambitious in the venture strategies which would be required to launch them, and will have a large profile when drawn on the pentagon. Those with lower degrees of investment, risk, reward, change and short-medium timescales can be described as more 'defensive', with a tightly grouped profile on the pentagon. There are also many combinations which have elements of both.

A defensive profile, scoring low in most aspects, would not require sophisticated entrepreneurial strategy or skills. An aggressive profile, scoring higher, indicates that a strategy to exploit it would require much more advanced management capability to be successful. Each opportunity therefore has its own profile, representing a view at that moment of its potential. If a venture is launched to exploit the opportunity, each of the variables has its own dynamic and may shift in either direction at any stage in the life of the venture.

activity

- Look at the opportunity assessment questionnaire in the toolkit and read through the questions in each dimension.
- Apply the pentagon model to the opportunity you have developed.
- Do you have all the information required? If not, what additional information would you need to gather to be able to answer the questions? You can either make estimates, and complete it again when you have more reliable information, or you can work on it as you develop the opportunity over the next few chapters.
- If you have completed the market research in the market focus funnel, will this provide the information needed to complete the assessment?
- How could the opportunity be changed to increase its attraction as an investment?
- Add the completed pentagon to your opportunity evaluation report.

In search of the better business model

Within existing industries, there are opportunities to introduce new business models which create superior value or cost efficiency. Over the past ten years many of these have used Internet technology to radically reduce transaction costs. Examples of new business models which have challenged or transformed existing industries include Glassesdirect in selling spectacles online, ING in personal savings banking, Dell in personal and business computers, and Ryanair in the low-cost airline sector. There are also many examples of new business models being introduced as a key aspect of an innovative service or product which did not already exist. Examples of these include eBay in creating new markets for online auctions and trading, Skype in providing Internet telephony, and Betfair in online gambling.

What these businesses have in common is their success in creating a business model which was much more cost-competitive than those used by existing players in the industry, and using this to offer customers a service with distinctive features – usually cheaper, possibly also faster, more convenient, personalised, or with features that existing providers simply did not offer. Whilst these are successful examples, there are many cases of less successful or failed attempts to introduce a new business model, and the model itself should be seen as one highly important aspect in the overall business concept, rather than the 'whole deal'.

Here are suggestions for recognising opportunities for a better business model:

- Look for industries which are dominated by large, high-price and high-profit operators who provide indifferent service.
- Analyse the business process being used: where is the value being created for the customer? Where are the costs being incurred?

example

Example: Glassesdirect.co.uk

James Murray Wells recognised that high-street chains of opticians were charging £150 for spectacle frames and lenses which actually cost a fraction of the price. They were providing eye examinations and prescriptions at a fixed cost which encouraged customers in, and then charged a high profit margin for the supply of the frames and lenses or contact lenses to support their expensive retail premises and staff costs. In 2004, Wells set up Glasses Direct to offer a low cost alternative and sell glasses from around £15.

Glassesdirect uses Internet technology to radically reduce transaction costs and offer much lower prices to customers. The website asks customers for their eye prescription from an optician and offers a wide range of spectacle frames and lens options. At their central laboratory they assemble frames and lenses sourced direct from the manufacturers and send the finished spectacles to the customer, with credit card payment online. The customer can save as much as 60 per cent of the cost in comparison with high-street opticians. By eliminating the premises and staff costs, stripping out all unnecessary costs, and trading on the requirement that opticians had to provide a prescription that customers could use online, Glassesdirect pioneered a new, low-cost business model which took the competition by surprise – and about which they could do little to respond.

- How can you provide what the customer really wants whilst eliminating as much of the costs as possible?
- Think radically about how essential activities can be provided at less cost, for example:
  - online and automated rather than by people
  - using advanced technology more effectively to deliver cost and speed or service performance improvements
  - offshore in a low-cost economy
  - in bulk by a specialist provider.
- Get the customer to do the work rather than providing the service for them
- Develop the new business model, comparing it with the competition to find vital features where it provides superior cost efficiency, and other features the customer will value over existing providers.

Creating a business model is demonstrated in Chapter 6.

Assessing high and low-value opportunities: the business opportunity model

The aim of opportunity assessment and evaluation is to distinguish between opportunities with high potential for value creation and those with lower potential, which are less attractive investments for effort and resource. The term 'value' means the prospective return from the venture, which may include these forms of value:

- profit stream and share dividend
- return on capital employed
- value of the business, e.g. through valuation of shares and prospective exit strategy
- ability to lead or dominate the market
- value of assets such as brand, intellectual property or innovation
- creative, community, environmental or social value added.

There can be no one way of establishing the potential return with a high degree of certainty. Instead, tools are used which give a degree of predictive judgement based on experience. Even venture capital funds with extensive experience in investing in many enterprises know most of the investment decisions they make will turn out to be ones that, with hindsight, they would not have taken because the ventures fail or under-perform. Their funds gain an investment return from the small number of businesses which perform very well and aim to exceed the losses made on the poor performers. In assessing opportunities, prospective judgements are made about the potential for venture growth and success, based on many variables, and aiming to reduce risk and uncertainty as far as possible. But judgement and intuition still entail an element of risk that is inevitable and comes with the territory.

There is clearly no simple way to find the best business opportunities, only tools which can better inform decision making and planning. The following model, the business opportunity or 'hexagon' model, is based on research with entrepreneurs running successful, high-growth ventures in the United States and UK, to find out how they chose between high-value and lower-value opportunities (Rae, 2004c).

The hexagon model shown in Figure 5.2 consists of six decision-making clusters, each of which includes a number of specific factors which can be used to assess an opportunity, enabling you to judge whether it is high value (as judged by profit and growth potential)

FIGURE 5.2 **The business opportunity hexagon model**

or lower value. An outline is included here and the full version is included in the toolkit. It is different in nature from the pentagon model because it is based on 30 decision-making constructs, or scales, in which an opportunity is considered to have either high or low potential in relation to each construct. Its application is in making decisions on venture strategy, especially on which factors are most likely to produce a higher potential rather than lower-value opportunity.

The factors in each of the six clusters are listed in Table 5.5 (overleaf). In reading through these factors, you might think that they are 'obvious', because they are based on the decision-making factors which entrepreneurs actually use. The full model enables the reader to judge whether an opportunity is characteristic of higher or lower-value potential on each of the relevant factors, noting that all of the six clusters and some, but not necessarily all, of the factors are relevant to every opportunity.

activity

- Read through the opportunity recognition model in the toolkit.
- Score your opportunity using the model.
- In which of the six clusters does it appear to have high potential?
- In which clusters does it appear to have low potential?
- Overall, what does this indicate about the potential for your opportunity?
- What new factors did the model prompt you to consider?
- How could you modify the opportunity to enhance its high-value potential?

TABLE 5.5 **Factors in the opportunity recognition hexagon**

1. **Market potential**
   1. Market growth – ability to access markets of growing size and value
   2. Customer base – extent of known, identifiable customers in defined markets
   3. Customer reliance – degree of customer reliance on the product
   4. Customer interaction – quality and compatibility of customer relationships
   5. Partnering – strength of supplier and technology networks
   6. Competition – advantages and strengths in relation to competitors

2. **Innovation**
   1. Innovation leadership – use of prior experience to lead the market
   2. Innovation providing a solution to a customer-defined problem
   3. Use of differentiated technology providing performance and cost benefits
   4. Strength of intellectual property protection – vulnerability to copying
   5. Speed and likelihood of being first to market
   6. Feasibility of implementation – extent of challenges to be overcome

3. **Strategy**
   1. Business growth – purpose, scope and strategy to create and grow a business
   2. Strategic options – single or multiple options for strategy and exit
   3. Value creation – profit margin and cash generation
   4. Innovative business model – superiority to existing models

4. **People**
   1. Chief executive officer (CEO) – ability to show leadership and innovation
   2. Management team effectiveness – skills, compatibility and motivation
   3. Contextual experience – ability to use prior experience and knowledge of industry
   4. Staff capability – ability to recruit experienced people from the industry

5. **Investment**
   1. Investment-reward: financial return and profitability in relation to investment
   2. Investor attraction: based on projected increase in equity value
   3. Risk: acceptability of loss in worst case scenario
   4. Commercial viability, break-even and predictability of cash flow
   5. Timescale: short/long-term income stream and exit strategy

6. **Learning**
   These factors feature the entrepreneur's individual learning in relation to opportunities
   They inevitably vary between individuals, and those included are illustrative
   1. Independent control of business direction
   2. Personal vision and confidence in business potential
   3. Incremental learning – being able to find 'what works'
   4. Intuition – knowing what is the 'right thing to do'
   5. Ethics – ability to practise ethical framework and values

The opportunity recognition hexagon is a guide to help in making decisions on business opportunities and the strategies for exploiting them. By paying attention to the relevant factors, aspects of a business idea which might have been overlooked and which might either strengthen or weaken it can be addressed. Using it as a thinking tool can help you decide where best to invest limited time and resources, and how opportunities can be reconfigured to create higher potential value. It can also identify (and help you steer away from) lower-value opportunities which are unlikely to provide a satisfactory return.

example

Case study: Nantero: a small company pioneering nano-electrical switch technology

Nantero is a nanotechnology company at the forefront of using carbon nanotubes for the development of next-generation semiconductor devices. Carbon nanotubes have the quality of conducting electricity combined with strength and flexibility. The wall of a carbon nanotube is only one carbon atom thick and the tube diameter is approximately 100,000 times smaller than a human hair. Nantero is developing NRAM™, a high density non-volatile Random Access Memory using carbon nanotubes as the active memory elements. This will provide a universal memory product to replace all existing forms of memory, such as DRAM, SRAM and flash memory. The potential applications include the ability to enable instant-on computers and to replace the memory in devices such as cell phones, MP3 players, digital cameras and PDAs. The value of these applications adds up to over $100 billion in potential revenue.

Nantero will license complete technology transfer packages to enable manufacturers to produce, market and sell its nanotube-based semiconductor products for use in both stand-alone and embedded memory applications. The packages will include a process module and the associated process knowledge, intellectual property rights and the necessary nanotube materials.

The co-founders of Nantero are Dr Thomas Rueckes, the Chief Scientific Officer, who is a former Harvard research fellow; Dr Brent Segal, Chief Operating Officer; and Greg Schmergel, President and CEO. They combine corporate, entrepreneurial, scientific and high-technology expertise. NRAM was invented by Dr Rueckes, whose pioneering design takes advantage of the unique properties of carbon nanotubes while cleverly integrating those nanotubes with traditional semiconductor technologies for immediate manufacturability.

Nantero has innovation leadership in a highly competitive field and is aiming to be first to market by managing implementation speedily and overcoming technical challenges 'so that competitors become customers'. The business is creating and exploiting a strong base of intellectual property, both legally and technically hard to copy, including over 80 patent applications, a growing number of which have been granted. This will be applied in a series of follow-on products and is focused on solving industry problems through differentiated technology, making it easy to sell to customers by offering an optimal combination of performance and cost benefits.

Nantero has selected a large market showing potential for exponential revenue growth. It will create long-term customer reliance and convergence, by entering partnerships to licence the technology to major manufacturers. Strategically, it has set out to create a high-value, high margin product from the various options available. This is expected to provide a high financial return on investment over a long timescale; with over $30 million invested in the venture, the return is attractive to investors, with well-defined and acceptable degrees of risks.

The CEO's background in starting two previous technology-based companies has provided important prior learning and enabled him to develop skills in leading an innovative business with an effective management team. Nantero has set out to recruit the best people in a young industry with a limited talent pool of highly skilled expertise, creating a further entry barrier for competitors.

www.nantero.com

activity

- Use the opportunity assessment (pentagon) in the toolkit to assess the attractiveness of the opportunity Nantero is targeting. You will need to estimate answers to those questions where you do not have complete information.
- Use the opportunity selection (hexagon) to identify whether this is a higher or lower-value opportunity.
- What do these assessments suggest about the overall strength and attractiveness of opportunity identified by Nantero?

locating clusters, networks and resources for opportunity development

The entrepreneurial economy operates in a highly social, networked way. Entrepreneurs and firms participate intensely in different kinds of social activity, including buying and selling, collaborating, competing, and copying. Industry clusters are based on groups of companies in a single industry being closely co-located and operating interdependently, by competing, co-existing and collaborating. In the process they develop a skilled workforce, attract specialist suppliers and a social and support network, so that particular regions become known as centres of expertise or 'the place to go' for a particular service or technology. Examples include the high-technology area of 'silicon valley' close to Stanford, California; the biotech industry around the University of Cambridge, UK; and the software industry in Bangalore, India.

The notion of clusters is based in part on the theory of 'industrial districts' first developed by the economist Alfred Marshall, which described an intense concentration of firms in specific and related industrial trades. For example, in the Black Country of the UK West Midlands, each town specialised in a particular product: Willenhall in locks, Tipton in chains, Walsall in leather aprons for the metalworkers. The industrial district concept has progressed and been updated beyond being simply geographical, with a particular emphasis on the role of social networks and the connections between networks and innovation (Pittaway et al, 2004). Lave and Wenger (1991), in writing about 'communities of practice', described these types of social networks as communities where participation, the creation of social identity, and social learning are important processes. Learning, the exchange of information and ideas, and innovation, can all occur more rapidly in clusters because of the improved available of information through social connections, when compared with firms working in isolation.

These ideas are highly relevant to the exploration of opportunity. One traditional stereotype of the 'the entrepreneur' has been as the 'lone wolf' – the individualistic, solitary achiever who builds a business independent of society or social connection (Ogbor, 2000). Increasingly this is a myth, neither valid or effective in building a business, since entrepreneurship is an intensely social and networked activity which depends for its existence on social networking (Birley, 1986). Industry clusters attract intermediaries, such as investors and financiers, specialist experts, technologists and consultants, legal and accounting professionals, as well as building up a social capital of experienced and well-connected company owners and managers. It has been found that the same people can be involved in forming and investing in a succession of businesses over a long period, and this 'genealogy' factor can be traced in clusters such as Cambridge, UK.

The cluster and the social network can be seen as a spawning-ground and hatchery for business opportunities. The concentration of related firms creates new opportunities, attracts customers and stimulates interaction between innovations and the resources needed to develop them. The social connections mean that people work with, find, talk to and develop ideas with other, like-minded or compatible people. This socialisation means that people get acquainted, form human bonds of friendship and trust (as well as rivalry, dislike and distrust) and the formation of new business ventures occurs. So clusters and networks can be seen as 'hotspots' for finding opportunities, resources, and the human, social and financial capital for entrepreneurship. It is easier to start a computer software business where there is already a cluster of similar firms, and probably easier to attract staff and customers, than when starting in 'virgin territory' where the long-term growth prospects may be greater.

However, some clusters and industrial districts are more supportive to entrepreneurship than others. The clusters of hi-tech companies around Boston and San Francisco in the United States, for example, resulted from such factors as the presence of research-intensive universities, including MIT and Stanford, with a high rate of producing industry-disrupting innovations and spin-out companies. Major customers such as defence industries or film studios stimulate cluster growth and these areas have become intensive and self-sustaining centres of innovation, entrepreneurship and business growth.

The concentration of a particular industry in a district does not necessarily lead to such activity. Many industrial districts in the UK and Europe have declined and shrunk or died, including centres of coalmining, steel making, shipbuilding, textile production, heavy engineering and so on. These became uncompetitive in cost and productivity, primary resources ran out, they failed to innovate, renew or migrate into new technologies, and market needs changed faster than the industries. State ownership or regulation often played a part in their decline.

For the new venture, assessing the opportunities, resource and support available in a cluster is important. Among the indicators to look for are the numbers of new-firm starts, the survival rate of longer established firms, the attraction of new clients and investors, and the productivity of innovation (e.g. number of patents registered) as well as the presence of entrepreneur networks and social connections, and enterprise-friendly universities, research or enterprise development agencies. This connects with the concept of the negotiated enterprise and the role of industry networks, which were explored in relation to entrepreneurial learning in Chapter 3.

It is much harder to work on an opportunity in isolation than it is when support, ideas and resources can be gained from participating in a relevant industry or social network. New entrepreneurs often fear they may lose their business ideas by networking, but generally there is much more to be gained by locating and participating in such activity. Previous experience and relationships in an industry can be of great assistance, and this is where the student or person with less experience is at a disadvantage and therefore needs to work harder to develop a base of contacts.

This aspect of opportunity exploration is concerned with the social network and industry cluster dimensions of the opportunity. These networks and clusters are zones where ideas, opportunities, resources and social contacts are available much more intensely than elsewhere. Even though there will inevitably be some competition, participating in these networks will enable you to learn more quickly, for example, what different people and organisations are doing, what ideas and technologies are 'hot', and what resources are available. You can meet people with complementary skills, interests and experience who are likely to 'speak the same language' as you, and explore possibilities for collaborating. You can also start to develop ideas of how you can make a distinctive contribution to groups you may want, or find it useful, to become part of. There are likely to be needs and opportunities within the group where your interests, skills, expertise and experience can be of use to others, which can be a good way of becoming accepted by them as a participant.

activity

- Which social networks, formal and informal groups are associated with the type of opportunity you are exploring?
- Is it related to industry clusters which you can identify?
- How can you identify any members and gain entry to these networks? For example, do you already know anyone who participates in any of these networks, and can you use these contacts to become involved?
- Can you identify any groups of innovative companies, where new opportunities are being worked on and new ventures are being formed?
- Who could you talk to find out more about these networks?

One approach to building up a picture of these networks is to draw an opportunity map of the opportunity's social domain. As an example, Figure 5.3 is a map of the creative industry networks in one city in the UK.

FIGURE 5.3 **Opportunity map of creative enterprise networks**

corporate entrepreneurship: connecting opportunities with organisational strategy

The interface between entrepreneurial and corporate organisational strategy and culture is increasingly significant. Traditionally, 'the entrepreneur' was simply the sole operator who founded and built an independent business, but this concept is now too limited to be of continuing validity. Opportunities and resources increasingly depend on the interconnections between entrepreneurial activity and the strategies, needs and resources of existing organisations, including corporate businesses, those in the public sector, and those with other missions such as universities, research institutes, professional bodies and charities. Entrepreneurs need to be able to relate the opportunities they recognise to the organisational context. This is seldom easy.

Corporate entrepreneurship has developed into a specialist field of its own, and whilst this book contains information and methods which are applicable to the corporate sector, that is not its main function. There is increasing literature available and Burns (2004) has used a structured approach to explore corporate entrepreneurship in depth.

There is a strategic movement in many corporate organisations, especially in the United States and in a growing number of cases in Europe, to buy-in innovation from entrepreneurial ventures. However the move to create start-up and spin-out businesses from within large organisations has also increased. Very often the intellectual property, technical capacity and expertise, market access and financial resources required to exploit an opportunity are controlled by large organisations which may lack the entrepreneurial culture and dynamism to take advantage of it, even if they have the strategic intent to do so.

Dr David Albert, a serial entrepreneur in the medical field with long experience of the corporate–venturer interface in the United States, emphasises the need for ambitious start-up companies to plan to 'intercept the strategic vector' of corporate organisations. They need to identify opportunities, develop technologies and grow businesses with the explicit intent of future acquisition or investment by targeted corporate organisations. On the basis that corporates have published strategies, known areas of expertise, intellectual property and core-product ownership, the entrepreneur can research and build a scenario of strategic development, including identifying opportunities for new products, services and processes which will have a synergy with the corporates' strategy. A new company developing such an idea for a corporate client can become attractive for future acquisition or investment. Dr Albert stresses the need for planning, dialogue with managers in the corporate sector, and keeping options open. The venture which plans to exploit the corporate opportunity can also be an attractive investment for venture capital in the early stages, offering better than average prospects for a profitable exit strategy and lower risk for investors.

Organisations such as General Electric, Pfizer and Cisco have a track record of acquiring growing technology-based businesses where there is a strategic synergy. Others, in what can be described as corporate partnership, invest or provide technological input, intellectual property licences or other support for compatible new ventures. Examples include Raytheon, 3M, Rolls-Royce, Nokia, Sony and Ford. Corporate venture capital (CVC) has been widely used in the United States by corporates to take equity stakes in high-growth new ventures since the 1960s, with organisations such as Exxon, Dow and DuPont being active, either making direct investments in specific ventures or investing indirectly via venture capital funds. Some corporates have established major venture capital divisions, notably GE and several Japanese electronics firms, including NEC and Fujitsu.

There is a growing range of such forms of corporate–entrepreneurial interaction, adding to the basic corporate-venturing form where an opportunity is identified within the organisation and a new venture launched from within it, as practised with varying degrees of success by DuPont, Siemens, and France Telecom. The entrepreneurial venture brings innovation, talent, market focus and potential new market opportunities to the corporates, enabling them to increase sales growth and future profits. In return the corporate needs to be able to invest time in investigation and relationship-building, financial equity, technology, expertise, and marketing and distribution capability.

It is important for the entrepreneurial person, who may be an independent agent or employed within a corporate organisation or an intermediary such as a venture capital firm, to understand and be able to work effectively within the dynamics of the corporate–entrepreneurial nexus. This is frequently complex and can involve slow and bureaucratic processes in dealing with corporate decision making. Some of the key questions to be addressed at the opportunity exploration stage include:

Identification

- Who are the potential corporate partners, investors or clients for the opportunity?
- What resources and input is required or desired from corporate organisations, and which ones can potentially provide this?

Selection

- Which corporates have a strategy which potentially provides convergence with the direction the new venture could take?
- Which corporates have a track record and culture of successful engagement with entrepreneurial businesses, including investment, knowledge sharing and acquisition?
- What benefits could they see in a potential relationship?
- What is the business proposal or 'pitch' from the entrepreneur?
- How and when can dialogue with these organisations be developed?
- Which clusters and networks do they participate in? Who do we know?

Relationship-building

- What form of relationships are optimal? Options include financial and non-financial, direct investment, IP licensing, technology partnership or transfer, marketing branding and distribution partnership, etc.
- How can a long-term win–win deal with the right organisation be created? How can trust be established on both sides?

The process of creating successful and durable corporate–entrepreneurial relationships cannot be expected to be straightforward or easy, since there are many understandable fears and risks on both sides, despite the advantages the 'right' deal may have. The entrepreneurial team may fear having their ideas, opportunities and market lead being stolen, copied or wasted, they may become impatient with slow corporate processes, inertia and politicised decision making, and the risk of changes in corporate strategy or ownership, or of the relationship being terminated without regard to the quality of the business. All of these things have happened. However corporate managers face similar anxieties which may make it easier and simpler not to open the door to entrepreneurial partnerships unless these achieve a strategic goal which has top management support. Corporates fear their investment in a small company may be a bottomless pit for funds and technology with little prospect of return; they fear their resources, technology, ideas, and even people will disappear into a small firm which itself may well explode; and they may not appreciate ideas and technologies 'which weren't invented here!'. These things have happened too.

However the reality is that entrepreneurs and corporate organisations are mutually dependent in technologically advanced industries; they need each other and have to learn to work effectively together, for the winners will be those that do. The losers those who cannot: the entrepreneurs who are tied down to running small firms and the corporates that stagnate for want of innovation and dynamism. Here are some guidelines for developing effective corporate–entrepreneurial interaction:

- Identify areas of shared potential which can be exploited on a medium/long-term basis, identify clear expectations on both sides and know your goals.

- View the potential corporate partner as a strategic investor who needs to see a credible investment proposal and business strategy; in return it will help you build the business.
- Identify and protect your intellectual property.
- Be prepared to invest time and patience in the partner search, relationship-building and decision-making processes.
- Demonstrate personal confidence, integrity, transparency and competence in all interactions; know your own value.
- Use professional help in the negotiating and contracting stages.
- Aim for a relationship based on trust on both sides, underpinned by a win–win contract; avoid marriages of convenience or exploitative relationships.
- Aim for a long-term relationship, and build in exit options for both parties.

activity

For your opportunity, consider:

- How would you identify potential corporate partners?
- What benefits does your opportunity offer to them?
- How would you initiate a potential partnership?
- What risks or constraints would you need to be aware of and to manage in the relationship?

critical questions to consider from this chapter

At this stage you should aim to bring together the information you have collected for your opportunity evaluation report, to collate this and review it.

- Overall, what is your assessment of the opportunity?
- What has the application of the tools covered in this chapter revealed about the strength of the opportunity?
- What have you learned from working through the opportunity evaluation process?
- Do you intend to go to the next stage of venture planning, and do you have sufficient information to do this? If not, what are the gaps and how could you fill them?
- How would you identify and gain access to the clusters and networks relevant to your opportunity?

chapter 6

planning to realise opportunities

chapter contents

introduction

The purpose of this chapter is to provide a practical guide to planning how to realise the opportunity. In many cases this will take place through planning the formation of a new business venture. However, many opportunities will also be realised to achieve growth within existing organisations, or in informal ways such as social enterprises within community groups. Therefore 'opportunity planning', is not always synonymous with business planning, and can be undertaken independently in relation to any opportunity.

The learning goals of this chapter are that you will be able to:

- generate the information to use in preparing a plan to exploit an opportunity
- develop a business model to show how the business will generate revenue
- create a plan for a new venture
- critically evaluate a venture plan and business model
- prepare to present a venture plan to potential stakeholders.

While waiting for a plane at Stansted airport, drinking coffee next to the airport bookshop I noticed that people were buying fiction much more than, for example, the business and management books on offer. Fantasy fiction, such as Philip Pullman and Terry Pratchett, seemed to be especially popular. So why does fantasy fiction outsell business books? Because people find it more interesting and entertaining, and it engages with their imagination. Yet the entrepreneur, in creating a new opportunity or venture, is also using imagination, but in a more practical way. We are trying to achieve a balance between creative and rational thinking, but the conventional approaches to planning often overemphasise the rational and miss out the inspirational. So what can we learn from storytelling and how can this be used to improve our opportunity planning?

There is a huge amount of literature on 'how to write a business plan', which this chapter does not aim to duplicate. Guidance on writing a business plan can be obtained from many banks, business support agencies and other sources listed in the resources section. However, many business ventures are set up without a written plan, and research does not show a clear relationship between business success and having a business plan. It may be that the orthodox advice to 'write a business plan' quite often misses the target.

This chapter therefore takes a different approach. It offers a flexible and imaginative, future-oriented approach to planning the opportunity, in which working on the 'design' for the venture and producing a viable business model are necessary skills and activities. A key task for the entrepreneur is to sell the business concept to third parties, be they investors, partners, customers or suppliers. Creating a credible and persuasive plan is generally an essential stage in doing this. Experience of working with many entrepreneurs in new and small businesses shows that they are often asked to produce a business plan by a third party, such as a bank, potential investor, customer or grant-providing agency, and the plan is written to unlock these resources. Chapter 8 includes the Aquifer case study of this type of venture planning.

The chapter covers the questions in the third quadrant of Opportunity-Centred Entrepreneurship, shown in Figure 6.1.

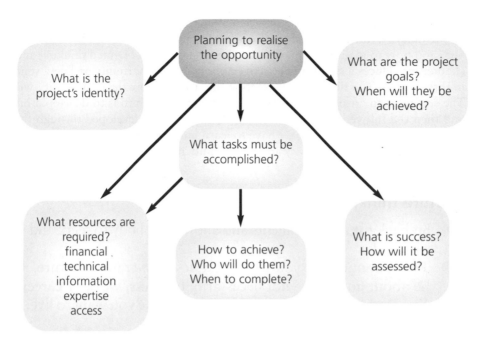

FIGURF 6.1 **Planning to realise the opportunity**

why plan and how to plan

Why plan? A professor of entrepreneurial studies often remarked wryly to business owner-managers that 'men make plans to make God laugh!', because the unexpected always happens. The serious point is that planning is about future-thinking, and envisaging the future as you intend it to be. However, while we must try to implement our plans and make them happen, as will be covered in Chapter 7, the reality is that we are not in control of the future, and what we intend through a plan will often be different in reality. Business plans usually end up being wrong.

This may seem like a good argument for not planning but, as with democracy, what is the alternative? The alternative is not to plan, to muddle along from day to day, being reactive or at best opportunistic. This is how many people, and indeed small business owners, do behave. The problem with this approach is that success, if it is achieved at all, becomes dependent on chance, circumstance and 'being in the right place at the right time'.

There are strong reasons for planning as a key aspect of the entrepreneurial process. Planning makes us think strategically and purposively about what we intend to achieve and how to realise this: it is planning for success as a clear statement of what the venture aims to achieve. Through planning, we can envisage different scenarios, anticipate and prevent problems. Planning helps put us in control rather than simply reacting tactically to events, and enables us to monitor the variations between the plan and reality and to re-plan accordingly.

Planning is necessary because we are making the connections between knowing what the opportunity is, having defined, explored and evaluated it through the activities in Chapters 4–5, and how to realise it. Opportunity planning is future-oriented thinking and acting. This chapter introduces a simple but effective approach to opportunity and new venture planning in three stages. The first involves creating the story of how the opportunity will be realised. The second is to create a plan for the opportunity. The third is to develop a business model and then the full venture plan, using much of the work developed through the activities in previous chapters. To do this, we have to learn how to think in the future. This builds on the work in Chapter 4 on creativity and opportunity mapping.

activity

Future thinking

- Sit back for a few moments and allow your body to relax and your mind to wander.
- Think about what you would *like to happen* in the future. This could be about anything – not necessarily business, work or career oriented. You could imagine your next holiday, where you want to live, your ideal evening out.
- What do you see? What does it feel like? What are sounds and sensations you experience? Spend some time thinking about 'what it would be like'.
- Have a piece of paper, preferably blank and unlined, and a pen or pencil to hand. Use this to note down the ideas in your mind. These might be words or pictures. You could draw a mind-map of what you imagine.

This exercise might seem strange or unproductive at first. However time spent developing your ability in 'future thinking', about what you would like to happen, which we can term 'vision', or about 'scenarios' or 'contingencies' which could happen, will be worthwhile. Humankind is, so far as we know, the only mammal able to think prospectively and imagine the future. This is probably the most valuable capability we have in entrepreneurial working, so it is worth investing time in developing these skills; even if it seems like 'daydreaming', it can be productive. Everyone can think creatively, and does so in different ways. Walt Disney, for example, had a creative space in his office where he went to develop ideas.

creating an opportunity plan

This section uses future thinking to develop an opportunity plan. We will use a 'storyboard' approach to develop prospective future-thinking and vision, and to plan the actions needed to make it happen. One of the problems of conventional business planning is that it has become dominated by highly rational and often numbers-based thinking, which creates an illusion of certainty through detail. There is nothing wrong with this in its place but it should be seen as one outcome, rather than the whole point of the planning process.

Instead, we can think of a good plan as being like a story. A story takes us into a different reality which may be the future, the past or an alternative version of today. A story has a plot or storyline, characters, actions and movement. A story is narrated in a way that holds the listener's interest. Even if the story is a fantasy, if it works it is 'believable' or credible and convincing in its plot, characters and narration. Increasingly the academic literature, both on entrepreneurship and business management more generally, is taking storytelling and narrative seriously (Hjorth and Steyaert, 2004). We can use the 'art' of storytelling to develop our ideas for the opportunity and to communicate these to other people more effectively than through a detailed plan alone. If you aim to use a venture plan to gain partners, investors or customers then it is essential that they believe your story.

Shaping the story

- The story has a structure including a beginning, a middle and an end.
- There is a plot or storyline which involves change and movement, so we do not know at the beginning what will have happened by the end.
- The story has characters – believable people who make things happen – and things happen to them which they do not expect.
- There is a storyteller or narrator.

example

Blue Fish Creative Media

Here Tony tells the story of how he set up Blue Fish Creative Media with his associates:

Blue Fish was established by myself, Mike and Darryl in 1991. We had lost our jobs when the design agency we worked for went into liquidation. We decided to start on our own, selling our motorbikes and renting a single room to work from. During this pioneering stage we worked ludicrous hours to get off the ground – survival was the name of the game. We spent every waking hour in the office. We didn't believe we were working hard enough unless we were working past midnight, we'd often work until 3 a.m., supplying our clients with pizzas and Coke whilst they checked and signed off text. We'd take on any work, agree to any turnaround, and built our reputation for service with a huge number of people.

We turned over £57k in the first year, then we turned over £220k in the second year and made £50k profit. But we were all working long hours and became busy fools, like prisoners in our own company, and we realised we wouldn't continue to enjoy work if we carried on like that. We knew we had the seeds of something good but needed help in getting to the next stage. We had to work out what we had done wrong and more importantly what we were doing right. So for the first four or five years we were messing around, trying to find our feet, establish our credentials, starting to understand how we made a profit or a loss. After five years we had seven people, turning over £400k.

We went to see our accountant. He ripped our business model apart and showed us how we make a profit. We assumed we made a profit on buying print and marking it up, but we were only charging 18 per cent of the hours that we worked. We analysed everything to see exactly what we were doing; we now know what our key performance indicators are. He showed us how to double our salaries and our profits but halve our hours within two years and we did it.

We all agreed we wanted to be out of the business by the time we're 50 with about £2m each, so we wrote a 20-year plan of the profitability levels we had to hit to get ourselves out of the business. We've put in a strong management team who can run the business for us; they can either buy us out or we could sell to a third party with the management team in place.

We're bang on target, we've set ourselves 30 per cent growth targets and this year we'll do just over a million, from £782k last year. We've set a target of around £1.3–1.5m next year but the main thing is the profitability levels. Now we work 40–50 hours per week, never more than that. Salaries have trebled, we've doubled our fee rate and profitability is still going up – we know where it all comes from now.

Tony's story tells us why they formed what has become a successful business, what they wanted from it, a good deal about how the business has changed and how the founders have learned, and what their strategy and goals for the business are. This is a story, not a business plan, which communicates something of the innovative, sometimes manic nature of their business that you would not gain from a conventional business plan. But they needed a plan to enable them to define and then realise their ambitions.

creating a storyboard for the opportunity

The purpose of this activity is to think creatively about how the opportunity will be realised in the future and to generate strategic thinking to inform the opportunity plan, by starting to create the story of your opportunity. You can use several sheets of blank paper to create the storyboard and draw mind-maps and 'rich pictures', putting down key words and ideas using marker pens. Alternatively you can tell the story orally and use a tape recorder.

Where you are

- On the first page, describe the beginning, where you are now. What is the opportunity, and the potential as you see it?
- What is your current situation?
- Why do you want to make the opportunity happen?
- Who are the other characters involved?

Where you aim to get to

- Now try moving to the end.
- What do you want the end of the story to be? When will this be – months or longer, two, five or ten years?
- What will you have achieved?
- How will the future reality be different?
- What will have changed for you? For the other characters involved?
- What will 'success' look and feel like?

How to get there

- Now work on the middle. You have an image of the end. What will you need to do to get there?
- What are the actions, the stages in the story that move you from current to future reality? What is the flow of events which need to take place?
- What are the good things and successes you think will happen?
- What could be the bad events and misfortunes which might take place?

Now you have a storyboard for the opportunity. This may be a voice recording, in which case you can play it back and write down the key ideas into a story, or it may be three or more pages of a written and drawn storyboard. This can be the basis for your opportunity plan; you can always come back to improve and work on it. Like any story it will improve every time it is told and this is certainly true of venture plans.

This activity aimed to help you to future-think about the opportunity and how you can make it happen. This material can be translated and used in a more formal plan which will be prepared later in this chapter. Future-thinking is creative strategic thinking, focusing on what you intend to achieve, where you want to take the opportunity, and what this means for you and others involved with it. The storyboard is about the story, the progression from now to the future and being able to identify the activities, events, people and possibilities which are involved in going from 'now' to realise the future goals.

planning from idea to venture

If you have used the storyboard exercise to map out the overall story, now you can start to work on it in more detail. The devil, as they say, is always in the detail! The next stage is to create a plan to make the opportunity happen. We have already moved from 'idea' to opportunity through completing the work in Chapters 4–5. We will use this information to create the opportunity plan, a template for which is shown in Figure 6.2.

The introduction to this chapter mentioned that an opportunity could be realised within an existing organisation, outside a formal organisation, or through creating a new business venture. The question is what type of organisation is needed to make the opportunity happen – formal or informal, existing or new, single or joint venture (e.g. two existing organisations forming a third jointly owned one). Any plan, decision and action to make an opportunity happen is a 'venture' in the sense that a venture is 'an undertaking of a risk, a risky enterprise, a commercial speculation' according to the *Concise Oxford Dictionary*.

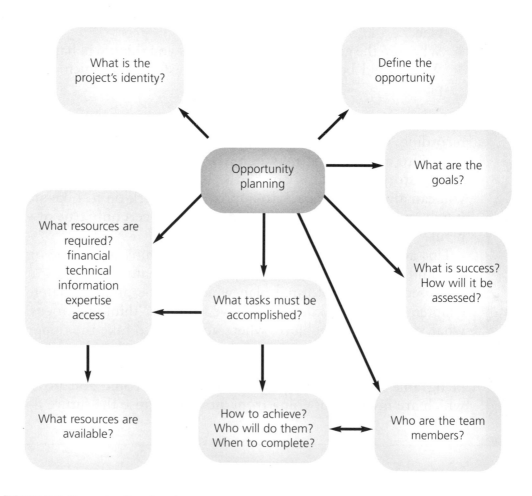

FIGURE 6.2 **Opportunity planning**

One feature of planning is that as well as being creative, it is a way of forcing out questions and decisions which need to be made, and of 'problem solving in advance' by identifying potential problems and finding ways of preventing, eliminating or dealing with these situations.

Here are key questions to be addressed in the opportunity plan:

- Restate what the opportunity is.
- Is there a name or title for the opportunity or business venture? What will you call it?
- What is the single most important goal to be achieved through the opportunity?
- When will this be achieved? How will you measure it?
- What are the other goals which need to be achieved?
- How do these relate to the overall goal, and are they compatible? What are their timescales?
- How will the success of these be measured or assessed?
- What tasks or activities need to be completed to achieve each of these goals?
- Who are the people who will make the opportunity happen?
- Who will take responsibility for each goal?
- Do they have the skills, information and time to achieve these goals?
- What resources are needed to achieve these goals?
- Which resources are already available and which must be obtained?

activity

Opportunity planning

- Work from your storyboard to develop an opportunity plan to make your opportunity happen.
- Use an opportunity map to develop answers to the questions in the previous section.
- Review the map: how feasible is it?

Identifying key themes, strategies, activities and tasks

The opportunity plan is not simply a 'to-do list' but the beginning of a strategic plan to develop the venture. Once you have a draft plan then review it, not just once but regularly to update and improve it. If you have a team then talk about each aspect to ensure that everyone has the same understanding and is committed to make their part of it happen. If you are working alone then reflect on it, or if you have an adviser, coach or mentor, share and discuss it with them. In this way the most important goals, themes and activities will become clear. Look for synergies and connections between different aspects of the plan: for example, how can you move from consumer research into test marketing and trial sales of a product?

defining the project and its identity

One vital aspect of an opportunity is to establish its unique identity. This can take different forms depending on the type of opportunity and the strategy for its exploitation; for example, whether a new venture is to be formed. Here are different ways in which the identity of the opportunity can be expressed:

- name of the business venture – e.g. company name
- name of the product, service or experience to be provided
- website domain name, URL and e-mail address
- brand identity which can include all of these.

Identifying, securing the rights to use the identity and exploiting it are an important step, already referred to in the section on intellectual property in Chapter 4. Here are guidelines for establishing the identity for the opportunity. The identity should:

- communicate the opportunity and its benefits to the target customers
- be distinctive, preferably unique, and memorable
- not be easily confused with similar offerings
- be hard to copy or to 'pass off' imitations of.

The concept of branding and identity is well established, so none of this is new, meaning that creating and protecting new brand identities has become much harder. Many of the readily available names and words in the English language have been registered as trademarks or Internet domain names. The identity has symbolic and linguistic importance, and being memorable is essential. It may be worth finding and using a creative consultancy which specialises in business identity to help develop your ideas.

example

The Hive

Nottingham Trent University was developing a new facility to support graduate business innovation projects and start-up business ventures. They had located a site and sources of funding, and needed an identity which would appeal to the target market – entrepreneurial students and graduates. The project team came up with 'The Hive' as a name, choosing this because it was short, memorable, and expressed ideas of busy-as-bees, hive-of-activity and honey = money. Even though the project team included a designer, they brought in an external design agency to create a vibrant visual identity as a brand, with co-ordinated marketing materials and website, ensuring that these brand values were carried through into the décor of the building. The ideal domain name was not available but they chose the closest available: www.businesshive.ntu.ac.uk

The Hive has become highly successful in stimulating university enterprise and the identity has been an integral aspect of its appeal. In its first five years of operation, over 60 businesses have been created and around 90 per cent of start up companies formed with the help of The Hive have remained in business. The Hive was rated 'A' star in a regional accreditation process for business incubators, and is recognised nationally for the success and rigour of its support programmes for graduate entrepreneurs.

activity

- Do you have an identity for your opportunity?
- If not, start to collect ideas, words and images which could be used. Aim to come up with a range of possible ideas, not just one. While a 'brain-storming' session can be helpful in coming up with ideas, it is just one stage in the process.
- Spend time putting possible combinations of words and images together, associating ideas in new ways which could appeal to the target customer. If there is a project team, everyone should be involved in this activity. Aim to come up with several combinations which can be checked out to see which brand names and website URLs are taken and which combinations are available.
- Aim to find one which meets the guidelines provided earlier, as far as possible – and which you think will have the maximum customer appeal. Try this with some limited consumer research – ask people in the target group which of the available combinations 'speaks to them' with most positive impact.
- Once you have chosen the identity, protect it by registering the website domain name (and different combinations of these) and a trademark if you think this could be of potential value.

creating a business model

What is a business model? The business model demonstrates as clearly and simply as possible how the opportunity will create revenue and financial value from its operations. This is at the heart of the opportunity plan and needs to show who is doing what; for whom they are doing it; and the financial assumptions and results on which the plan is based. Here are some deceptively simple questions we ask people with ideas for new business ventures:

- Who are your target customers?
- What value will you create for them?
- Why will they buy from you?
- How is this superior to competitors?
- How will the business generate cash flow through sales?
- How will the business generate profits?
- What financial investment does the business require?
- Can you draw a simple diagram to show the business model?

One format for a simple business model is shown in Figure 6.3. This starts to include basic financial measures. If you are not familiar with these, they are explained in the financial toolkit. The business model includes:

- the target customer group, intended product or service, and customer benefits
- sales targets and revenue
- variable costs (costs attributable to each customer)
- fixed costs (costs which apply at any level of sales)
- total costs, gross and net profit before tax
- gross and net profit margins and break-even sales figures
- projected sales growth in years two and three.

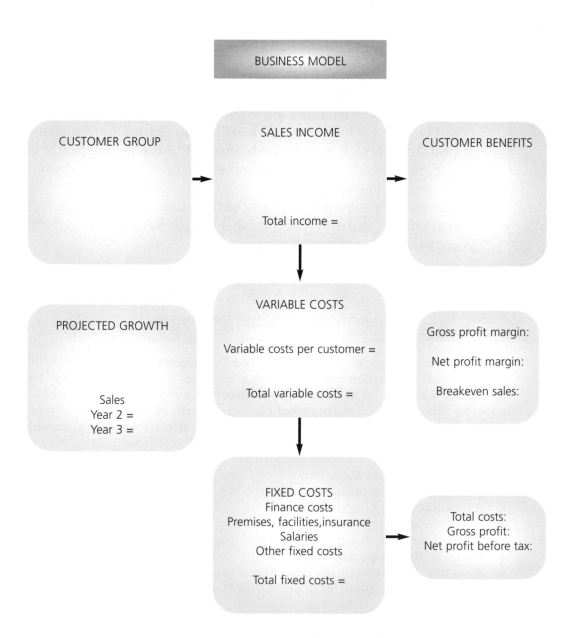

FIGURE 6.3 **Business model template**

Evaluating a business model

A business model such as this can be completed and presented to give a readily understandable one-page overview of the opportunity to potential investors and lenders. It can also be revised easily to account for different scenarios. It is important to be aware of the criteria which potential investors and other decision makers may use in evaluating a business model:

● Are the assumptions and information on which the model is based realistic and reliable? Or are, for example, your expectations of the rate of customer acquisition and sales growth over-optimistic?
● Are fixed costs kept as low as possible (e.g. avoiding unnecessary expenditure – hire or lease rather than buy)? Are costs controlled overall?
● At what point are break-even sales reached?
● Are the levels of gross and especially net profit both realistic and attractive?

preparing the venture plan

This section covers the development of the venture plan; the business model is an integral part of this plan. This activity will use the work you have done in Chapters 4 and 5 on exploring the opportunity and the work from earlier in this chapter on future-thinking, opportunity planning and business modelling. By now you should be familiar with the use of mind-maps for key concepts and we will work on the venture plan in the same way. Figure 6.5 (page 143) shows an overview of a venture plan, and a template is included in the toolkit. It is suggested that you work on the venture plan using flipchart paper on the wall or a white board. The advantage of working on the venture plan in this way is that you can start from the 'vision' of what you aim to achieve through the venture in the centre, and then work on each of the other boxes, starting with the opportunity, then the strategy, and the plans for marketing and sales, operations, finance, and people. The final step is the action plan which summarises the priority actions which need to be completed. Additional information under each of the headings can be pasted up and the venture planning map can become a 'header' or summary of the information in the plan. Notes on what to include in each section of the plan follow in the next section.

Table 6.1 (page 142) builds on the map of a venture plan by showing the headings and sub-headings of a typical venture plan as they might be used on the contents page, with links to where the information can be obtained from activities in this and preceding chapters. This will help you as you develop your venture plan in the next section.

Vision and strategy were covered earlier in this chapter. Opportunity was covered in Chapter 4. Guidelines on completing the other parts of the venture plan are given in the next section.

Marketing and sales plan: key questions to address

● What are the vital success factors which you have to get right? These factors will differentiate the venture from competitors. They may include superior technology, service, choice or other benefits to the customer. Beware of claiming to offer lower cost unless the business model really provides a lower cost structure.
● Who are the target customer segments? This was covered in Chapter 4.

activity

An example of a business model using this format is shown in Figure 6.4. This is for an IT services business to be set up by two people.

- Review the business model using the evaluation criteria in the previous section.
- What problems or weaknesses can you identify in the business model?
- What suggestions would you make for improving it?

What problems did you identify? Here is a selection:

- Customer group and business opportunity: how competitive is the sales proposition given the reducing cost of IT services to the small-business market?
- Sales income: the pricing appears high for the same reason. It assumes all 200 customers will pay for full 12 months, yet in reality they would sign up at different points during the year.
- Variable costs: who is doing the marketing? Is the spend to attract each customer realistic? Are variable costs really as low as £50 per customer?
- Fixed costs: why borrow £100k to spend on IT systems which will depreciate quickly when more flexible options include leasing or renting space on a server? Are other fixed costs realistic?
- As a result, sales, gross and net profit figures are over-optimistic and need to be reconsidered before a sound basis for growth in years two and three can be envisaged.

Clearly this is a flawed business model which needs revision from the basic assumptions onwards. However too many businesses are started using poor business models which have never been written down and do not work well. This can lead to the failure of the business, so it makes sense to chart, evaluate and improve the business model as a starting point.

- Marketing matrix: the marketing matrix is a simple concept which can be used in many different ways to plan and analyse the relationship between customer segments and product types. It relates customer segments to specific product or service offerings, and is useful if there are two or more segments or product/service combinations – see Table 6.2.

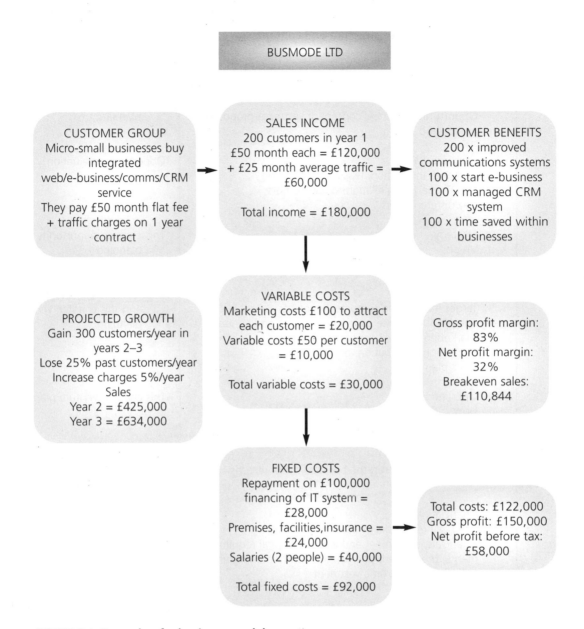

FIGURE 6.4 **Example of a business model**

- Develop a business model for your opportunity. You can use the template in the toolkit.
- Evaluate your business model using the criteria listed above.
- What problems can you identify and how could you revise the model to correct these?

TABLE 6.1 **Venture plan structure and contents**

Section	Source of material
1. Executive summary Opportunity, business concept, investment proposition, anticipated return	This chapter, opportunity planning
2. Opportunity Demand, innovation, feasibility, attraction SWOT analysis in relation to competitors Key differentiators	Opportunity evaluation, Chapter 5
3. Strategy Vision, Direction, goals, sales targets	This chapter, opportunity planning
4. Marketing plan Target market and customer segments The product/service concept – features and benefits Marketing matrix Promotion, distribution, pricing Sales plan	Market research, Chapter 4 and this chapter, venture planning
5. Operations plan How the business will operate: capabilities, resources, people, processes	This chapter, venture planning
6. People plan People: who will run the business, track records	Capabilities assessment, Chapter 3 This chapter, venture planning
7. Financial plan The business model or process Financials: investment and working capital requirements, break-even, pricing, gross and net margins, cash flow, return on investment	This chapter, venture planning and toolkit
8. Action plan	This chapter, venture planning and toolkit

The example shows that some customer segments form a strong core market for certain products and services, but make few purchases of other offers from the same business. The marketing matrix can be used for the following applications:

● matching products and services to customer segments
● identifying client types and the 'triggers' which cause them to buy a product/service
● matching product features and benefits to each client type
● forecasting the sales value from each customer/product combination

FIGURE 6.5 **Map of venture plan**

- forecasting the profitability of each combination
- identifying the marketing activity needed to connect with each customer segment
- analysing strength of competitive position.

TABLE 6.2 **Marketing matrix of product sales distribution to customer groups**

Customer segments Product/service types	Customer group 1	Customer group 2	Customer group 3	Customer group 4
Product A	60%	30%	10%	0%
Product B	20%	30%	40%	10%
Service A	55%	40%	5%	0%
Service B	10%	10%	10%	70%

Complete a marketing matrix to show the relationships between customer segments and product service types: which customer groups do you envisage will buy which types of products? Even if you only plan to offer one product initially, you can project which types of customer you expect to buy it.

Operations plan: key questions to address

Here we plan how the venture will provide its product or service to the customers.

The business needs to be designed effectively so that it can exploit the opportunity. It can be designed in the same way that a product, a building or a website is designed for effective use, so that it operates effectively and efficiently, enabling it to adapt and grow. Here are guidelines for designing a new business venture effectively.

- Form follows function – so make it easy for the customer to find, interact with and buy from the organisation through well-designed selling processes.
- Processes are kept simple, flexible and robust.
- Responsibilities and functions are defined clearly to avoid overlap.
- The organisation is lean and flat, avoiding unnecessary hierarchies.
- The effectiveness of each aspect of the business can be measured using simple, useful metrics.

The key to operations planning is to use simple, step-by-step processes, for example through process mapping or flowcharting. The aim of a business process is to make it simple to follow for both the customer and worker within the business, to minimise the scope for it going wrong or for introducing variability which affects quality, and to

TABLE 6.3 **Example of sales order process**

Step	Time taken (minutes)	Information record
Log customer enquiry	5	Enquiry form and set up customer log
Assess customer requirement	30	Enquiry form
Prepare and send quotation and terms of business	50	Quote
Check acceptance by customer	10	Customer log
Plan job into work schedule	5	Work schedule
Initial design work	420	Design file
Check approval by customer	30	Customer log
Make modifications	60	Design file
Check final approval by customer	30	Customer log
Commission website	120	Design file
Invoice customer	20	Customer log
Follow-up to check customer satisfaction, payment and assess further requirements	20	Customer log

make it as efficient as possible so that costs can be controlled. The most important process for a new venture is probably the sales order process: what are the steps in taking and fulfilling a customer order? The sales order process for a website design consultancy is shown in Table 6.3 and is typical of a generic process in a small service business.

As part of planning the process, consider what information is generated and

- Design the sales order process for your venture.
- Map out what you think the key stages will be from enquiry to completion and payment.
- What information would be generated/retained at each stage?
- What variations would you expect there to be in the process?

retained. This could be as simple as a customer record 'job card' on a computer, with an invoice being generated. This basic process will be developed using the 'business resource process' technique. There are relationships between the business process, information and people's skills and capabilities which are needed to manage the service or product delivery. Questions for the people plan are considered in the next section.

If the business depends on supplier, subcontractor, distributor or reseller relationships, then these need to be identified in the operations planning:

- Which suppliers, subcontractors, distributors or resellers does the business depend on?
- Is the business entirely dependent on any of these or do alternatives exist?
- How reliable are they known to be?
- What are the contractual relationships with them for delivery and payment?
- Which types of new suppliers etc. will be required and how will these be selected?

A new venture often depends on establishing a reputation for high quality and customer service. Putting this another way, it is hard to grow a new business if it gains a reputation for low quality and poor service! Quality and service standards do not happen by accident and need to be planned. Simple service standards may include maximum response times to customer enquiries, time intervals between order and delivery, and targets for customer satisfaction.

- What standards of product and service quality will the target customers expect? If these vary between segments or product types, use a marketing matrix to chart them.
- How do these compare with competitors' standards for quality and service?
- How can the consistency of quality and service be maintained, e.g. by minimising variability or inconsistent standards?
- What measures or records of quality and service need to be maintained (some may be contractual requirements)?

Use the questions in the sections on suppliers, quality and service to plan how the business will ensure consistent quality and service, both from third parties such as suppliers and within its own operations.

People plan: key questions to address

It is important to demonstrate that the venture has the people with the skills, expertise and experience to start and manage the business successfully and to provide the service expected by customers. The experience of the venture team and especially the chief executive or lead entrepreneur is an essential aspect of this.

- Who are the key people in the business?
- What are their track records relevant to the venture (this can be important in reassuring investors and reducing the perception of risk)?
- What are their roles? For example, who will be responsible for: general management (chief executive); marketing and sales; operations; finance; information; people?
  - The business is unlikely to have one person responsible for each of these, and an owner-managed business may start with one person responsible for all of them. How can responsibilities be shared most effectively within the team?
- What are the key skills, capabilities and expertise required by the venture? Which need to be employed within the venture and which can be bought-in when needed?
- Which people have these, and what training and development is needed (e.g. to meet external requirements for qualified staff)?
- What recruitment of staff is likely to be needed to fill gaps in skill or capacity?

Use the questions in the people planning section to develop a simple people plan for the venture.

Financial plan: key questions

The financial plan is a vital part of the venture plan and will be scrutinised closely by potential investors and lenders. It needs to demonstrate that the business is viable, that it will show a satisfactory return on the investment to be made in it, and that the financial projections are realistic, being based on valid costings and data. It may well be written to meet investors or lenders requirements, as outlined later in this chapter. The key financial aspects normally included in the plan are:

- Business model: include the business model prepared earlier.
- Sales, pricing and income projections.

- Investment: what investment is required in the business?
- When is this required (at what points and over what timescale)?
- How this will be spent, e.g.:
  - in fixed capital assets
  - start-up capital to cover launch expenses
  - working capital to finance cash flow and trading.
- What combination of equity investment and loan finance is required?
- What investment are the venture team making and what percentage of share ownership do they intend to retain?
- From whom is the investment/finance required?
- What is the projected repayment of loan finance?
- What is the projected return on equity investment? (For example, an investor would require a share in the equity of the business with an anticipated exit strategy through sale of the shares and a capital gain, or a share in the profit stream through dividends on shares, or both.)
- Cash flow: show a cash flow projection for at least 12 months, or until the business reaches positive cash flow (cash income exceeds expenditure) if this is longer than 12 months.
- Profit and loss: show a profit and loss projection for the first 12 months.
- Balance sheet: include a projected balance sheet if investment is required.
- Key ratios: include anticipated:
  - break-even sales figure
  - gross and net profit margins
  - gearing and other ratios.

activity

The activity is to prepare a financial plan for the venture plan. This may involve significant work so it is suggested that you read through the financial planner in the toolkit. Identify any terms which are unfamiliar to you and check that you understand them. Then gather the financial information on the venture which you have already prepared, as listed in Table 6.1. Identify what additional information you require and gather this, by research to collect costing or pricing data. Once you have the information then prepare the financial plan.

If you have not prepared a financial plan before, the recommended starting point is:

- Start with your business model.
- Prepare a cash flow forecast for months 1–12.
- Identify what start-up capital is needed to launch the venture.
- Identify what working capital is needed to finance operations when trading.
- These will show the funding required for the first year.
- Profit and loss, balance sheet and key ratios can be worked out from this.

Rather than being considered in detail here, these highly important components of the financial plan are included in the finance planner section of the toolkit. Further reading of financial planning texts at an appropriate level for your knowledge and confidence is also recommended in the resources section.

An important consideration in financing a new venture is the point at which break-even and financial viability is reached. Any venture which involves either innovation (new product, service or process development) or market development is almost certain to have a period in which funds need to be invested prior to trading, and even once trading has started, further working capital will be needed to finance operations. Entrepreneurs are usually optimistic at the planning stage and often do not realise that there are three golden rules governing this period of innovation or market development and early trading:

● Development costs are higher than you expected.
● Development takes longer than you expected.
● Because you have under-estimated the investment needed at the planning stage, you will find it much harder to raise second-round funding part-way through this process.

This is known as the 'death valley curve' and is shown in Figure 6.6.

Action plan

The action plan pulls together the business goals, sales targets, immediate priorities, actions and responsibilities. This can be in the form of a project plan (e.g. a Gantt chart) or of the template in the business action planner section of the toolkit.

● The action at this stage is to bring the various parts of the draft plan together and to review them. Are they integrated to support each other?
● Confirm the business goals – is everyone in agreement?
● Decide on the priorities which must be achieved to start the venture.
● What actions must take place, by when, and who will be responsible for each?

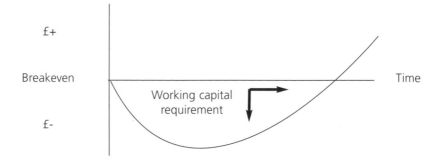

FIGURE 6.6 **Death valley curve**

establishing and accessing resources

The venture planning process is likely to identify that a range of resources are required to enact the opportunity. Some of these may already be available, but unless you are very fortunate or are planning a venture of quite limited scale, other resources will be required. The types of resources were outlined in Chapter 4 and the networks through which they can be attracted or captured were considered in Chapter 5. Resources can come, for example, from corporate organisations; public sector organisations, including regional development agencies; research institutes; including universities; and investors, including business angels and venture capital funds. It makes sense to invest capital only in purchasing assets which are known to be of long-term and appreciating value to the business, and to aim to gain the use of other assets at least cost, for example by renting, leasing or borrowing. Large organisations, including corporates, public sector bodies and the military, often buy and then do not fully utilise capital assets, which may then be targeted by entrepreneurs to use on a 'pay as you go' basis. These can include premises, printing, payroll, manufacturing and distribution facilities.

The types of resources required may include, for example:

- *Knowledge*: specialist knowledge, expertise or information not held by the venture team which needs to be researched or bought-in.
- *Human resources*: skills, expertise and capability required in the venture.
- *Finance*: investment or lending for capital asset purchase or working capital.
- *Technology*: product or process technology which needs to be bought-in or licensed.
- *Intellectual property*: permissions or licences which need to be negotiated to provide the rights to use them.

activity

- Review the resources which have been identified as being required in the sections of the venture plan prepared so far.
- Use the resource identification grid in Table 6.4 (overleaf) to identify which resources are already available to the venture.
- Which resources will be required, but are not currently available to the venture?
- For each of these, identify the options available for obtaining this resource, e.g.:
  - Which organisation/person has this resource and could it be borrowed at no/minimal cost? (these may include existing organisations including public and corporate organisations, which often have under-used assets)
  - Can it be bought-in or rented on a flexible pay-as-you-go basis?
  - Cost of purchase?
  - What alternative options are available if the resource cannot be obtained, e.g. substitutes or effect on the venture of the resource not being available?

Table 6.4 **Resource identification grid**

Factor	Resources available	Resources required	Potential sources
Knowledge			
Human resources			
Finance			
Technology			
Intellectual property			
Physical resources			
Capacity			
Networks			
Other			

- *Physical resources*: equipment, plant, buildings or land which the business needs to access or control.
- *Capacity*: facilities which need to be bought-in, e.g. subcontracting manufacture, packaging, despatch or call-centre operations.
- *Networks*: for access and distribution to customers or resellers.
- And any other resources not included in the categories above.

planning as a dialogue

Venture planning is not a solitary exercise but can be a way of connecting the venture team who are promoting the opportunity with the network of investors, resource providers, customers, and others. This can explore how their needs can be met through the venture, to the mutual benefit of all parties. Venture planning is part of the process of the negotiated enterprise, as outlined in the entrepreneurial learning model in Chapter 3. It therefore includes conversations and negotiations, both informal and formal, with the network of interested parties around the venture whom we can term stakeholders. Key stakeholders connected with the venture are likely to include:

- the venture team
- investors and lenders
- technology and other partners

- suppliers, sub-contractors, distributors and resellers (as appropriate)
- customers of potential significance (e.g. corporate clients)
- public sector, grant providing and regulatory organisations.

The venture planning stage is often a good point to contact, seek out and consult people and organisations to get their input into the plan. However they will expect you to be able to 'pitch' an outline of the plan to enable them to understand the nature of the opportunity, so as a minimum you should have completed the business model and a one-page outline of the venture plan, as shown in Figure 6.5.

In addition, expert business and professional advisers, such as lawyers, accountants, technical and intellectual property specialists may be involved where their expertise and advice can benefit the venture. But beware, there are sharks out there who feed on little businesses, so select advisers with care and take up references on them from other entrepreneurs.

- Look back to your network of industry and related contacts from the activities on networking in Chapters 3 and 5.
- Identify the most useful contacts who could guide the venture towards resources or other networks such as potential customers.
- Shortlist these contacts.
- Consider how you could contact them to successfully engage their interest in the venture.

presenting the plan: pitching the idea

The venture plan is 'the sales document for the business'. As well as the venture team requiring a plan, it is needed to convince potential investors, partners, supporters and clients that the venture is credible and able to meet their requirements. This involves strategies and skills of presentation, communication and influencing.

The venture plan is a slim-line, easily revised document which communicates all the necessary information about the venture, as outlined in this chapter. It could also be termed a 'business proposal'. A useful analogy is that the venture plan or business proposal is rather like the 'trailer' for a film at the cinema – it is designed to excite attention and provide as much information as necessary to stimulate the target viewer to want more. For those who do want more, then the full business plan becomes the 'main picture'. Table 6.5 shows the characteristics of an effective venture plan.

The venture plan may be all that is needed for an opportunity where the client does not require more information. However some organisations, including some in the public sector, corporate and institutional sectors, equate the thickness and weight of a business plan with its value and ability to minimise risk. If one of these organisations requires a more detailed plan and you require their support, then it is important to obtain specific information from them about their detailed requirements so that you can follow this.

In presenting the plan or 'pitching' to potential investors, partners or customers, preparation and planning are the key. You need to 'know your audience', having researched

TABLE 6.5 **Characteristics of an effective venture plan**

> *Here are 12 features of an effective venture plan:*
>
> 1. It demonstrates a clear opportunity which has not yet been exploited.
> 2. It displays strong customer attraction and differentiation from competitors.
> 3. There is significant, quantified growth potential in identified markets.
> 4. There is a credible strategy and plan to exploit the opportunity.
> 5. It deploys innovation which can be shown to work effectively.
> 6. It has unique aspects which can be prevented from copying (control of IPR).
> 7. There are success factors with risks identified and minimised.
> 8. Investment required is shown with realistic return on investment.
> 9. Timescale to break-even and anticipated profit stream are realistic.
> 10. Financial planning is accurately costed and realistic .
> 11. Potential exit routes and timescales for investors are shown.
> 12. The venture team demonstrate capability and motivation.

their interests, track record and likely goals. You need to anticipate their questions, and particularly those related to areas of weakness, such as customer demand, product readiness, financing and venture team capability, which will be probed remorselessly. So you need to 'put yourself in their shoes' to prepare convincing responses which use factual data rather than excessive confidence. If you are seeking financial or other investment such as technology, prepare your negotiating position: what do you want, and what are you prepared to offer in return.

Key questions in 'pitching' or selling the idea

- Who is the plan written for?
- What do you aim to achieve from presenting the plan? What are you prepared to exchange to gain what you need?

activity

- Prepare your venture plan and a short presentation of no more than 15 minutes.
- Review your plan against the 12 features of an effective venture plan shown in Table 6.5.
- Rehearse this. If possible video it and view the feedback to enable you to correct mannerisms, hesitation, repetition or over-confidence.
- Invite a small group of your contacts from the previous exercise, preferably including at least one third party such as an entrepreneur, investor or business banker.
- Present the venture plan and invite their feedback on how you could improve the venture plan and your presentation; give them the above list of features and ask them to review the plan against this.
- Use their feedback to revise and improve your venture plan and presentation.

● What are their needs and expectations? (e.g. are they looking for investment or lending opportunities, technology or distribution partnerships?)
● How can you fine-tune your presentation of the plan to meet their needs?
● Do you know your audience? What is their investment history, in which types of ventures? What are their investment objectives or lending criteria?
● How can you reassure them of your credibility and capability to make it happen?

critical questions on venture planning

This final section highlights key questions on venture planning to consolidate your learning in this important area. There is also a case study in Chapter 8 for you to read later. Venture planning is one skill-set which you are highly likely to use a number of times during your career, so it is worth reflecting on what you have learned so far.

● What do you think are the objectives of venture planning?
● How would you go about preparing a venture plan: what are the main stages?
● What are the key components of a venture plan?
● What are the main factors which make for an effective venture plan?
● What are the key skills you have developed and learning points you can use in planning opportunities and venturing?

chapter 7

acting on opportunities

chapter contents

introduction

The purpose of this chapter is to demonstrate how to act on an opportunity by implementing the venture plan and by applying skills of entrepreneurial management and strategic thinking. It shows how knowledge of critical success factors and ways to avoid the causes of failure can be applied in early-stage business ventures. This chapter covers the final quadrant of the Opportunity-Centred Entrepreneurship map: acting on opportunities to make them happen, as shown in Figure 7.1.

The learning goals of this chapter are to enable you to:

- implement the venture plan in order to act on the opportunity
- apply and learn from critical success factors and causes of failure in early-stage ventures
- develop, implement and review strategies for the new venture
- analyse and reflect on entrepreneurial management capabilities and practical theories of 'what works', both personally and in relation to venture management.

The outcome of this chapter will be to assess and enhance your awareness and ability to translate venture plans for opportunities into action. The limitations of entrepreneurship theory in acting on opportunities are outlined and helpful approaches identified, including sensemaking and action learning. The chapter proposes that enacting the opportunity involves a process of real-time, dynamic learning by discovery, in which the models, tools and ideas from previous chapters are applied in making the venture happen. Factors in implementing the venture plan include going beyond planning, responding to new opportunities, and handling setbacks and failure. Essential activities in an early-stage business and reasons for success and failure of businesses are considered. The practical theory approach

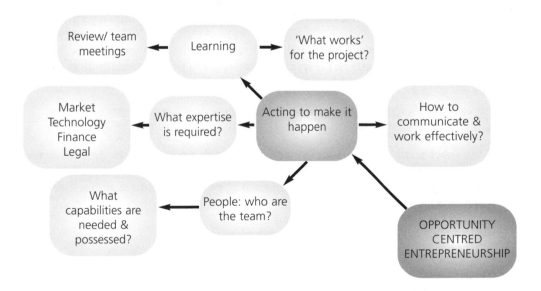

FIGURE 7.1 **Acting to make it happen**

is applied to establish both 'what works' in businesses and what happens when it doesn't work, and to demonstrate how this can contribute to organisational sustainability.

The development of entrepreneurial management as a means of connecting entrepreneurial and managerial skills with a strategic focus is explored. Strategic decision making, types of entrepreneurial strategy, and methods of reviewing the effectiveness of strategy are explored. The final exercise prompts experiential learning, through problem solving, reflecting, using experience and moving forward both personally and organisationally.

making it happen: implementing the venture plan

Rationally, you would expect that the action required to implement a venture plan would simply be to operationalise what had been planned, and that a well-researched plan, well implemented, would be successful. There may well be 'textbook' examples of this occurring, but the implementation of the plan is likely to be both considerably more complex and – crucially – different from what has been planned. Alan Gibb talks about the 'lifeworld' of the entrepreneur, a lifeworld characterised by uncertainty, complexity, independence yet interdependence with stakeholders, control and ownership (Gibb, 1996). In this lifeworld, planning is a continuous activity which interplays between planning and acting, and which is more important and useful than slavishly implementing a plan which may quickly be superseded by events and environmental change. What happens is always different from what was planned.

Implementing the plan is therefore most usefully seen as a process of real-time learning by discovery. The entrepreneur discovers which aspects of the plan are effective and useful, and which were founded on incorrect, partial or outdated assumptions. For example, it makes sense to conduct market research to test out demand and consumer reaction to a new product. But the mere fact that this shows a positive result, with potential customers saying they would buy the product, does not guarantee that this will in fact occur. Many students organising events such as club nights and trips to sports or entertainment have conducted surveys of their friends who always *said* they would buy tickets – the reality was often different.

In the process of enacting the plan and acting on the opportunity, it is therefore helpful to take a dynamic learning perspective in relation to this continually changing reality. The next section sets out guidelines for how the opportunity can be enacted successfully.

six essential activities in the early-stage venture

This short section sets out six key activities which are essential in the early stages of most new ventures. Whilst these are necessarily general, they contain practical steps to assist in relating them to the specific nature of each opportunity, and are summarised in Table 7.1 (opposite).

Managing holistically: see the whole picture

The art of managing a new business successfully is first to realise that you, as the manager or part of the venture management team, are responsible – there is no-one to delegate to, blame or pass on the unwelcome tasks to. You cannot simply concentrate on your 'comfort zone' of tasks you enjoy and are good at, but must take holistic responsibility for

TABLE 7.1 **Six essential activities in the early-stage venture: action points**

Activity	Action points
Managing holistically: see the whole picture	Set targets for the business: sales, finance, innovation and development Collect and use information to monitor results (see operations below) Review performance and adjust business targets Ensure you assess business performance from all aspects
Communicating effectively to build up the customer base	Talk to customers to build close customer relations Collect customer comment, feedback and ideas Use these to create new sales opportunities Build the brand through consistent and effective communication Use public relations and media to get your news stories out Attract people to use your website
Build a fan club around the business by working effectively with people	Attract, select and manage a fan base around the business Carefully select employees and associates who have the passion, values and skills you need and who can grow with the business Make them feel part of the business by sharing rewards and success stories with them Develop your staff so you can delegate essential tasks to them
Widen the talent pool, accessing and using expertise	Identify critical areas where knowledge and expertise will be needed Identify and contact people and organisations who can provide this Develop a network of trusted advisors
Managing business operations	Define the basic business process Identify what information will be produced on sales, customers, operations, people, suppliers and finance Plan how this will be analysed to monitor business performance Ensure business data is secured and backed up Aim to minimise dependence on any single element: customers, staff, suppliers, product, technology
Managing financial resources effectively	Plan and control cash flow to maintain a positive cash position Control costs, especially fixed costs, by growing the business on a variable cost basis Ensure customers pay promptly and debt is collected Assess and monitor the break-even position to establish profit or loss of the business, of each activity and major customer. Maintain personal supervision of business finance Employ a competent and trustworthy person to maintain the business accounts using a standard accounting package

the whole business. This means connecting all the different aspects covered in the venture plan, of marketing, sales, finance, operations and people management, to make sure that they happen. Self-organisation is essential in order to plan, to prioritise and allocate time for all the essential activities, and to work sustainably. It may feel necessary to work 80-hour weeks just to get through everything which needs to be done, but after a few weeks or months it will become clear that this is not sustainable, efficient or very enjoyable. So managing personal time and energy is vital.

Communicating effectively to build up the customer base

The customer is the reason the business exists. The first rule of business is never to trust someone else to find your customers for you; you, and everyone in a new business, have to be a sales representative, able and confident to call up, go out, meet and get to know potential customers. Selling requires confidence, communication skills, and interpersonal skills or 'likeability'. So a confident approach to finding prospective clients, opening a dialogue with them to find out what they require, how and when they want it, building rapport, listening and learning from them, and developing effective selling skills, is vital. Marketing and selling are means of attracting and communicating with customers, and satisfying their needs.

Behind this business process there are real human relationships, and the early life of a business is a vital and sometimes scary period of talking to some people you already know – and, it is recommended, to many you do not – to establish their needs, interest them in your selling proposition, and in some cases to start a business relationship with them. The business will depend on developing a positive reputation for quality and delivery among customers, so it is essential to get to know your prospective and actual customers by valuing and appreciating their business. Not only do these habits make running a business more enjoyable, they develop social capital and make it easier to find new customers, to develop more business from existing clients, to deal with problems and complaints, and to get paid reliably.

Build a fan club around the business by working effectively with people

Running a business is a social activity, and in this negotiated enterprise you achieve results through and with other people. Therefore finding, selecting and working effectively with people both inside and outside the business are essential. The capabilities of interpersonal interaction, leading and managing people, are vital ones to develop. Some entrepreneurs adopt a 'hard', instrumental approach to working relationships, in which they use people for their own ends, but this is not necessarily the way to get the best from them. Others have adopted a more social approach of 'building up credit in the favours bank' and 'giving without expectation of return', which can be more productive. Again the concept of developing social capital within networks is helpful. The aim should be to create a network of 'recommenders' based on staff, customers, suppliers and other contacts: people who will advertise the business to others.

Widen the talent pool, accessing and using expertise

This leads into the fourth activity. Building up the business will present problems, opportunities, decisions and issues which you have not met before. Frequently, these will not have 'textbook' answers and you cannot know the answer to every question, but you need to be able to find out the options quickly. However it is certain that similar situations have occurred many times before, and the collective expertise to deal with them exists out there. There are many situations, from dealing with large bad debts and negotiating with potential investors to defending your intellectual property, which you would face for the first time and possibly not handle in the best way. It is in your interests to develop a network of experienced and expert advisers whom you can trust and learn from. Some of these should be professional advisers such as a lawyer, accountant and possibly technical expert, whilst others can be experienced and battle-hardened business owners. As the business grows there may be merit in having one or two trusted advisors as non-executive directors.

Managing business operations

Small businesses have a habit of growing organically, adding activities and products in response to opportunities. It is easy to lose focus in this way. The basic business process needs to be planned, organised and managed efficiently, to ensure customer requirements are progressed quickly and efficiently, whilst people and resources are working productively. The business resource process included in Table 6.3 is a recommended technique for planning, organising and measuring the business process from sales enquiry to fulfilment. This analyses the relationship between the business process, information, and people's skills and capabilities which are needed to manage the process efficiently and effectively.

Managing financial resources effectively

In an early-stage venture, effective financial management is crucial in five respects:

● First, by planning and controlling cash flow you can achieve and maintain a positive cash position and minimise unplanned borrowing requirements, whilst keeping in contact with lenders or investors.
● Second, it is needed to control costs, especially fixed costs, and grow the business on a variable cost basis, except where committing fixed costs is essential and makes business sense.
● Third, it helps ensure customers pay promptly (preferably in advance) and debt is chased and collected.
● Fourth, it is important to assess and monitor the break-even position to establish profit or loss of the business, of each activity and major customer.
● Fifth, maintaining personal supervision of business finance keeps you aware of the risk of theft or fraud, although employing a competent and trustworthy person to maintain the business accounts using a standard accounting package is recommended.

reasons for success and failure in early-stage ventures

Why do new ventures succeed or fail? There are of course many reasons for this. However if the new venture can recognise the reasons for failure and their possible causes this can help in planning, managing the venture and solving problems. Similarly, and more positively, if the characteristics and behaviours of successful businesses can be identified these can act as positive exemplars to learn from.

It is important to note that in the UK, for example, a high proportion of new businesses – as much as 36 per cent – do not survive until their third anniversaries. Not all of these businesses fail; a surprising proportion close voluntarily, as a result of lifestyle changes, the founders finding alternative employment, or for other reasons.

Reasons for business closure

Common reasons for failure and early closure include the following:

Financial

- cash flow shortage/exhaustion
- inability to obtain financial loan or investment
- bad debt incurred by customer
- insufficient sales revenue
- costs of running the business higher than expected in relation to income.

Competition, marketing and selling

- failure to secure sufficient customers
- size of market too small to sustain business
- action by competitors or lack of competitive advantage
- loss of customers
- over-pricing or under-pricing and lack of viability.

Operational

- failure to satisfy customer quality or delivery requirements
- high rates of complaints, rejects or re-work
- unreliable suppliers, subcontractors or distributors
- inability to obtain essential items or services
- essential data or information lost or unavailable.

Legal

- failure to protect intellectual property
- costs of defending or losing legal action
- costs or difficulty of complying with legislation or regulation.

Human

- insufficient skills and expertise to manage the business
- inability to find or retain employees with necessary skills or experience
- disagreement or incompatibility between people in the business
- ill health or death in the business.

Environmental

- economic downturn or recession
- loss or unavailability of premises
- fire, flooding, weather damage or effect on seasonal business.

These 25 reasons for business failure illustrate the diversity of events and problems which can disrupt a business and result in failure or closure. Some of them could not be predicted. The Indian Ocean tsunami wave and New Orleans flood disasters in 2005 destroyed thousands of small businesses. However many business failures result from incorrect or over-optimistic assumptions or decisions made by the founders, or from lack of skills and preparedness.

Most of these problems could be prevented by better planning and research, or are capable of being managed to enable the business to survive. Only the factors connected with environment and health-related events are reasons for closure which the business can do little or nothing to prevent or manage if the effects are serious. It is unrealistic to plan for every contingency, but financial planning should enable most of the financial, marketing, operational and human problems to be prevented or identified early enough to be resolved, so long as the business is being run in a competent way. Therefore, management skills are critical in reducing the exposure of the business to normal events and contingencies. They are addressed in more detail in the section on entrepreneurial management skills.

Reasons for business success

The National Business Awards in the UK observed the characteristics of the entrants for and winners of its awards, including entrepreneurs, start-ups and micro-businesses, growing businesses and larger public limited companies (Forrest, 2004).

They identified ten characteristics: five enabling characteristics which are required for success, and five operational characteristics which are also required for effectiveness, but can only be optimised if the enabling characteristics are practised in the business.

> Successful companies exhibit most of these characteristics most of the time. The blend and proportions vary according to the business, its state of development and the market conditions in which it operates, but regardless of size there is never any abatement in the quest for success. Successful businesses want continued success and those that lead them and work in them want to sustain that position.
>
> (Forrest, 2004)

Enabling characteristics

- *Good leadership*: the most important success factor, with leaders who deliver results, show vision of the opportunity available; execution to direct, organise and resource the opportunity; and personal commitment to achieve it.
- *Strong culture*: company values practised by the leaders which are backed up by consistent actions and behaviours in the business.
- *Clarity of purpose*: mission or strategic intent focused on achieving a clearly defined objective, e.g. the capability to create or meet a market-identified need.
- *Real customer focus*: the business is directed to meet clearly identified customer needs – understanding the customer's world drives the business management, processes, and product or service proposition.
- *Readiness to reinvent*: businesses make fundamental strategic changes to reposition themselves in their chosen market, by changing business models, product and process innovation, and customer interaction.

Operational characteristics:

- *Engaging people*: ensuring the right people for the business are recruited, developed and managed effectively; providing the skills, resources and freedom for them to work effectively.
- *Courage*: leaders and people in the business are prepared to adopt new strategies and change with determination to achieve significant growth or improvement.
- *Persistence*: in achieving goals, to overcome adversity, failures and setbacks.
- *Creativity*: everyone is encouraged and stimulated to bring about innovation.
- *Focus on growth*: desire and determination to grow sales revenue, through clear market understanding, a sound business model, available resources, clarity of purpose, staff engagement and waste prevention.

activity

business success and failure

Consider the business opportunity you are exploring in relation to the reasons for business success and failure.

- Which of the list of reasons for business closure and failure do you think your business could be most exposed to? What steps could be taken to reduce the risk or impact of these?
- Which of the characteristics of business success do you think will be most important to your business? How could you develop these characteristics in the business?
- How could you use the six essential activities for early-stage businesses to help you in managing the launch and early trading of the venture?
- Overall, which of these factors do you think are most critical to the success or failure of a new business venture?

example

Case study: Michael – Phoenix Fabrications

Michael started his career in the family business in the West Midlands, which manufactured bespoke aluminium fabrications for the construction industry. In his words, the business had become 'tired', lacking innovation and its margins were being eroded as it chased orders. After ten years experience in the fabrication industry, he left, frustrated by the lack of development in the business, having decided to start his own venture; it was, he says, 'a career move'.

Michael realised that there was a growing demand for architectural aluminium fabrications in the construction industry as building projects became more complex and made increasing use of aluminium shapes in cladding and roofing. Existing manufacturers had not kept pace with architectural designers and he saw the opportunity to bridge this gap, starting his company, Phoenix Fabrications and Accessories Ltd, in 1999.

From the beginning, constant innovation has been the key to the business with over £1m invested in technology. Phoenix designs and manufactures 'anything in aluminium' – a growing range of aluminium roofing, cladding and detail components including louvres and bullnose fascia products. It responded to demand by being first in the sector with its technology, improving speed and efficiency through production innovations such as automated production using robotics and powder-coated finishing. The business has expanded to include a holding company which owns the three trading companies of fabrications and accessories, structural supplies which trades as a one-stop supplier of tools and fasteners, and Acme self-storage which responded to the growth in this market by fabricating self-storage units.

A major innovation has been the company's approach to marketing. The visual identity, website and brochures project a strong, confident corporate image which has been used successfully to target top clients in the construction industry. The website provides a facility for customers to create fabrication drawings online, calculate and place orders as well as responding to questions, making the technology easy to interact with. Michael pays close attention to working with key clients, ensuring good communications and looking after both new and existing customers, being aware of the 'residual value' of the client. The company's products have been used in high-profile projects such as the Selfridges' store in the Bull Ring, Birmingham, and the new Wembley Stadium.

The company started in 2000 and its first year sales were £1.9m with operating profits of £135k, growing steadily to £5m sales in 2004 with profits of £182k and a forecast of steadily increasing sales. The low growth of profits in relation to sales indicates the significant re-investments made in the business to support its growth. The future strategy is to maintain and steadily increase sales whilst improving profit margins by cost control and better purchasing, adding new business units where strong opportunities are identified, and aiming to be the best rather than the biggest.

A vital aspect of the success of Phoenix has been the approach taken to managing people. The company employs 70 staff, and aims to give them ownership and responsibility for managing their part of the business, by defining costs and expectations clearly; as Michael says, 'they work with you, not for you'. This encourages people to 'shine in their own roles'. Initiatives have been taken to train apprentices, to find and retain people, to promote family–work time balance, and to give employees responsibility for their own machines, resulting in better care and reduced maintenance. These are all facets of the strategy to attract employees and to instil the 'feelgood factor' at work.

This concern for people is also reflected in the company's community involvement; there is engagement with schools, sponsorship of football events, and environmental impact reduction and waste recycling and control which have also helped to reduce costs.

Phoenix completed its first five years not only with the success of being a supplier to several high-profile projects, but also winning a Shamrock award for their marketing and website, and Michael being a finalist in the Entrepreneur of the Year award by the National Business Awards. As well as success for the company, this represented a personal achievement for Michael, who had realised his vision to create a design-led brand identity rather than simply a metal-bashing business; to lead by example in finding people to complement his own skills; and to use his communication and marketing skills to focus on the key profit opportunities in the industry. He had realised his 'modest but realistic ambition' to create his own business through self-belief and motivation, and was well placed to add new business ventures to the group.

www.phoenixfab.co.uk

activity
- What constraints or problems do you think the business may face?
- What significant opportunities which could be open to the business?
- What recommendations would you make to take advantage of these to enable Phoenix to continue its growth?

sensemaking in entrepreneurship

The vital task of entrepreneurship is to make opportunities happen. Yet it is often difficult to apply the general theories and principles in the literature on the subject to the specific nature of real situations. Textbooks and journal articles refer to 'implementation' of the business plan or the 'exploitation' phase of an opportunity but making opportunities happen is a practical, real-world activity rather than a theoretical domain. So it is helpful to introduce approaches which enable us to develop skills of discovery learning and practical action in opportunity exploitation.

Karl Weick, in *Sensemaking in Organizations* (1995), described sensemaking as a way of making sense of complex and changing environments, which explained surprises, and individual and social behaviour. Sensemaking is how we continuously interpret the world around us and create new meaning through our interaction with it. Weick's notion of sensemaking is generic and not limited to entrepreneurship, although it has been connected with entrepreneurial opportunity recognition (Gartner et al, 2003).

Sensemaking, Weick proposed, is a process with seven characteristics. It is:

- grounded in identity construction
- retrospective
- enactive of sensible environments
- social
- ongoing
- focused on and by extracted cues
- driven by plausibility rather than accuracy
  (Weick, 1995).

What does this mean, and how does it help in understanding how to act on entrepreneurial opportunities? The seven properties of sensemaking are outlined in Table

TABLE 7.2 **Sensemaking in entrepreneurship**

Sensemaking property	Entrepreneurial application
Grounded in identity construction: the discovery of who I am through how and what I think, in relation to others	Becoming and behaving as an entrepreneur in society – personal and social emergence, Chapter 3
Retrospective: creation of meaning from reflection and conceptualisation of meaningful lived experience	Reflecting on learning to work effectively – 'what works for me' as an entrepreneur, the concepts of 'practical theory' and the entrepreneurial learning model, Chapter 3
Enactive of sensible environments: constructing reality and order from creating, acting, and relating; producing part of the environment we face	Recognising opportunities and innovating to create new products, services, ways of working and organisations within an existing environment which impact on that environment, Chapters 4–5
Social: contingent on conduct and interaction with others in shared learning, meaning construction and negotiated or joint action	Working with others through the concept of the 'negotiated enterprise' and entrepreneurial teams, Chapter 3
Ongoing: 'in process' and emergent, in-flow but subject to interruption and emotionality	The real-life process of making things happen and making decisions in unpredictable environments, Chapter 7
Focused on and by extracted cues: selective structuring of experience and meaning, dependent on context	It is important to pay attention to clues and to what we have learned , such as market signals, opportunities, competitor behaviour – contextual learning, Chapter 3
Driven by plausibility rather than accuracy: coherence, reasonableness and emotional appeal are important in producing socially acceptable accounts or 'good stories'	The message or story, for example of the business plan or marketing presentation, must be plausible to be accepted, Chapter 6

7.2, and possible applications in entrepreneurship are listed in relation to each of them.

The seven properties of sensemaking in entrepreneurship

The following short case study illustrates how an entrepreneur in the media industry noticed an opportunity and developed his business to act on it. Read the case overleaf, and then the following activity asks you to interpret this using the sensemaking properties.

example

Newsline: online business news service

Guy used his skills and experience in industry journalism, editing trade journals and public relations to start a business providing a new type of media service for corporate organisations. He termed this 'press marketing' because it used a targeted marketing approach to achieve press and media exposure. It became a small, profitable business which fed business news stories from corporate organisations to selected journalists and media outlets. This matched product news from companies with the need for news stories in the trade press. The business innovated by applying leading-edge technology, using computer-based profiling of journalists and individual editors in specialist media. It was able to rifle-target material to the right person in the ideal publication with the readers it wanted, using the right language.

Guy recalls that 'I made an applied process out of a black art. We used technology, skill and expertise to manage an unmanageable process. We closed the loop and made it measurable, so businesses could see the return they got for their media spend.'

In the early 1990s the company started to lose customers and turnover. Guy realised early on that the Internet would revolutionise the media industry:

> I wanted to innovate where nobody had been before. I'd always been intrigued by technology and how technology can impact on my sector of the market. I realised that major data transmission networks were being built across Europe, from local to wider area and metropolitan area networks – why not global area networks?
>
> We carried out a survey to find out the demand for an online news service. This showed a very clear requirement for an online pull rather than push news service which was just not available, where journalists could access news as it's broken, personalised to their requirements.
>
> I knew I had to get into the market quickly, re-engineering my business because technology was starting to move so fast. I realised that the business was chicken and egg – egg and chicken. You didn't get the journalists if you didn't get the companies putting news onto the network, if you didn't get the journalists.
>
> The business was complex because it had to balance the revenue-generating part of the business with the non-earning part of the community, how would that work? No-one knew. We figured it out. What we did was to give the journalists what they wanted, how they wanted it and we showed we cared about them as clients.
>
> We had to sell this new service to the key movers and shakers in the market, so we went to the big early adopters at the top of the pyramid and got IBM, Hewlett-Packard, Digital, Compaq, Microsoft interested in using us. Once you get those signed up they bring in the whole market.
>
> We demonstrated our online service at the big IT network trade shows by taking the new technology onto the trade show floor and into the press office and demonstrating to journalists how it worked. We put a modem into a laptop and walked round the press offices remotely accessing news on the Internet without any connection – they couldn't believe it. We started to change the

paradigm of the industry, because we eliminated the need to distribute news in hard-copy format.

Guy pioneered the Newsline business, building it up successfully and profitably during the 1990s, gaining media accounts with major communications and IT corporations. The business innovated constantly, developed radio and video newslines, and became a pan-European, pan-American business. He realised that it needed major investment to achieve the scale required to grow into other industry sectors and to fulfil his vision of transforming the industry through technological innovation, and sold the business to a major news media organisation.

activity

Use the following questions from the sensemaking framework to interpret the case study:

- How does Guy use *identity* in exploiting the opportunity?
- How does Guy use *retrospection* to make sense of the opportunity?
- How was the opportunity *enacted*? How does Guy describe the *environment*?
- How does Guy develop the opportunity in a *social* context?
- In what ways is his sensemaking *ongoing*?
- What were the *cues* he *focused* on?
- Do you think the story is driven more by *plausibility* or by *accuracy*?
- Which of the seven properties do you think are most significant in entrepreneurship? In what ways?
- How could you use the sensemaking approach as an entrepreneur?

There is no single way of 'making sense' of a case, but here are some of the points you may have picked up:

- *Identity*: Guy uses identity in several ways in creating the business – inventing the concept of press marketing to differentiate this from PR, then branding the Newsline, Virtual Newsline and Radio and Video Newsline businesses. His own identity as a journalist/media entrepreneur is also deployed to create the media personality of the business.
- *Retrospection*: retrospectively, with the benefit of hindsight, the story makes sense. At the time, people did not know the Internet was going to revolutionise the news industry and foresight – prospective sensemaking – was needed to imagine this. However the retrospective capabilities of applying technology to the market need and staying close to the customer to find out and provide a solution for their unmet needs were applied effectively to achieve this.

- *Enacted in sensible environments*: the changing economic environment of the recession and its effect on his business prompted Guy to explore opportunities and to carry out research. By creating and launching the Newsline concept successfully he started to affect the environment and to change the industry paradigm.
- *Social*: Guy found out what journalists and corporate organisations wanted as clients and paid close attention to their unmet needs to gain their acceptance of the innovation. The 'chicken and egg' business model of the online community created a new social dimension for a media business, and demonstrating the technology at trade shows was a social enaction of the business.
- *Ongoing*: Guy was motivated partly by fear of losing the existing business, partly by ambition to use technology to change the industry. The pace of technological change meant that he had to either move faster than the industry to change it, or become obsolete as a result of change driven by others. He used a series of innovations to create a distinctive space for Newsline.
- *Focused on extracted cues*: the cues Guy mentioned, to which he responded, included declining revenue and loss of clients in the recession. Feedback from market research, clients and competitors, and the use of technological innovation to accomplish change, such as making press-packs obsolete, are examples of focusing on extracted cues.
- *Driven by plausibility rather than accuracy*: is the story accurate or merely plausible? You can decide. Certainly it is a selective rather than complete account of the business which may be convincing (it is 'true'), but equally Guy's telling may omit mistakes, what went wrong, and apparently unimportant detail through which the reader could construct alternative interpretations of the case.

Using sensemaking in entrepreneurship

The sensemaking framework is useful in entrepreneurship, not only in textbooks but in the reality of businesses. We all use the skills and properties of sensemaking without necessarily being aware of them. Having a heightened awareness means that our skills in assessing and working on opportunities can be enhanced. The concept of enactment is especially useful here. Through enactment we generate interpretations of the changing world and act in ways which cause further change. By acting, we create new reality and change the environment; however this environment can constrain further action. So for example, Guy identified the opportunity for a new service which he enacted through Newsline, causing change in the competitive environment. This innovation was noticed by other media businesses which responded with their own innovations, accelerating change and reducing the potential scale of opportunity for Newsline. Rather than compete, Guy decided to sell the business.

Learning to make it happen

In Figure 7.1, the map of acting to make it happen, the most important word is 'learning', because it is the speed and effectiveness of real-world learning which often makes the difference between the success or failure of a venture. This is related to 'action learning', originally developed by Revans (1980), which is the exploration of problems or questions which arise in everyday practice and which do not have evident solutions. Action learning investigates the causes, effects and possible actions through investigative and problem-solving skills, and is generally a group-based activity. In a new venture, the quest is to find 'what works' as quickly as possible and this is explored further in the section below on

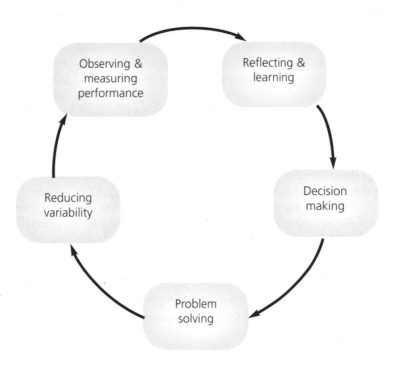

FIGURE 7.2 **Problem solving, decision making and learning**

practical theories. The connections between decision making, problem solving and learning in launching and managing a new business venture or an innovation project in an existing enterprise are vital.

Decisions to be made in establishing a new venture can include, for example:

- *Choice of organisation type*: company, partnership, sole trader.
- *Company ownership*: control and allocation of shares.
- *Financing*: self-funded, sale of equity, or loan of investment or working capital.
- *Target market*: single or multiple market segments.
- *Production/service provision*: make in house or subcontract (buy-in).
- *Capital equipment*: purchase, lease, hire or pay-to-use.
- *Venture team*: roles, responsibilities and authority to act.
- *Workforce*: employed, self-employed or agency (commitment or casual).

These are only examples of the many types of decision to be made in starting a new venture. Just as evidently, there are no automatically or normally 'correct' answers, since this always depends on the context. However it is important for the entrepreneur or venture team to have a decision-making framework or principles which they can use and which will help them to arrive at the best decision in the situation. Some successful entrepreneurs use rational argument and logical reasoning, others base their decisions on intuition and experience, and a combination of rationality and experience-based intuition may well be the optimum balance. These factors are likely to be helpful in decision making:

- What are all the possible options – both creative and rational?
- What are the intended outcomes of these, positive and negative?
- What could be the unintended consequences? How likely are these?
- What are the risks? What are the upside and downside? Can you live with the downside if it happens?
- How do we know the decision will work? Can it be implemented? What is the likelihood of success?
- What future options are opened up or closed down by this decision?
- Is the course of action in line with the strategic, longer-term direction of the enterprise?
- What short-term tactical advantages does the decision create?
- Are the short and long-term consequences of the decision compatible?
- What resources does the decision commit? What are the opportunity costs?
- How can the effectiveness or impact of the decision be measured – financially and non-financially?

<table>
<tr><td rowspan="2">activity</td><td>Consider the opportunity you were exploring and planning in previous chapters. Use the list of factors above to help you develop your response to these questions.

- What are the key decisions which would need to be taken in the early stages of acting on the opportunity?
- What factors would you use in developing a decision-making framework?</td></tr>
</table>

finding what works: practical theories for the venture

The key factors of strategy, skills, business model and product-market fit which can result in success are an individual combination for each entrepreneur. Every business is in a quest to find out 'what works' in its specific circumstances. This section addresses how to generate practical theories of 'what works' for a business using the practical theory grid shown in Table 7.3. Mike in Shires FM described his approach to running local radio stations:

> This is part-art, part-science, this is part what-feels-right. What do I know works? I can tell you what works because I've done it a number of times. I know what works, by gut feel and how people feel. Is there a list of rules? No, there's an approach, a style, a feel – I suppose it's things we believe in front of the business.

Entrepreneurs such as Mike produce practical theories in their own words from their experiences of their own practice, together with observation and social exchanges with other practitioners. Shotter (1995), described 'practical theories of action' as analytical tools which enable the manager as a 'practical author' to develop 'knowledge in practice'

TABLE 7.3 **Framework for practice-based theory**

Question	Explanation
What works? (or 'what happens ?')	What practices generally 'work' or occur and are effective? In what application?
Why does this work? (why does it happen?)	What is the logical explanation? What are the theories, factors or variables which explain it and which cause or define its effectiveness?
How does it work? (how does it happen?)	What are the activities, processes or conditions which are necessary for it to occur? How can we tell that it works? How do we know?
Who does it work for? With whom?	What are the social conditions and relationships within which it occurs?
What are the boundaries within which it works?	When, where etc. is it known to occur or not to occur?

Source: Rae, 2004b.

as 'special, contextualized forms of knowing', enabling them to see connections and create meaning between aspects of their lives and practices.

Practice is simply 'what we do', and entrepreneurs as effective practitioners discover 'what works for me', reflecting and making sense of their experiences to develop these 'practical theories' to explain or *account for* 'what works' and why it works. These theories govern such issues as decision making, dealing with recurrent situations, problem solving and the routines of managing relationships with others.

This knowledge can be used to develop an enhanced understanding of entrepreneurial practice. Through trial, error, and reflecting on action, people discover and adopt the practices, rules and routines which they describe as 'what works', often described as 'gut-feeling'. This is intuitive and tacit 'know-how', 'know-what' and 'know-who'. This social knowledge and acquired wisdom is practical, contextual, experiential, hard to analyse or test, and is formed and shared through social interaction, for example through the 'war stories' entrepreneurs share.

Practice-based theory is derived from interpreting entrepreneurs' practical theories at a more general level above the level of the individual case. Practice-based theory not only provides an understanding of 'what works', or what happens, but goes beyond this to explain why it works or occurs, how it works, with and for whom it works, and the conditions or boundaries within which it works.

Practice-based theories especially relevant to entrepreneurship have been identified in the following areas:

● personal learning and development
● transition from pre-entrepreneurial to entrepreneurial action
● opportunity recognition and selection

- creating and starting business ventures
- decision making
- risk spreading and minimisation
- developing entrepreneurial managers and management teams
- employee attraction and retention
- market and customer relationship development
- innovation development
- managing growing businesses.

Here are two examples of practice-based theory which illustrates the concept of negotiated enterprise which was introduced in Chapter 3.

Guy (Newsline) said that:

> The business was very complex because it meant balancing the revenue-generating part of the business with the non-earning part of the community. How does that all work? No-one knew. We figured it out. What we did was to give the journalists what they wanted, how they wanted it and we showed we cared about them as clients.

Mike (Shires FM) said that:

> In radio you have to start big time, because you spend a huge amount of money winning an audience before you get a single penny in revenue. You're winning customers who don't pay you a penny to listen, and it only comes when you can turn round to advertisers to say 'Hey, all these people can listen to you if you advertise with us.

Practice-based theory: negotiated enterprise

What works?

The creation of value in media businesses involves a negotiated exchange between paid-for information and content by advertisers or content providers with media producers who can show, in measurable ways, that they are gaining their required exposure by attracting targeted groups of non-paying customers.

Why does it work?

The media enterprise meets the needs of the advertiser to gain exposure and of the customer to have information or entertainment in ways which create cultural value.

How does this work?

The media enterprise provides a media channel which attracts both advertisers and their target groups of customers in a culturally distinctive way through the mix of programming, style and services.

Who does it work with?

With advertisers or content providers who are prepared to invest consistently in gaining exposure for their message among target groups they wish to attract, and who are receptive and culturally attuned to their messages.

What are the boundaries within which it works?

Independent commercial media including print, radio, TV and Internet.

- Identify a business or organisation which you are familiar with, for example as a customer, and which is successful or effective in what it does.
- Apply the practical theory framework to it and use this to identify:
  - What works for them? How does it work, and why? Who does it work for and with? What are the boundaries within which it works?
- Is this practical theory transferable to other organisations?

Having a base of defined and understood practical theories gives a business important advantages. These include being able to grow, by being able to recruit managers and employees to work or be trained in ways which are known to work. The practical theory may be used to franchise or license the business model, or to sell the business as an effective going concern. Practical theory is therefore an aid to growth strategy and a means of reducing risk; you would not be likely to invest in a business which did not know 'what worked' for it.

entrepreneurial management

Entrepreneurial management connects entrepreneurial and managerial skills to enact opportunities. This section proposes that both are required to start and more importantly to grow and sustain an organisation over time. This builds on the model of entrepreneurial and managerial skills introduced in Chapter 3 (and available in the toolbox) which we will return to at the end of this section.

The academic literature on entrepreneurship started to find points of convergence with strategic management during the 1980s, for example through Kanter (1983), Drucker (1985), and Burgelman (1983). These proposed that established corporate organisations could rejuvenate their fortunes by systemising entrepreneurial behaviour and innovation, as conceptualised in Guth and Ginsberg's integrative model (1990). Although the related concepts of corporate entrepreneurship and corporate venturing were developed partly to meet the needs of large corporations, the literature reflected a tension between the qualities of corporate strategic management and of entrepreneurship. Aiming to reconcile this, Stevenson and Jarillo (1990) advanced a set of propositions for corporate entrepreneurship, focusing on the pursuit of opportunity regardless of resources controlled; the orientation of employees towards detecting and exploiting opportunities; connecting resource networks to opportunities; and organisational risk-taking. Kanter (1983) more recently proposed a dynamic model of innovation within a networked organisational context as a framework for corporate entrepreneurship, advocating cross-functional working within very small business units.

These are principally North American perspectives on the transformation of corporate organisations through adopting entrepreneurial approaches; British writers have also explored this territory. Watson (1995) argued against a 'fatal distinction' between entrepreneurship and professional management, suggesting in accord with Drucker (1985) that entrepreneurship requires the application of complementary management practices, especially in the area of strategic exchange of organising, shaping and giving direction to people's work. Carr (2000) offered a critique of the culturally produced discourse of entrepreneurial management, stressing the role of government in creating this. She also noted the dialectic contradiction, yet necessary co-existence, between entrepreneurial freedom and rational control-centred management. More recently, Burns (2004) has explored corporate entrepreneurship in depth.

Significantly, Gibb (2000), like Kanter, advocates the virtue of 'smallness' in organisational thinking to stimulate entrepreneurial behaviour, arguing that large organisations are agglomerations of small ones. In enacting the 'entrepreneurial lifeworld' concept, he proposes the need for autonomy in strategy making, ownership, linking responsibility with reward, holistic management and networked, trust-based, rather than hierarchical relationships.

These perspectives still leave a gap in the literature on entrepreneurial management. Entrepreneurship theory continues to focus on creating opportunities and new ventures, whilst corporate and entrepreneurial management literature concentrates on how established large firms can become more effective in achieving corporate renewal through innovation and new ventures. The gap is in an understanding of how the new venture, whether independently or corporately owned, is managed in order to exploit the opportunity and to grow the business to its full potential. This requires an understanding of how management principles and practices can be applied to the growth of the entrepreneurial business.

A simple conceptual framework for entrepreneurial management is shown in Figure 7.3. This demonstrates the relationship between entrepreneurial and managerial working in which both modes can work in synergy within an organisation to create new value by stimulating and meeting customer demand in new ways, without the tension identified between the implicit values of each mode (Stevenson and Jarillo, 1990; Carr, 2000). The two modes are successfully integrated, with an entrepreneurial focus on customer attractiveness and rapid innovation in response to new opportunities, whilst managing the direction, processes, relationships and resources of the business organisation.

Entrepreneurial working

In this model the business has a strong *opportunity focus*, constantly searching to anticipate and identify potential opportunities by being close to its chosen market. It *innovates rapidly* to create and implement new business models, products and services, which are presented as attractive buying propositions to stimulate the customer demand. The business behaves dynamically in the market, *challenging the orthodox* business models, often being first to introduce change or responding swiftly and energetically to competitive or environmental threats. It uses new and existing ideas and technologies to engage the customer in new ways, to reduce costs and continually improve efficiency or service, while approaches which do not work are quickly rejected.

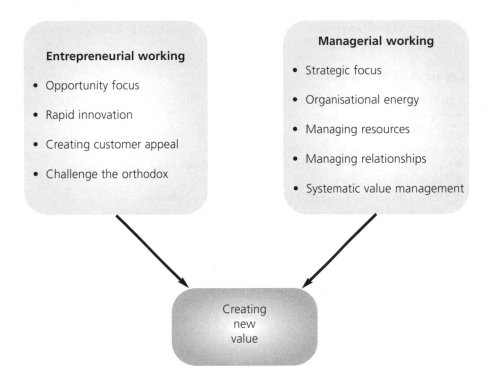

FIGURE 7.3 **Entrepreneurial management**

The business creates a strong *customer appeal*, using its own images, myths and stories to personalise the brand identity and using public media effectively to meld an affinity with its customer base, knowing that their loyalty is temporary and can quickly be lost.

Managerial working

The business is managed with a strong *strategic focus* through which the mission, strategic goals and business values are tightly focused, interdependent, mutually consistent, and communicated effectively. Staff enact the strategy and values through their everyday actions in managing the business.

There is *organisational synergy*, co-ordinating and communicating effectively between all parts of the business. Hierarchy is minimal and people are empowered to make operational decisions, with self-managing teams and a no-blame culture of dealing with problems quickly as they arise. Attention is paid to *managing relationships* effectively both within the organisation and externally, with groups such as investors, suppliers, customers and government agencies.

The business focuses on capturing and *managing resources*, of people, finance, technology and those related to capacity, which are needed to grow the business and to meet customer demand. At the core of the business there is a robust economic model of *systematic value management*, which optimises demand, resources and profit through making pricing and cost control decisions which enable the business to operate more efficiently in the market place than its competitors whilst offering 'best value' to the customer. Operational processes are robust, simple and designed to achieve maximum efficiency at least cost.

Creation of new value

The result of entrepreneurial management is the creation of new value, which may take multiple forms, including:

- developing new market opportunities
- introducing product, service or process innovation
- growing sales revenue and profit stream
- increasing asset value and share value of the business
- increasing demand for employees and supply chain businesses.

The practice of entrepreneurial management is demonstrated in the low-cost airline case study in Chapter 8.

Entrepreneurial management capabilities

Entrepreneurial management capabilities are essential for the effective development and management of the entrepreneurial venture over time, and as the scale of the business grows, the level of management capabilities required will become more advanced and sophisticated. The type of strategy pursued, as shown in the next section, will affect the balance of capabilities required, but both entrepreneurial and managerial skills are needed. However few people could justifiably claim to be equally capable in both these forms of working, and there is the need for venture teams to include a combination of both. The map introduced in Chapter 3 is repeated in Figure 7.4 to remind you of these capabilities.

activity

- Use Appendix 1 in the toolkit to assess your management capabilities.
- How does your self-assessment of entrepreneurial and managerial capabilities compare? Which are stronger?
- How could this preference be explained? In what ways could it affect your career choices?
- What roles would you be most capable of adopting in a venture management team?

strategic business growth

In acting on an opportunity, the decisions and actions required to pursue a strategic direction are vitally important. It is assumed that, in exploring and planning the opportunity, decisions will be been taken regarding the market segment, product or service

FIGURE 7.4 **Entrepreneurial management capabilities**

combination, the fit between the product/service offer and the market opportunity, the differentiation from competitors, pricing, the business model and other issues. These are all strategic decisions, even if they did not appear to be so at the time they were taken. It is surprisingly easy in starting new ventures to make what seem to be 'natural' or 'obvious' choices without realising the strategic implications these can have later on.

It is therefore important to be able to evaluate how effective these decisions are and to confirm, modify or re-think the business strategy. You may remember that two of the features of successful companies identified earlier in this chapter were their readiness to reinvent themselves together with courage to change. It makes sense to review the effectiveness of the business strategy regularly, and the framework in Table 7.4 provides a means of doing this.

Strategic framework

A regular review of the strategic framework should inform and evaluate the business strategy. The scope of key items from the review can be determined by the characteristics of the business and many will review the operational issues of sales and financial perform- ance weekly. It may not be necessary to review the vision every month, for example, but the effectiveness of strategies in achieving the vision should be reviewed. This applies even in the smallest business where it is normal for the founders to be so enmeshed in the tactical day-to-day issues that they feel unable to 'work on the business rather than in it.' Yet it is essential to do so regularly. Perceptions from customers, employees, community and intelligence on competitor behaviour should be reviewed because no business can afford to be isolated from these stakeholders.

TABLE 7.4 **Framework for strategic review**

Scope of review	Information available	Review process
Vision Purpose or mission Strategic direction Goals or objectives Actions to achieve these Business model Sales targets Financial targets Key decisions: Market segments Product/service development Customer perceptions Competitor strategy Employee feedback Community feedback	Quantitative measures of progress against perform-ance targets or indicators (e.g. sales targets, market share percentage, cash flow, profit) Qualitative information or feedback (e.g. customer and community feedback – compliments and complaints, staff sugges-tions, intelligence on competitor behaviour)	Is progress as planned? What has changed? If different is this better or worse? What are the reasons for variation? What decisions or changes are required? What options for action are available? Which will be most effective? How will this be measured?

The information gathered for the review should include both quantitative data and qualitative information. The former enables achievement of targets to be measured, while the latter is likely to include suggestions, feedback and ideas from customers, employees and community. It is a mistake either to run a business by purely 'managing by numbers' or to ignore quantitative data, because vital trends will only be apparent through this analysis. The risk is either of managing minutiae or of paying attention to the bigger picture and missing crucial detail.

The vital factor lies in how the information is used in the review process. The starting point should be to compare progress with the projections in the venture plan, and to identify whether this is as planned or has changed. The reasons for variation, whether 'better' or 'worse', need to be established as clearly as possible, since these could reveal either assumptions which have turned out to be incorrect or changes which have taken place. The decisions which need to be taken and the options available should be estab-lished. Both creative and rational approaches are needed – creative thinking to turn problems into opportunities or open up new possibilities, and rational thinking to ensure that implementation and implications are considered. It is important that tactical decisions which seem right at the time do not exclude or 'lock off' future options, and that they are congruent with the strategic direction of the business. The most effective options should be selected and success measures, responsibility and timescale decided for review at the next meeting.

This activity of reviewing the strategy is a learning process which every business will undertake differently, but which is vital in order to check the effectiveness of decision making and implementation. It needs to be as factual, objective and emotionally neutral as possible because egos, personal pride and vulnerability will fog analysis and decision making. So the key factor is always: 'What do we know now that we did not know before, and how can we use this knowledge?'

Here Mike in Shires FM describes how he reviews business strategy for the group of radio stations as well as monitoring key information in three vital areas of the business – costs, income and audience figures:

> I sit down with all the senior managers responsible for programming, sales, finance, administration and human resources once a week besides company board meetings. At that meeting we review sales and expenditure, we talk about the overall strategy. I had previously been involved in meetings with individual stations, but now I've stepped back to focus on strategy.
>
> I still see the sales figures for each station and every sales executive every single day; it only takes me two minutes to look at them. I sign all but a very small number of invoices, I do look at them carefully so I still know exactly what we're spending. Our currency is audience, and I still deal directly with all the audience research for each radio station. So although I've stepped back from the individual man-management, I am still managing our three principle things: audience, revenue, expenditure.

The entrepreneurial business needs to seek opportunities for strategic business growth, based on future and emerging markets and product/service/technology possibilities. There is a very wide literature on business strategy but this section uses just one model to illustrate how entrepreneurial strategy often differs from conventional business strategy, and introduces the

TABLE 7.5 **Opportunity, resource and relational strategy**

Strategy mode	Resource-based strategy	Relational strategy	Opportunity-based strategy
Organisational priority	Efficient allocation of existing resources to opportunities	Profitable matching of short-term opportunities and resources	Identifying future opportunities and finding resources to exploit them
Activities	Capacity planning Cost control Addition of new resources Innovation	Market and capacity planning Sourcing decisions Innovation	Customer segment development Strategic innovation Partner acquisition
Examples of types of business	Capital intensive manufacturing, health, process and utility industries	Consumer electronics manufacturing, air travel, hotels, financial services, trading, retail fashion	Next generation technology Design and media Knowledge-based business

concept of resource-based, opportunity-based and relational strategy. As shown in Table 7.5, resource-based strategy is used when an organisation decides its forward strategy on the basis of the most efficient allocation of its resources to opportunities. Opportunity-based strategy is the opposite: it identifies and selects the most promising opportunities first, and locates the resources required to exploit them. A relational strategy seeks to match resources and opportunities in optimal ways. Both entrepreneurial and managerial capabilities are required – for example, an opportunity-based strategy will require enhanced capabilities of investigating opportunities, whilst a resource-based strategy will require rather more operational and organisational management capabilities.

This model demonstrates that, for many organisations, their priority will be to make the optimum use of the capital-intensive resources they already own. So companies in industries such as processing and manufacturing will allocate the existing resources they own to opportunities which they can accommodate in the most efficient way possible. Their potential is limited by the need to manage resources economically and to 'fill the factory'. The scope for entrepreneurial strategy is constrained by resource optimisation, although the addition of new resources to add value by complementing existing ones is one strategic approach. They need to create new opportunities by innovating and finding new combinations and applications for both existing and new resources. Whilst the targeted customer segments may be either existing ones or extensions of existing markets, they may need to develop new market opportunities in which they can exploit their products and capacity, as in the case of automotive manufacturers selling mature vehicle model types into developing-world economies.

An example of resource-based strategy is a UK hospital trust which has to work with primary care organisations to provide the most economic acute health care service for its community, and has to allocate its limited clinical and financial resources to meet ever-growing needs, leaving minimal scope for entrepreneurial innovation or for developing new income streams.

The opportunity-based strategy is much more creative in identifying potential and emerging opportunities in line with the strategy, and finding resources required to exploit them, which will very often not be owned or controlled by the organisation. This approach lends itself to the nimble and fleet-of-foot business which is adept at finding and deal-making with partner organisations who control the productive, knowledge or other resources required. Ownership of capital intensive resources restricts this, and there are surprisingly few organisations able to pursue a purely entrepreneurial strategy. For a business which has a significant resource base to adopt an entrepreneurial strategy, it must be prepared to see that base simply as a potential resource, which in future may either not be fully used or even not required at all and be divested.

It may well be easier for individual entrepreneurs to pursue serial entrepreneurial strategies than it is for entire businesses. An example is George Davis, who after leaving the fashion chain Next, which he founded, first worked with Asda to set up the George clothing brand based on wearable fashion, value for money and low-cost production, and then set up the Per Una mid-market fashion brand with Marks & Spencer. The Virgin group, led by Sir Richard Branson, is an exceptional case of a portfolio of businesses under a single brand pursuing an entrepreneurial strategy.

Most organisations find themselves in a relational strategy of trying to match opportunities with resource allocation in the most profitable way, and of shifting internal resources and buying in external capability in 'make or buy' decisions. Major brands such as IBM and Rolls-Royce have moved away from ownership of manufacturing capacity to focus their resources on the customer relationship and technology innova-tion, and buy in hardware and services they require. Relational strategy may seem a sensible middle way, and even inevitable for many businesses, but the disadvantage is that it can become a series of short-term compromises which consume a significant amount of management time, which is therefore not invested in opportunity develop-ment. One way of countering this is to have a director and team within the business that are responsible for identifying and developing new market opportunities, and to separate this from the part of the organisation that manages current business operations. Innovation can result from converging internal capabilities with external opportunities.

example

Lumus Lighting

Lumus Lighting is an independently owned business in the UK which designs, manufactures and installs exterior lighting systems for sports, industry and retail sites. The lighting sales, design, manufacturing and installation business units are managed efficiently and profitably, using a resource-based approach. However for 30 years the business has been active internationally, and pursued a relational strategy of finding clients and identifying suppliers of lighting components outside the UK with whom it could form partnerships to broaden its product base and differentiate its service from competitors. The potential of the Asian market was identified and a joint venture set up in China to manufacture lighting equipment for the rapidly growing Pacific market, and to import this into the UK where the domestic factory was not price-competitive on commodity products.

activity

Can you identify examples of organisations pursuing resource-based, relational and opportunity-based strategies? Alternatively, if you cannot identify organisations which fit neatly into each category, then think of organisations which are moving between resource-based and relational, and relational and opportunity-based strategies.

What do you think are the advantages and limitations for these organisations of these strategies?

critical questions on opportunity enaction

- What do you consider to be the most important activities in enacting opportunities?
- In creating a new business venture, what factors would you pay most attention to?
- What lessons do the reasons for success and failure of early-stage business ventures provide for entrepreneurs?

- How can the concept and skills of sensemaking help you in enacting an opportunity?
- How would you establish 'what works' in a business venture?
- What approach would you take to strategic decision making and reviewing the effectiveness of the strategy?
- How would you achieve balance between entrepreneurial and managerial effectiveness in the organisation?

opportunity-centred entrepreneur-ship in action

The purpose of this chapter is to provide case studies which include examples and illustrations of Opportunity-Centred Entrepreneurship in action. These demonstrate different stages, facets and types of entrepreneurial working in three distinctive environments, each of which has unique characteristics. They also provide more generally applicable ideas which can be used beyond their specific context. These case studies are designed to help you to apply techniques, tools and approaches covered in earlier chapters. They encourage you to use strategic and creative thinking to enable you to analyse the situation and to decide 'how you would act' in each case. Each of the three sections can also be used for teaching purposes, and suggested activities are included for this purpose.

This chapter should enable you to:

● appreciate the application of entrepreneurial working in different contexts
● identify how the concepts, methods and techniques covered in previous chapters can be applied to real situations
● stimulate you to think of the decisions you would make in each case.

The aim of the chapter is to develop an understanding of how entrepreneurship works in different national, cultural and economic environments, and to recognise that whilst these factors affect the way in which an enterprise is developed within that situation, the practices and approaches used in Opportunity-Centred Entrepreneurship remain generally applicable.

The first section explores an example of social entrepreneurship which is of increasing interest worldwide, and the case is especially relevant to developing economies. Social entrepreneurship is a means of rejuvenating communities, generating employment, providing valuable social and other services, and contributing the coveted 'triple bottom line' of economic, social and environmental value. The case describes the development of an innovation to purify drinking water in Kenya, and provides an example of venture planning for an international social enterprise.

The second section focuses on the creative industries, in which there is growing interest and expectations of economic resurgence. An increasing number of students have started businesses based on creative ideas and skills, and this section introduces the concept of cultural diffusion to a creative enterprise. This provides a framework for the analysis of how creative enterprises transform ideas into commercial activity, and includes questions based on the five processes of cultural diffusion for use by students and early-stage creative entrepreneurs. This will be of value to businesses outside the creative industries, for example in hospitality and service industries.

The third section discusses the development of the low-cost airline industry in the UK, and explores the significance of entrepreneurial management in the development of this industry. It includes the formation of easyJet and Ryanair, the entry of corporate spin-out businesses in the guise of Go, Buzz and bmibaby, and the move towards consolidation in the industry. One of the significant themes in this case is the relative performance of independent and corporate ventures.

aquifer: innovation and venture planning for social enterprise

Recognising the need

Jomo Chichongo was a water systems engineer. Born in Kenya, he had experienced at first hand the effects of water scarcity in African rural areas. It was normal for women to have to walk for several miles to collect water for the family and carry it home in jugs on their heads. Periods of drought caused major problems, and the lack of water affected health and sanitation, and limited agriculture and economic development. Jomo had realised through his education that science and technology could be used to benefit people's lives, and his motivation was to apply his understanding of water engineering to make a difference to people in developing countries, by solving some of the problems of water supply. He felt that in the twenty-first century people should not have to endure the hardship and uncertainty caused by lack of water or unsafe water.

Jomo had become professionally qualified and worked as an expert in water supply for communities, government bodies and non-government organisations as well as water supply companies. He had found that even where borehole, river or lake water was available, it was often unsafe for drinking because of the presence of minerals or other substances. The water could be tested by engineers such as himself, but in rural areas such expertise was not easily available and the quality of the relatively small supplies of water was not known. People tried the water and stopped using it only if they or their animals got sick. There was a need to find a way to test water at local level and find out if it could be filtered or treated to make it drinkable. This was the problem Jomo set out to solve.

Developing the innovation

Jomo's idea was to develop a simple kit to test any source of water for drinkability, and a filter kit which could filter enough water to supply a family for a day. The test kit would identify the type of filter or additives needed to purify or treat the water; these would need to be easily obtainable and would form part of the filter kit. In this way, potentially drinkable water could be tested and treated at family or village level. The test and filter kits would be robust, only requiring a battery for the test, and using gravity for the filtration process. The technology had to be easy to use, requiring only demonstration training, low in cost and reliable. People would have to want to use the system, and not reject it as unsuitable. If these conditions could be met, the market for it would be enormous.

Jomo realised he could not develop the system alone, and needed expert assistance. Through his professional institute, he made contact with a university department with expertise in digitising information on water quality and chemical composition. They researched the problem over a period, experimented with various ideas and technologies, and found a way of giving a simple digital readout of water quality on a small hand-held device. This also identified the filtration or treatment required and indicated unsafe water which could not be treated. The professor suggested this was a technological breakthrough which could be patented, and he and Jomo worked with the university technology transfer office and a patent attorney to file a patent application in their joint names.

The testing technology was only part of the solution, however, and a filter and treatment system needed to be developed to accompany it. Jomo designed a process where water was pumped or poured into an upper tank, and then passed through a filter and treatment cartridge into a lower tank from which it could be decanted through a tap. The water quality was checked by the testing device, and filter cartridges would be obtained and inserted depending on the test readout. In most areas, once the composition of the water was known, the same filter kits would be required each time. The capacity of the tank and filter system ranged from 20 litres, sufficient for a family for one day in rural conditions, up to 500 litres which could supply a small village through a supply pumped from a bore-hole or diverted from a stream. Prototypes were built, tested in village conditions and improved until the system worked perfectly.

Protecting and exploiting the technology

Jomo had investigated existing research, technologies and products, and concluded that the filter technology could not be patented as the process had already been discovered. However, the design for the system could be protected as a registered design. Also, a trademark could be registered to brand the process. Jomo knew that if he did not protect the technology, it would be open for others to do so and they would be able to restrict its use by imposing high prices. By protecting it, he would be able to control the application and be better placed to ensure that it was made available for rural communities in developing countries as he intended. So he registered the design and the trademark of Aquifer, which means water-carrier. This meant that for every system which was supplied, the university, its researchers and Jomo would receive a share of the rights for the patent on the testing device, and Jomo himself owned the design rights and brand identity of the range of systems he intended to produce. He financed this from his income as a water systems expert. However, at this point he was thinking hard about the different options for making the systems available. He had never run a company and had no experience in manufacturing, distribution, or marketing. He wanted the technology to be widely available as a generic solution at reasonable cost, and a reasonable return to be made for his family and the university research team.

At this point, having defined his rights to the technology, he made contact with other entrepreneurs who had started technology-based businesses. From these contacts, he realised he had four basic options. The first was to start a solo venture, in which he would manufacture, distribute, market and sell the system himself, but he realised this would limit the take-up of the system and probably expose him to imitative technology he would need to contest. He lacked the time, experience and skills to do this. The second option was to set up a partnership in which he would seek out people with complementary expertise to found a business and exploit the product, but this would involve some of the disadvantages of the first option. The third option was to set up a company to own the rights to the technology, and to licence this through distribution and agency deals. The final option was to sell or licence the rights to the idea to a major company. He was advised that, for whatever option he chose, he would need a business plan and high-quality legal and financial advice. He also realised the venture needed financial capital, to which he did not have access. Going it alone was not a good option and the question was which strategic option and set or relationships would achieve his goals.

activity

- What do you consider the advantages and disadvantages of each option?
- Can you identify any other options for exploiting the innovation?
- Which option would you advise Jomo to take? Why?

Jomo was in touch with various non-governmental development agencies and charities who shared his concerns for improving water supplies and were interested in using his system. He decided that the best option was to set up a company which would own the design rights, trademark and share of the patent, and would negotiate contracts for the manufacture, marketing, distribution, and field support for the systems. The revenue stream into this company would be re-invested into further research and development as well as paying a reasonable return to the founders and investors. There was strong potential for the supply of the systems into many rural areas to be grant-aided by development agencies and charities so long as the product and field support were effective and the price structure was equitable. In the business model which emerged, the distribution and field support would be provided by setting up a network of social enterprises, in which local people would be trained in water purification and in testing, installing and maintaining the systems. This had the potential to create sustainable employment, to retain income at local level, and to ensure ownership and continuity of the systems. Jomo's problem was that he had never done any of this before, and could not do everything himself. Yet he could not afford to employ experts or consultants for the development work which was now required, and he needed to see an income stream from the business. He was aware that this was a vulnerable stage for his business idea, because the innovation had been protected but he did not have the capital to exploit it, and he was aware that corporate vultures were eyeing up the opportunity.

The opportunity map Jomo prepared is shown in Figure 8.1 (overleaf).

Planning the venture

It was clear that nothing could happen without a business plan. Jomo started to put together a plan to raise money from non-governmental agencies and possibly private sector investors with compatible values and objectives. He was aided by Chris, an experienced entrepreneur who had recently sold his business. The plan covered a five-year period. The business model was for a company to hold the intellectual property and overall control of the business. The product manufacture and distribution to local level would be subcontracted. Licences for distribution and field support would be negotiated for specific territories, in collaboration with specific NGOs who would grant aid for systems supplied to disadvantaged rural areas and support the development of social enterprises to undertake training, installation and support. Other clients would pay the full market price.

The business plan segmented the market, set out the business model and predicted the growth over the five years they felt it would take for the product to become established. The investment would fund a management team to set up and run the business until break-even was reached in the third year. A total investment of $2m was predicted. This would enable an office to be set up with a development budget, and directors responsible for science and technology, finance and legal affairs, and marketing and operations to be recruited, with Jomo as chief executive officer and Chris as non-executive chairman. Jomo and Chris registered Aquifer Pty in South Africa, where the most developed business, communications and technology support they required could be found.

Jomo and Chris prepared to present the plan to a range of NGOs, investment organisations and charities as well as corporate organisations with the distribution and field support capability. They proposed that Aquifer would issue shares such that Jomo would retain 40 per cent, Chris would hold 10 per cent, a further 15 per cent would be reserved as share options for the directors to be appointed, and the remaining 35 per cent would

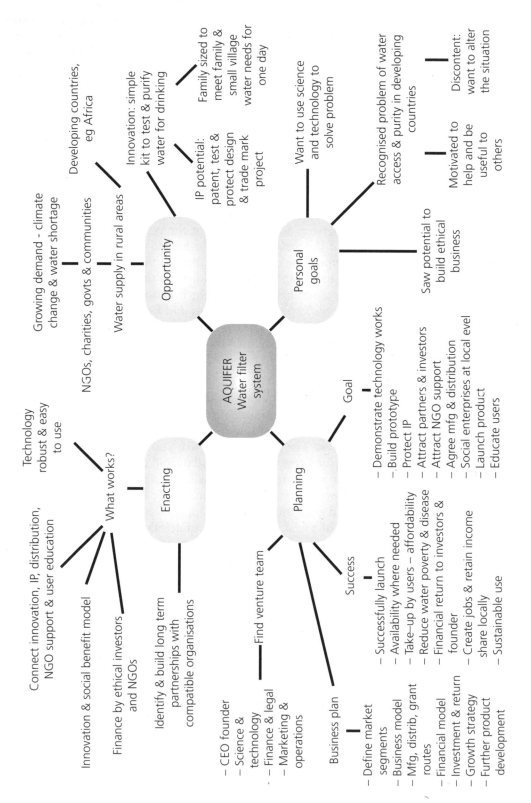

FIGURE 8.1 **Aquifer opportunity map**

be sold for $1m to an investment company, possibly one backed by the South African government. Up to $1m loan finance would be sought from the World Bank, to be repaid from year three. Finally, Aquifer would be able to hire the management expertise it needed, and negotiate deals to manufacture and distribute the product.

The venture plan they prepared is shown in outline in Figure 8.2 (page 192) and the business model in Table 8.1 (pages 186–7).

Aquifer case study

Assessing the opportunity

- Use the opportunity assessment (pentagon) and business opportunity (hexagon) models in the toolkit to evaluate the opportunity.

Entrepreneurial and managerial capabilities

- What entrepreneurial capabilities did Jomo develop or use in establishing the venture? You can group these under the headings given in Chapter 7, using Figure 7.4 – entrepreneurial management capabilities.
- What skills and expertise does the venture require which Jomo has not demonstrated, and will need to be provided by others? Does Jomo have all the capabilities required to act as CEO?
- What risks does Jomo now face as a result of the decisions which have been taken in establishing the venture?

The venture plan

- Assess the venture plan and business model in relation to the criteria in Chapter 6, 'Characteristics of an effective venture plan'.
- What do you think are the weaknesses, and how would you overcome them?

activity

TABLE 8.1 **Aquifer business model (figures in $000)**

Sales	Year 1	Year 2 Volume	Year 2 Value	Year 3 Volume	Year 3 Value	Year 4 Volume	Year 4 Value	Notes
Village kits		220	440	880	1760	2200	4400	
Business kits		80	160	320	640	800	1600	
Family kits		200	160	800	640	2000	1600	
Filters		400	800	1500	3000	5000	10000	
Total	0		1560		6040		17600	Assumes $200 revenue from 50% kits sold each year
Variable costs		*Per unit*	*Value*					
Kits	100 test kits	500 units		2000 units		5000 units		
Manufacture		$600						Includes subcontract profit margin for mfg, distributor, installer
Distribute		$120						
Install		$120						
Train		$60						
Total	10	$900	450		1800		4500	Average unit costs
Filters	*Test filters*	*Per unit*	*Value*					
Manufacture		$80						Includes subcontract profit margin for mfg, distributor, installer
Distribute		$20						
Install		$60						
Total	5	$160	64	1500 users	300	1500 users	1000	Average unit costs
Total variable costs	15		514		2130		5500	
Gross profit	-15		1046		3940		12100	
Fixed costs								
Employment	150		300		500		1000	
Premises	20		30		50		200	
IP & legal	30		30		50		80	
Marketing	20		50		80		100	

TABLE 8.1 Continued

	Year 1	Year 2	Year 3	Year 4	Notes
Travel	30	30	60	120	Product development & testing
Other	200	50	100	200	
Interest	50	250	240	230	
Total fixed costs	500	740	1080	1930	
Total costs	515	1254	3180	7430	
Net profit	-515	306	2860	10170	
Gross profit margin	0	68%	65%	68%	
Net profit margin	0	19%	47%	57%	
Breakeven sales	0	1088	1661	2838	
35% profit share	0	107.1	1001	3559	
Return on $1m	0	10.00%	100%	355%	Return on 35% equity share

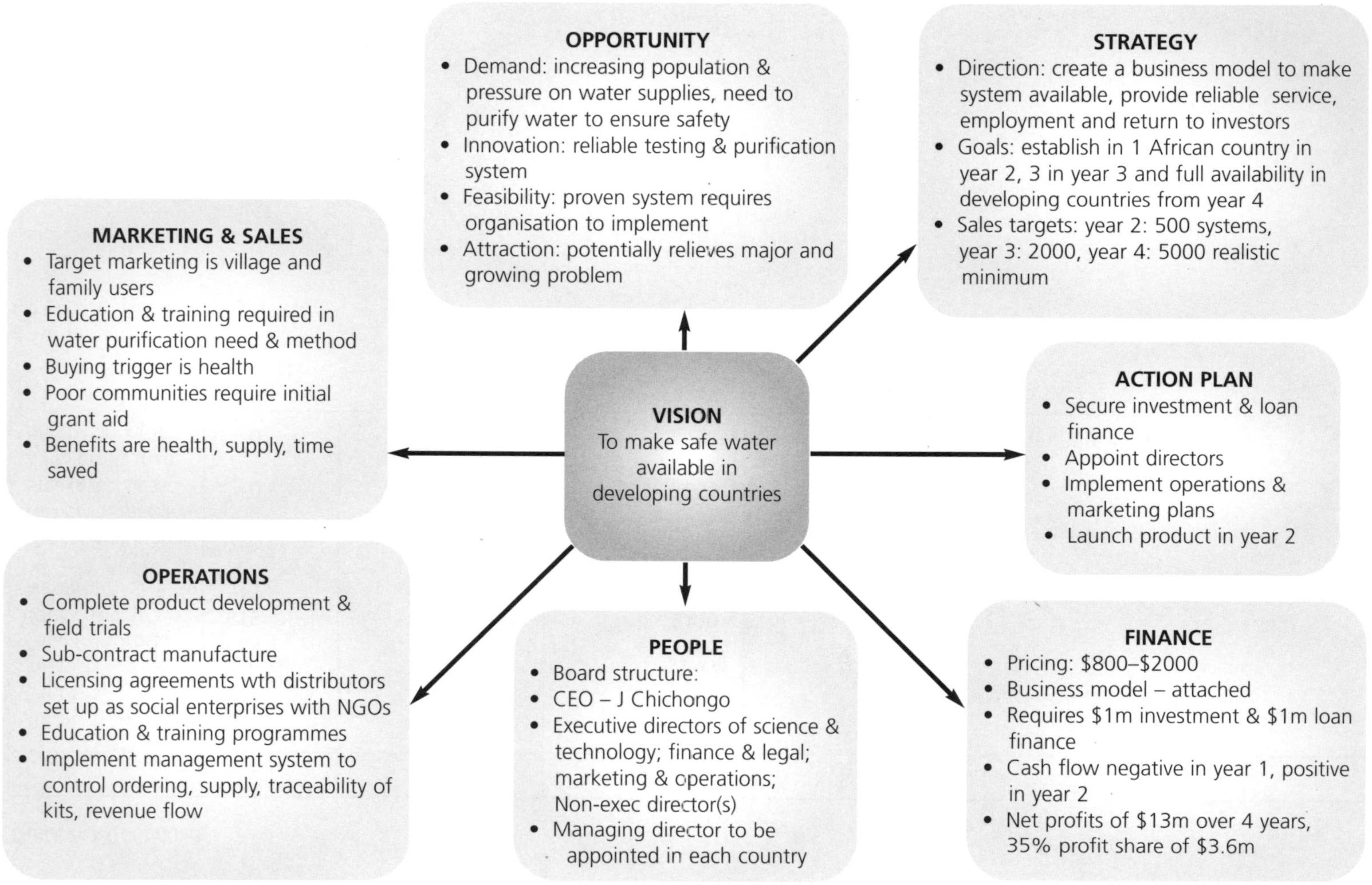

STRATEGY

- Direction: create a business model to make system available, provide reliable service, employment and return to investors
- Goals: establish in 1 African country in year 2, 3 in year 3 and full availability in developing countries from year 4
- Sales targets: year 2: 500 systems, year 3: 2000, year 4: 5000 realistic minimum

OPPORTUNITY

- Demand: increasing population & pressure on water supplies, need to purify water to ensure safety
- Innovation: reliable testing & purification system
- Feasibility: proven system requires organisation to implement
- Attraction: potentially relieves major and growing problem

ACTION PLAN

- Secure investment & loan finance
- Appoint directors
- Implement operations & marketing plans
- Launch product in year 2

FINANCE

- Pricing: $800–$2000
- Business model – attached
- Requires $1m investment & $1m loan finance
- Cash flow negative in year 1, positive in year 2
- Net profits of $13m over 4 years, 35% profit share of $3.6m

VISION

To make safe water available in developing countries

PEOPLE

- Board structure:
- CEO – J Chichongo
- Executive directors of science & technology; finance & legal; marketing & operations; Non-exec director(s)
- Managing director to be appointed in each country

MARKETING & SALES

- Target marketing is village and family users
- Education & training required in water purification need & method
- Buying trigger is health
- Poor communities require initial grant aid
- Benefits are health, supply, time saved

OPERATIONS

- Complete product development & field trials
- Sub-contract manufacture
- Licensing agreements with distributors set up as social enterprises with NGOs
- Education & training programmes
- Implement management system to control ordering, supply, traceability of kits, revenue flow

FIGURE 8.2 **Aquifer venture plan**

cultural diffusion: entrepreneurship in the creative industries

> So how do you go about turning creative ideas into a business? It's not as if you're just making a product, is it? How do you attract people to creativity and make some money out of it?
>
> (Kevin, founder of Loudmouth Music)

Creative entrepreneurs are diverse, ranging from self-employed artists to owners of global businesses (Björkegren, 1996). The growth of the creative sector beyond state-subsidised arts is largely a result of creative entrepreneurs identifying opportunities to provide cultural products, services or experiences, and bringing together the resources to exploit these as enterprises. Many graduates have set up creative businesses, but often struggle to make them viable.

Cultural diffusion is a distinctive approach to running a creative enterprise through applied creativity. The concept is used in this section to explore the social and creative processes of interaction between the creative enterprise and its audience or customers, to show how the creative enterprise can work successfully as a business in the cultural economy. The five key processes of cultural diffusion in creative enterprises are outlined and this framework is used to analyse a case of a creative enterprise. Questions based on the five processes of cultural diffusion are included to help you apply the concepts to early-stage and existing creative ventures.

The emergence of enterprise in the 'creative industries'

The 'creative industries' are of growing social and economic significance within the United Kingdom (Leadbeater and Oakley, 1999). The Department of Culture, Media and Sport estimated that they generated a revenue of £112.5 billion in 2000, and employed almost 1.9 million people in 2003 (DCMS, 2001). The 'creative industries' are broadly defined, and embrace activities ranging from fine and applied art, design, dance and entertainment to advertising, publishing and electronic media, including films, book publishing, popular music and computer gaming. Their growth has accelerated through the mass appeal of digital media over 20 years from introduction of the compact disc to include digital video, cable and satellite media.

The creative economy embraces the entire process from creating the artefact to its marketing, retailing and consumption, as the DCMS shows in its 'production chain' concept (DCMS, 2004). This creative economy is synergistic, requiring the involvement of many agents, some large and capital-intensive, some small and skill-expert, in its productive processes. Any cultural production, whether a music or video recording, computer game or theatrical play, requires a group of independent enterprises to act interdependently in complex and specialised ways. The self-employed creative workers who sell their ideas, talent and skills have to join forces with production and distribution companies in a shared enterprise. The existence of these complex and tightly wrought informal and collaborative networks of workers and enterprises gives rise to the concept of the cultural cluster (Scott, 1999).

The term 'creative industries' indicates that creative activity is economically significant, but it must find a market and support viable enterprises to be sustainable. The environment for creative businesses is characterised by rapid technological and social change, intense competition, and transient relationships with customers. Given this complexity and the distinctive nature of cultural enterprise, it has been argued that the learning process involved in starting and running such businesses, and the characteristics of 'this new generation of entrepreneurs', are little understood by policymakers and that education fails to prepare them for entrepreneurial activity (Leadbeater and Oakley, 1999; Raffo et al, 2000).

From production and consumption to cultural diffusion

In the creative industries a distinction is traditionally made between 'production' and 'consumption' (Lash and Urry, 1994; Hall, 1997; Du Gay, 1997). For example, a computer games designer produces a game, and it is then sold to players who consume it. This perspective over-simplifies both the cultural significance of the activity and the intermediary roles which many enterprises in areas such as media, entertainment and advertising play. The activity of these intermediaries is neither simply producing nor facilitating cultural consumption. An online computer game such as *Runescape* attracts millions of players who interact with the product and with each other as a virtual community. The idea of diffusion goes back a long way; John Dewey (1934) rejected the notion of the artist as active creator and audience as passive recipient of art, arguing that the appreciator actively engages with the work. As Leadbeater and Oakley (1999) argue, cultural entrepreneurs 'blur the demarcation lines' between consumption and production, work and non-work, individualism and collaboration.

Many cultural businesses engage their audience with the cultural product or experience in creative ways, such as the 'art-house' cinema which offers a themed programme of films selected to appeal to a particular niche market, both meeting and leading their expectations, and also provides an ambience of café culture in which the films are experienced and given life by the audience. Culture is a live social experience, even when it is exchanged through digital media, being actively constructed with the audience as an interactive symbolic exchange, and not just consumed by them.

Cultural diffusion occurs where the primary activity is not simply the production of creativity but rather the distribution and sharing of cultural discourse – ideas, language, symbols, music – with an audience, either live or remotely (Rae, 2005a). Cultural diffusion explores the social and creative processes in which symbolic and commercial value is created through interaction between the audience and the creative enterprise. Cultural diffusion is a creative process applied to a business activity, communicated discursively with its audience. A creative business performs a narrative and often visual act, 'telling a good story' or 'putting on a good show'. Forming such a business is not only an economic but also a creative act, for it involves shaping a complex cultural web of identity, relationships, communication, language, and technology. Communications media such as design and print, audio and video broadcasting, and the Internet engage the audience creatively and reflexively with the cultural message. Cultural diffusion gains the attention of an audience and leads their expectations. The development of interactive media and the Internet enables this reflexive diffusion of culture to take place rapidly and in new ways.

The five processes of creative diffusion

Cultural diffusion distributes and shares a discourse of symbols, ideas, language and artefacts with an audience by means of diverse communications technologies, enabling a viable commercial enterprise to be developed and managed. The five generic processes of cultural diffusion are outlined below and illustrated in Figure 8.3:

● It creates a unique *identity* invested with a personality or branding, which appeals to individuals and networks of intended customers, and with which they can identify.

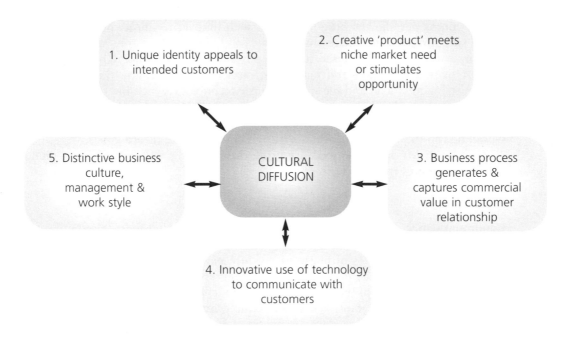

FIGURE 8.3 **Cultural diffusion in the creative enterprise**

● The creative *product, service or experience* meets a recognised market need or stimulates an opportunity, attracting a specific audience who interact with it in acts of symbolic exchange.

● A *business process* generates and captures commercial value in the symbolic and economic interaction between the business and customer.

● Innovative use is made of *technology* in engaging, communicating and interacting in creative discourse with the customer, especially use of digital media and Internet technologies.

● A *distinctive business culture* is enacted in managing the creative enterprise as a social organisation in which language, behaviour and work style interact to support the identity, product and process.

loudmouth music: a case study in cultural diffusion

Loudmouth Music is a business which aims to provide everything musicians need, from rehearsal studios to recording, production and distribution. The founder, Kevin Ellis, was a sound engineer who found talented and innovative musicians were often unable to find the rehearsal rooms and recording facilities they needed at a reasonable cost. He started Loudmouth to provide these in a town in the UK midlands, and attracted groups of young musicians to use the studios. These included musicians who experimented with crossing over and converging different styles of music, including punk, metal, rap, hip-hop and world music to produce vibrant sounds with a different edge. They developed their creative abilities and built up a fan base by performing locally, and sent demonstration CDs to major record labels. However the A&R (artist and repertoire) departments of the record companies showed little interest in such innovative music, preferring to look for bands similar to existing successful artists.

Kevin and his friends realised that the power which the major labels had enjoyed, of control over distribution and marketing, was changing rapidly through the Internet, especially by download and file-sharing music technology which the fans of the musicians around Loudmouth used constantly. They planned to develop Loudmouth as an independent music media business which would promote new music by using new technologies, and would be run to promote the artists better than the existing record labels.

Loudmouth Music is described using the themes of the cultural diffusion model, with illustrative quotes from the venture team.

Identity

Loudmouth appeals to young, 14–30 musicians and fans of 'alt-indy' (alternative independent styles of) music, especially those who are interested in the possibilities of combining different genres and styles of music to produce new and exciting sounds. The identity is summed up by the name: it is loud, with an aggressive, in-your-face, black-leather-jacket image. The personality of the business is independent, non-corporate and speaking for and to musicians and music fans, across all ethnic groups. Loudmouth aims to produce and release music quickly, with a constant stream of new sounds to excite listeners, and to keep them returning to hear new music every week:

> We encourage young people who are involved in music to come here. We involve them in helping to grow Loudmouth, make them feel special and they feel part of it.

Product

Loudmouth fills three gaps: it enables artists to rehearse and develop new material; to record and produce it; and to release and promote it in various ways. Rehearsal and recording studios are available with skilled sound engineers and producers. CDs can be produced, artwork designed, copied and distributed by independent networks, though Internet-based distribution is also becoming more common. Songs can be mixed and released in CD, MP3 and downloadable iPod file formats. The Loudmouth website is the focal point for browsing, downloading and mail ordering CDs. The music and the artists attract fans who want to hear different styles which experiment, challenge, sometimes subvert and give a voice to music which is not heard through the major commercial record labels and radio stations.

> People listen to us because we offer them music that they want to listen to with an attitude and style they can relate to, it speaks to them and is not just a manufactured pop product.

Loudmouth is also involved in creative projects with youth groups, giving it an educational role in the community. It runs workshops and access courses in music recording and production to encourage young artists to develop their musical skills. Song-writing encourages self-expression, whilst recording and production develop organisation and problem-solving skills.

Business process

Loudmouth started as a purely creative organisation but Kevin and his friends quickly learned that they had to operate as a business, by attracting and producing music as well as stimulating demand from listeners to buy the songs. They had to find ways of creating finan-cial value at each stage of the process, without this being seen as exploiting or 'ripping off' musicians or their fans, many of whom saw who file-sharing as a 'free' way of distributing music. The best way they could see of doing this was to maximise interest in their artists' music and therefore stimulate demand to buy it. They aim to identify and develop local talent and to promote this to a regional and national market. The musicians have creative control, working with the production team, and Loudmouth manage the commercial development. Their artists have the opportunity to build up careers and progress towards becoming major artists, even if this results in them leaving the label.

The rehearsal, recording and production services are all charged at commercial rates, with rehearsal rooms from £10 per hour and studios from £20 per hour depending on size and facilities. A song can be recorded, produced and mixed for download release for as little as £250 in studio costs. If this is downloaded at £1 a time, then the direct costs can be recov-ered by no more than a few hundred listeners. Each part of the business – the studios, production and distribution – aims to cover its full costs and to contribute revenue for further development.

Loudmouth also set up a music publishing company which protects the song publishing rights of its artists, unless they prefer to arrange this themselves. This ensures they receive royalty payments for radio airplay or recording of the songs by other artists.

> We have to make money from studio time, producing artists and selling their songs. We can't do it for free so we have to grow the demand for their work. Our way of working gives us real advantages over the major labels, we just don't have their marketing budgets or distribution networks so we have to use technology to our advantage instead.

Use of technology

Loudmouth aims to use new technologies to make it quick and easy for its creative output to get to the listeners. Listeners are encouraged to visit the website regularly and sign up for updates on artists and latest song releases, which are e-mailed to them. The aim is to release new music constantly, and free samples of each artist can be browsed. Tracks can be down-loaded onto MP3 and iPod players, and CDs can be ordered online. Listeners without credit cards can pay for downloads through their mobile phones. There is a fanzine section which includes news on artists, and listeners are encouraged to send in messages and reviews. The website includes gig schedules of performances by its artists and promotes their appearances.

Loudmouth artists have difficulty getting onto radio station playlists, with commercial radio stations having a limited output dominated by major artists and most BBC stations being conservative in their airplay. However the business was constantly being approached by young DJs who wanted to broadcast and play their music. Getting onto the crowded AM or FM radio frequencies was not possible for Loudmouth, but they investigated Internet radio and found that the start-up costs of an Internet radio station were low and Internet programmes did not have to meet the regulation requirements of a broadcast radio station. As Broadband grew, people could listen to online programming without worrying about dial-up costs. Loudmouth Radio was launched as an Internet station attached to the website. Initially this put out live programmes for a few hours each evening and weekend, when the target listeners were most likely to be logged on to their computers, and listeners could also download them at other times. They are available as 'podcasts' which attract growing numbers of listeners. The radio format gave new DJs the opportunity to develop their skills and attract an audience, while featuring tracks from Loudmouth and other independent producers. Take-up of podcasting and Internet radio downloads is growing rapidly and forms a major part of Loudmouth's strategy to expand its audience reach through new channels.

The radio programming, being free to listeners and initially not attractive to advertisers, was not commercially viable in its own right but formed an increasingly important part of Loudmouths's marketing, since it was unique, it attracted and held an audience, and could be accessed worldwide. It provided a further example of Loudmouth using new technology to develop its own listener base by going round the established 'rules' which had enabled the major commercial stations and music producers to dominate the market. Internet radio and podcasting will be a fundamental part of Loudmouth's growth although Digital Audio (DAB) is also a future option.

> Our listeners are technologically sophisticated; many are habitual Internet users with mobile phones, MP3 players, iPods and all those things. We use technology to make it easy for them to interact and maintain their relationship with us. Our website features the downloadable music range, you can sample tracks before buying them, and we have developed the Fanzine to enable listeners to tell each other what they think – within reason! The radio station gives them something new to relate to, to communicate with others, exchange ideas and form a virtual community online. It also makes it easy to update them with news and song releases. We will be introducing blogging [weblogging] into the Fanzine next to make it truly an interactive community.

Culture

The culture of Loudmouth is 'by music fans for music fans'. Their values are enthusiasm, creativity and support for new musicians, aiming to develop talent and to attract a fan base. This is coupled with a commercial realism: that everything they do must increase the fan base and offer them a unique new experience, and every new activity must achieve viability. All the facilities and creative output is priced commercially but keenly, so that young musicians and listeners will see it as good value. Loudmouth encourages musicians and listeners to be part of its community, and to tell their friends.

The core staff at Loudmouth is kept to a small production and management team, with creative, Internet and radio programming being provided by freelancers. This keeps costs down and makes it easy for dedicated and talented people to progress from being fans to creative producers.

> We keep it small, make it easy for people to feel they are part of Loudmouth and to develop and share their ideas. This gives everything we do an exciting, different edge. We are about being creative, having fun, producing great music and getting people to listen to it.

using the cultural diffusion model

This section includes questions on each of the five processes of cultural diffusion for you to use in analysing the Loudmouth case study. These questions can also be used by entrepreneurs and students who are developing creative business concepts.

- Use the questions in each theme of the cultural diffusion model, provided below, to analyse the Loudmouth case study.
- Take each theme in turn. You may find it helpful to use the themes to draw an opportunity map to do this, expanding on the map in Figure 8.3.
- How effective is Loudmouth as a creative enterprise? What do you think are its strengths and opportunities? What are its limitations and areas of vulnerability?
- How would you advise Kevin and the Loudmouth team to develop the business?

Unique identity appeals to intended customers

Identity attracts target customers to the enterprise and they express their affinity and loyalty by identifying with it. This notion of 'building a fan base' around the business can be seen in the emotional and symbolic connections which people form with creative enterprises, from the Rolling Stones to Harry Potter. This identity is jointly enacted and the business therefore needs to create ways which enable customers to identify symbolically with it ('wear the T-shirt').

- Who are the target customers of the business?
- What perception or message are they intended to form of the business?
- What is the 'personality' of the business? How will the business make itself memorable?
- How will the customer identify with the business ('join the fan club'), by relating to its values and personality?
- What motivates the customers to maintain their identification with the business?

Creative product meets market need or opportunity

The acquisition, consumption or experience of the product by the customer is a symbolic act which expresses a cultural or emotional need. However the enterprise must find ways to innovate and to engage the customers with new product ideas which retain their interest and loyalty.

- What is the existing need or emerging opportunity which the business will fulfil?
- What experience, service or product will be offered to meet this?
- Why will the target customers want to experience, consume or buy the product?
- How can the customers experience and interact with the product?
- What is the symbolic or cultural value to the customers?
- What makes the product unique and different from alternatives?
- How will the business keep in touch with customers' changing tastes and demands?
- What new product innovations can be introduced to maintain customers' interest?

Business process generates and captures commercial value

The business process is essential to generate commercial value and revenue from the customer interaction. Many creative enterprises, including radio, TV, galleries and websites, provide their product 'free' to customers so, unless they are subsidised, they must generate revenue from advertising or from selling affinity products. This is a growing challenge as people increasingly expect creative products to be available free of charge, and practices such as copying and file-sharing digital data are widespread.

- How will the business generate and capture financial value from interacting with the customers?
- What is the business process or model? Can you draw a simple diagram of this?
- What factors lead to risk, uncertainty or volatility in the business? (e.g. competition, customer taste, variable demand, seasonality, technological change)
- How can these risks be reduced, managed or prevented?
- What gross and net profit margins and break-even sales figures need to be achieved?
- What are the key success measures for the business? (e.g. sales per customer, sales and profit per month?
- How can performance be measured and improved?

Using technology innovation to communicate with the customer

The advance of communications technology enables the creative enterprise to engage its audience and to diffuse its message in increasingly sophisticated ways, for example through mobile phones, iPods and interactive Internet applications such as weblogging. Rapid innovation provides new possibilities but may also make the enterprise or its product redundant. Internet sites enable enterprises to provide newsletters for customers and to update them on events and new product offers as well as downloadable images, video and audio files using Broadband technology. The enterprise can reach an international audience, strengthening the customer interaction, and pervading their everyday lives.

- How is communications technology used to create relationships with potential and actual customers?
- How is technology used to update customers, lead their tastes, maintain their interest, and exchange information about their interests and needs?
- How can customers access information about the business and product via technology?
- Can customers access the product itself via technology?
- How can you use innovative technology to improve customer communications?

Distinctive business culture, management and work style

'Culture' is not simply a product of the creative enterprise but also a constant aspect of its lifeworld. Each enterprise develops distinctive social norms, behaviours, practices and modes of communicating. Founders and managers of successful creative enterprises understand how to foster the values, norms and behaviours which support creative production, effective customer interaction and commercial activity.

- What values are important in relation to the business, which staff and customers share?

- How are these values be communicated and enacted? (e.g. in design, language, processes, behaviour)
- What are the key roles in the business for creating the customers' experience?
- What attracts the staff who want to work for the business?
- How does the business 'keep the buzz' by innovating at a cultural and social level?

Conclusion

Cultural diffusion becomes intuitive in the creative enterprise. It works by combining the enacted values of innovation, emotional engagement and responsibility to people, with the 'feel' and 'approach' which the audience responds to. In a creative enterprise, the success of cultural diffusion depends on the interplay between the community of fans who provide the audience, the commercial activity which provides the revenue stream, and the creative producers. This fusion of creative and commercial strategies, which channels individual creative effort into commercial applications, is vital for success in the creative enterprise. Creative production alone has no intrinsic value, so finding opportunities to exploit it is essential. There may be tensions between creative activity and commercial exploitation, but only a minority of creative enterprises produce 'pure' or 'high' culture. Most apply a repertoire of creative ideas and discourse to exploit commercial needs and opportunities. The ability to do this successfully and to attract the chosen audience are vital aspects of creative entrepreneurship.

There is a quality of shared emotional engagement and energy in creative businesses which goes beyond rationality. People talk about their work using such words as 'buzz', 'excitement', 'fun' and 'passion'. The language, practices and repertoire of creative enterprises express the identities, emotional energy and abilities of the producers of creative work. This distinctive quality of creative businesses is culturally diffused and shared with the audience. The radio disc jockey, games designer, actor or musician, all share their creative production and emotional engagement with the audience. Their performance needs to be consistent and consonant with the ongoing expectations and values of the audience, aiming to gain attention, to entertain and in a marketing sense to result in a decision to buy.

Cultural diffusion engages the customer as an active participant, not simply a passive consumer. It offers the audience a narrative conversation of ideas and language through creative media, requiring new ideas to attract and maintain their interest. Innovation is a negotiated process which meets cultural needs in a different way, drawing customers with it, and distinguishing one enterprise from others. Cultural value is generated in the symbolic exchange between producer and consumer, and just as the producers are giving something of themselves, so the customers identify with the enterprise. The cultural identity of the enterprise is formed and enacted through the interactions between it and the groups with which it engages. Participating in selected networks, influencing opinion-formers, and being 'talked about' in the 'right' way are significant aspects of entrepreneurial working in the creative economy.

Although every creative enterprise is unique in some aspects, they face similar challenges in forging a business from cultural tastes and discretionary spending. This transformation of creative discourse into economic and social activity is more complex than simple 'production and consumption'. Cultural diffusion provides a practical and conceptual means of understanding the negotiated, interactive, informal and relational aspects through which the creative enterprise is enacted. Enterprises which enact the processes of cultural diffusion effectively are more likely to succeed, by working in dynamic and socially connected ways in a rapidly evolving environment, than those which persist with static notions of production and consumption.

> People give us ideas about what we could offer them, and they want it to work –
> they tell their friends! I think we meet a cultural need for our listeners.
>
> (Kevin, Loudmouth Music)

entrepreneurial management and corporate entrepreneurship in the low-cost airline industry

The third case study follows the rapid growth of the low-cost airline industry. It traces the success of independent businesses, in particular Ryanair and easyJet, in comparison with corporate ventures by existing businesses in the sector. It illustrates entrepreneurial management, especially in the form practised by these independent airlines, as an approach which is essential for success in the dynamic competitive conditions of this market (Rae, 2001). It analyses the reasons for the market leaders' successful growth and assesses the wider lessons this can offer to entrepreneurial organisations which aim to grow rapidly in a highly competitive industry.

The development of the low-cost airline sector in UK and Europe

A key to entrepreneurial management is recognising a potential market opportunity and acting to exploit this by creating a better business model ahead of competition. The opportunity for low-cost European airlines arose in the late 1980s when the European Commission began implementing staged 'open skies' legislation, full deregulation being achieved in 1997. This aimed to liberalise air travel within the EC and challenged the cartel of flag-carrying national airlines such as British Airways, Air France and Lufthansa which controlled 40 per cent of the available passenger-kilometres on scheduled intra-European flights through bilateral agreements. Progress in Europe from an oligopoly to a deregulated market was slow in comparison with the much faster transition in the United States, and seat prices remained high, being pegged to the fares of the flag-carriers, which had a high cost base and inefficient operating practices. Attempts by lower-cost operators to enter the market were blocked by denial of landing slots at main traffic hubs, or by anti-competitive and even illegal behaviour, as used by British Airways against Virgin Atlantic in the 1980s.

Southwest Airlines in the United States had developed a model of point-to-point short-haul commuter and leisure flying, and became the world's most profitable airline through highly efficient operating practices such as intensive fleet utilisation, fast turn-round times and crew flexibility, sharing the rewards with its staff by means of employee share ownership (Porter,1996). It continues to achieve revenue and profit growth, demonstrating the durability of its business model. Southwest Airlines provided a template for both easyJet and Ryanair to use in Europe. These two airlines created and dominate the low-cost airline sector in the UK; whilst there have been several moves by larger airlines to introduce 'no-frills' operations as corporate ventures, as well as new low-cost flyers which have entered the market, these have met with limited levels of success.

The independents: easyJet, Ryanair and Flybe

easyJet

easyJet was launched in November 1995 by Stelios Haji-Ioannou, with two chartered Boeing 737s flying between Luton and Scotland. Within five years it had grown into a leading European low-cost airline operating on 31 routes with 21 aircraft, and increased its fleet to 92 aircraft by 2004. The company's successful marketing and media relations initially focused on the flamboyant Mr (now Sir Stelios) Haji-Ioannou, who moved on to develop other easyGroup enterprises.

easyJet's mission statement is:

> To provide our customers with safe, low-cost, good value, point-to-point air services. To offer a consistent and reliable product at fares appealing to leisure and business markets from our bases to a range of domestic and European destinations. To achieve this we will develop our people and establish lasting partnerships with our suppliers.

The mission emphasises values of safety, low cost, efficiency and people development, whilst connecting with the operational business model. The point-to-point operation eliminated the complex hub-and-spoke model which causes disruption, customer dissatisfaction and extra cost. The easyJet model achieves optimum aircraft utilisation at maximum load factors (seat occupancy) on point-to-point flights, minimising overhead costs. This is achieved through simple, efficient business processes, 'no frills', dynamic pricing, and obsessive cost control. From its launch, seats were sold direct from a call centre, not via travel agents who demanded commission, which initially saved 30 per cent on booking costs. The passenger gets a booking number not a ticket, eliminating cost and unnecessary steps. From 1998, Internet-based sales were promoted and 80 per cent of bookings were online by 2001, branding easyJet 'the web's favourite airline'. The dynamic pricing model is a key element in the commercial operation; with all fares quoted one way, the earlier customers book, the cheaper their fare will be. All flight bookings are reviewed constantly to measure their popularity, with fast-booking flights having seat prices raised. The result is a highly efficient booking operation run from one call centre and website which consistently delivers high load factors on flights.

In the winter of 1995–6, easyJet flew on three routes from Luton to Scotland, and progressively added routes to continental European and to UK destinations. Low-price fares to exotic destinations on the French Riviera, Greece, Spain and Switzerland were highly successful with budget-conscious travellers who previously relied on charters and bucket shop agents, or simply did not travel. EasyJet created a new market of elective travellers who would fly if the price was right, and achieved significant growth by adding capacity and increasing its routes whilst attracting more new budget-conscious customers. In 1997 full European air deregulation took effect and easyJet was granted its own air operating certificate, demonstrating its operational and financial soundness, having previously operated under the certificates of other airlines. Now the European skies were open to easyJet so long as it could find the landing slots.

The selection and marketing of routes is a vital step for any airline, and new entrants face blocking tactics in gaining landing slots at prime airports such as London Heathrow and Paris Charles de Gaulle. These airports are also the most expensive and most congested, causing delays. EasyJet chose London Luton as its first base. This became a constraint as charges and competition from other flyers increased, and with the acquisition of Go in 2003 it developed operations from London Stansted and Gatwick.

easyJet had to fund aggressive growth in the face of competition from Ryanair and established airlines. Stock market flotation was the obvious route to finance its expansion, which aimed to increase capacity by 25 per cent by 2004 through buying 32 new Boeing 737-700s. As a privately owned company, easyJet made limited financial information available in its early years, but in 1998 turnover of £77m yielded a pre-tax profit of £5.88m. In 1999 turnover almost doubled to £144m but profit was negligible at £1.26m, whilst in the pre-flotation year to September 2000 turnover climbed to £264M with a pre-tax profit of £22.1m showing an upside for investors.

The easyJet flotation took place in 2000 and was highly successful, with £195m being raised at 310 pence per share, valuing the company at £777m. Staff were allotted 15 per cent of the shares, and a further 9.45 million shares were authorised and subsequently issued, yielding a total of £224.6m. The float was limited to institutional investors and individual applications were not accepted, despite which the shares were oversubscribed by nine times. The shares subsequently performed well and appreciated in value to 416 pence by January 2001, a rise of 25 per cent in three months, before falling in line with the market in March 2001 and trading as low as 118 pence a share, rallying to 418p in mid-2006 with a price/earnings ratio of 39.5.

A key factor in the share price is the credibility of the management and Board. Initially the business was fronted by the charismatic Haji-Ioannou, with the seasoned airline professional Ray Webster as Chief Executive. Together, they represented a combination of entrepreneurial flair and management competence, with Webster responsible for the highly efficient operating management of the airline while Haji-Ioannou created its public persona equally skilfully. When Haji-Ioannou withdrew from the Board to concentrate on new business ventures in 2002–3, this did not appear to affect the business growth or share price significantly, although the public persona of the business did become less ebullient, in marked contrast with Michael O'Leary of Ryanair.

Ryanair

Ryanair is the oldest-established low-cost independent. It started in Ireland in 1985 as a family business and broke the London–Dublin price cartel, then grew rapidly but unprofitably until 1990, when a relaunch headed by Michael O'Leary using the Southwest Airlines template saw it focus on five routes with six planes. Subsequent growth was profitable and in 1994, the year before easyJet started, Ryanair employed over 500 people, carried over 1.5 million passengers, offered low fares between Dublin and London, and was in profit for its fourth successive year.

Continuing growth in routes, fleet capacity and customers saw Ryanair achieve New York and Dublin stock market flotation in 1997 and initiate employee share ownership. In 1999, Ryanair announced a major investment programme of up to 45 new Boeing 737-800 series aircraft, with higher capacity than the Boeing 737-300 then flown by easyJet.

During 2000, Ryanair launched online bookings, quickly achieving 70 per cent sales online and over 90 per cent direct, making large savings in marketing and distribution by reducing commission on sales through travel agents. Since then it has competed and grown aggressively as the lowest-fare operator in the market, offering repeated 'giveaways' and flights from £1 return (plus airport taxes) as special promotions. Ryanair established 45 routes serving 11 countries by 2000, flown by 31 aircraft and with a workforce of 1400 people. It claimed to be the second largest airline in the UK, and Europe's largest low-fares airline. The target of carrying over 7 million passengers in 2000 was met, with a rising trend in traffic growth during the year and a 42 per cent increase in pre-tax profits over the previous year. Ryanair has demonstrated the ability to grow very rapidly, to compete with brutal effectiveness against other airlines by offering the lowest fares and high levels of punctuality, and filling its aircraft to turn in consistently growing profits.

Ryanair is the most ambitious of the low-cost flyers, becoming one of the 'big four' European airlines by 2003 and aiming to be the largest and leading European low-cost flyer. By 2001, it had positioned itself to grow the fleet capacity and routes to carry 9 million passengers in 2002 and 14 million by 2003, a doubling of its 2000 results. It developed very effective marketing, operating and cost-control models to achieve highly profitable operations, enabling a further share issue which financed increased capacity. Ryanair aims for continued growth, expecting to carry 35 million passengers in 2006, with a fleet of 115 aircraft operating from 12 hubs and a European market position ahead of British Airways and Lufthansa, challenging the merged Air France/KLM as the biggest airline in Europe by 2012.

Chief Executive Michael O'Leary based this forecast on the growth of the European low-cost market, together with the major flag-carriers concentrating on more profitable long-haul flights, leaving the bulk of European routes to one or two major low-cost carriers. O'Leary is the very public persona of the business, losing no opportunity to score points off the competition, declaring of easyJet that 'we're beating the crap out of them', to berate greedy or inefficient airport authorities, and to tell environmentalists, trade unions and even demanding customers where to get off. His mission is to deliver the lowest fares by squeezing out costs and to achieve growth and market domination profitably. By 2005 he had succeeded.

Flybe

Flybe originated from a merger of small UK flyers, Jersey European being formed in 1979 and acquired in 1983 by the Walkersteel group, operating from a base at Exeter. Jersey European established routes from London Gatwick to Guernsey and Jersey in 1991, adding routes to Belfast City, Dublin and Edinburgh from London City airport. It established a franchise partnership with Air France in 1996 with routes from London Heathrow to Toulouse and Lyons, and from Birmingham International to Paris Charles de Gaulle and Glasgow. These were not low-cost flights and used the more costly BAe 146 aircraft.

Following a change of name to British European, it rebranded itself as the low-cost airline Flybe in July 2002. It established a niche flying from the south coast to Europe, with a mix of low-cost and business-class ticketing. Flybe has major centres at Southampton, Birmingham and Exeter, and flies from 17 UK to 25 international destinations, having established itself as the third largest UK low-cost airline. Business flyers paying higher fares are an important aspect of its commercial model, and it offers them a frequent flyer scheme, more comfort and higher service levels. Flybe is profitable, having achieved net profits of £31.1m for 2003–4, and may consider a future stock market flotation.

● Refer to the entrepreneurial management model in Figure 7.3, which is reproduced below. Apply this to easyJet and Ryanair.
● What evidence do you see of the 10 characteristics of entrepreneurial management in each organisation?
● Which airline do you consider most effective in relation to these?

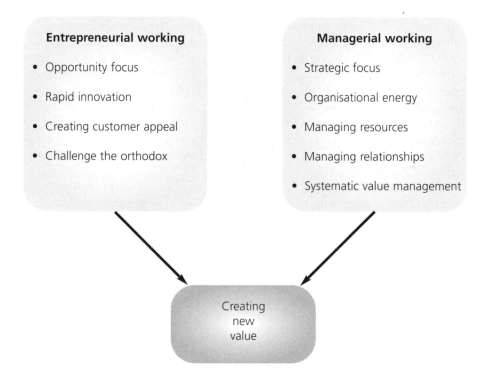

FIGURE 8.4 **The entreprenurial management model**

The corporate ventures: Buzz, Go, Virgin Express, bmibaby, MyTravelLite

The low-cost operators created a new market sector which challenged the dominated flights of the larger operators which were dominated by business flyers, and several existing airlines and travel organisations responded by setting up their own lower cost operations: KLM UK set up Buzz, British Airways launched Go, Virgin launched Virgin Express, and British Midland launched bmibaby. None of them found this easy, as it was difficult to cut their cost base by up to 60 per cent to achieve the same levels as Ryanair and easyJet. The different approaches they adopted provide an interesting comparison and have also provided opportunities for growth by acquisition.

Buzz

Buzz was launched by KLM in 2000 by rebranding Air UK, which it had acquired in the 1990s. This attempted to produce a low-fares airline but had the high cost base of a staff-intensive business commuter operation flying BAe 146 four-engine planes rather than the more cost-effective Boeing 737. It was estimated to be losing £100,000 per day, which was not sustainable for the loss-making parent airline, and it was sold in January 2003 to Ryanair for £15.6m, with cash assets of £12.4m and a net price of 3.2m. Ryanair immediately slashed its costly operations whilst gaining valuable landing slots.

Go

Go was launched by British Airways in 1998 after BA's offer to buy easyJet was rebuffed. Widely seen as a spoiler tactic, Go established an efficient and well-regarded operation with flights from Stansted, Bristol and East Midlands. After reporting losses of £21.8m and carrying 1.9m passengers in the year to March 2000, it achieved profitability on a monthly basis and declared a profit by the end of its third year in March 2001. Go was seen as peripheral by BA, which felt it competed with its own operations and did not know what to do with it, putting it up for sale in November 2000. Go was bought in a management buy-out funded by venture capital fund 3i for £110m in June 2001. It succeeded commercially for a year as an independent airline, led by the feisty Barbara Cassani whose entrepreneurial drive led it to make fourth year profits of £14m. However her airline was sold from under her by the equity owners, who were keen to find an exit route which offered them a short-term profit. EasyJet eventually acquired and absorbed Go in June 2002 for the much higher price of £374m.

Virgin Express

Virgin Express was an opportunistic move by Virgin's Richard Branson, based on the acquisition in 1996 of charter operator EuroBelgian Airlines. It was intended to take the Virgin brand, which had succeeded with Virgin Atlantic, into the low-cost European sector. It operated a network of routes based on the European hub of Brussels, but lost money heavily in its early years, and cut back to eight routes. Its failure to achieve profitability indicated that a hub-and-spoke model does not work in the European low-cost market, as it is inefficient and has high operating costs. In 2004 a merger with Belgian airline SN Brussels was announced, with Virgin losing overall control. Its last results for 2004, prior to the merger, showed turnover had declined by 13 per cent to £143m, with a corporate loss of £4.6m and operating loss of £2.9m, although the scale of its losses had been reduced by cutting the number of planes from 13 to 11 with lower leasing costs. Virgin Express was an uncompetitive failure in the tough conditions of the low-cost sector.

Bmibaby

Launched in 2002 as a subsidiary of the independent British Midland (BMI), bmibaby was a response by the parent airline to low-cost competition that was undermining its business-flyer base within the UK and Europe, especially when Go started flying from one of its bases at Nottingham East Midlands. It had to contend with the challenges of reducing its fixed cost base, which was 40 per cent higher than the low-cost competition, and of creating a new business model within an existing airline, the parent company being loss-making at the time. It has built a strong UK regional identity and operates effectively as one part of the BMI group, but does not appear to have the resources and drive to achieve significant growth. The future of its parent company is unclear as although the founder and largest shareholder, Sir Michael Bishop, has no apparent plans to sell the airline, which returned to profit in 2004, Virgin Atlantic has long been interested in a merger.

MyTravelLite

MyTravel Group PLC, an established holiday tour operator formerly known as Airtours, announced in 2002 its intention to launch a low-fares airline, MyTravelLite. It was concerned about the erosion of its business by travellers booking low-cost flights and holiday accommodation independently, and was experiencing a decline in profitability.

From August 2002 MyTravelLite flew from Birmingham Airport to Alicante, Belfast International, Geneva, Paris (Beauvais) and Malaga with prices from £15 one way including taxes. Strong initial sales resulted in extra aircraft and new routes to Amsterdam, Pisa, Murcia, Barcelona, Palma, Faro and Knock, Ireland, in 2003, together with twice daily flights to Malaga, Alicante and Dublin. Over a million customers booked with MyTravelLite in its first year, with over 90 per cent booking online.

For 2005 it added routes to Ibiza, Minorca, Tenerife, Gran Canaria and Lanzarote.

It has established a niche as a Birmingham–Europe airline, using TV celebrity David Dickinson to personalise its marketing, and added optional extra services including allocated seating, pre-bookable meals, more onboard shopping and seats with extra leg room. Whether it has the potential and resources to grow beyond its West Midlands base is not yet apparent.

The failures

A number of 'me-too' would-be low-cost operators have started or attempted to start but lost out in the ruthless and competitive market for low-cost flights. These were generally over-optimistic and under-capitalised ventures. Failures include Debonair, Ciao Fly and Goodjet, whilst other small marginal flyers such as Jet2 are vulnerable to increases in costs and competitive ticket pricing.

Strategic positioning of the low-cost airlines after 9/11 2001

In the mid-1990s a bilateral divide emerged between the operations of the regular fare airlines and low-cost operators. In the UK, 14 per cent of flight capacity in 1999 was in the low-cost sector, compared to 4 per cent of intra-European capacity and 10 per cent in the United States. Initially, the existing airlines responded to easyJet by selectively discounting fares on scheduled flights. In an intensely competitive period following the attack on the World Trade Centre on 9/11 2001, the flag-carrying airlines were hit hard by the drop in transatlantic and business passenger numbers, and several have either closed or merged (including KLM, Sabena, Swissair and Alitalia). The high cost base of such airlines, together with their limited ability to compete with the largest European carriers, British Airways, Lufthansa and Air France, led to their business being squeezed at both ends of the market.

The response to 9/11 by both easyJet and Ryanair was to reduce their fares to maintain load factors, but unlike the major airlines they did not make major reductions in scheduled flights and applied for landing slots at major airports which the flag-carriers were no longer using. This strategy was successful in that the low-cost flyers weathered the storm following 9/11 and it was evident that low-cost flying would dominate the European market. Similarly, in 2004–5, as British Airways imposed fuel surcharges to adjust for higher fuel costs, Ryanair maintained its prices, declaring it would never impose fuel surcharges, and exceeded BA's monthly passenger numbers in early 2005.

activity

- Refer to the 'reasons for business success' and 'reasons for business closure' in Chapter 7.
- Apply these to the low-cost airlines. Based on these, what do you consider to be the key factors behind the success of the market leaders and the failure or non-progression of the others?

The role of entrepreneurial management in the industry

The comparison of airline performance is affected by many variables, but one vital ratio for a low-cost operator is the net profit earned by each aircraft. Routes, schedules, fares and employees can be varied relatively easily, but when an operator has the fixed cost of owning or leasing and financing a fleet of aircraft they must be used as intensively and profitably as booking, scheduling and turnround will allow. In 2004, each of easyJet's 92 aircraft in the fleet earned a net profit before tax of £0.67m. In comparison, Ryanair's fleet of 72 aircraft earned £1.9m each in the year to March 2004. Factors which helped Ryanair's superior performance included their development of longer, higher-earning routes in mainland Europe, and introduction of the larger capacity Boeing 737-800. In 1999–2000, easyJet's net profit per aircraft had been £1.22m and Ryanair £1.74m, so that Ryanair has been able to increase the profit earned per aircraft whilst significantly growing the size of the fleet, number of passengers and destinations, but in contrast easyJet has suffered a drop of almost 50 per cent. This indicates that Ryanair is more efficient at growing and running its operations profitably in an increasingly competitive market with tight fares.

TABLE 8.2 **Low-cost airline comparative performance in 2003–4**

Airline	easyJet	Ryanair	Virgin Express*	bmibaby	FlyBe
Number of destinations	44	41	14	20	42
Aircraft	92	72	11	13	31
Load factor	84.4%	81%	75.7%	–	–
Passengers	24.3m	23.1m	2m	3m	4m
Net profit before tax	£62.2m	£137m	(£2.9m)	–	£3.1m
Net profit before tax per aircraft	£0.67m	£1.9m	(£0.26m)	–	£0.1m

*   Figures apply to scheduled services only.
–   Information not available.
     Figures in brackets denote losses.

Future prospects: open skies or turbulence ahead?

The easyJet story was extremely successful up to 2003–4. At that point, after it bought Go, and possibly paid more than it should have, the share price declined, Stelios Haji-Ioannou eased himself out of the business, subsequently returning as a director, and easy-

Jet increasingly lost its competitive edge to Ryanair whilst being assailed by waves of new price-cutting competitors. Although the company had been recognised as the 'best low-cost airline' within the industry, the successful formula of the early years with its combination of warm, informal image, efficient cost control and winning fares needed a boost. None of the opportunities identified by Haji-Ioannou for stretching the easyGroup brand through easyEverything cybercafés, easyRentacar and easyMoney, cinemas, hotels and cruise ships seemed to have the pace and growth trajectory once enjoyed by the airline.

The intense competition in the domestic UK and UK–Europe routes has squeezed prices and profit margins, especially outside the summer season. It is clear that the UK domestic market is already very competitive, but significant growth remains possible within mainland Europe. Ryanair has successfully established a network of flights and bases there; easyJet's establishment of operational bases in Geneva and Amsterdam had given it the opportunity to grow a mainland European operation to such popular destinations in Central and Eastern Europe as Prague, Berlin and Warsaw, but it failed to develop this successfully.

Independent airlines are always vulnerable to action by their larger competitors in an industry obsessed with scale, merger and global alliances, especially as they lose market share. However, both easyJet and Ryanair have survived and grown to be resilient and financially sound. Their principal challenges are capturing the maximum slice of the market and filling planes at reasonable margins in order to finance the large new orders of aircraft they are committed to. Because they do not control many of the variables, such as fuel costs, landing charges, taxes and sterling/Euro exchange rates, they are vulnerable to fluctuation. Increasing jet fuel prices and growing competition both from smaller fliers, some desperate to stay in business, and between the larger airlines, have squeezed revenues. There are growing environmental concerns about the impact of the increase in flying on air pollution and climate change, and it has been suggested that fuel could be taxed. However, there are no signs that the market's appetite for cheap flights is likely to be saturated in the near future, whilst economic slowdown across Europe placed higher cost operators under even more pressure as travellers traded down to the no-frills operators.

EasyJet and Ryanair are the two heavyweight, publicly quoted, and profitable low-cost operators in the market. Both have ambitious growth plans and achieved or exceeded their targets of doubling their traffic by 2003, which was essential in order to meet investors' expectations and to gain maximum return from the extra capacity of expensive new aircraft they had ordered. It is inevitable that their performance in growth, revenue, profits and share price will be compared.

Once easyJet acquired Go and Ryanair bought Buzz, the two airlines competed head-to-head with each other on marketing as the lowest-fare flyer and on key routes. The market is now entering a mature state rather than one in which rapid growth is possible, and the competition is for market share and to maximise load factors. Ryanair has a longer track record of profitable growth and is larger, with more routes, planes and passengers, and higher sales and profits. It is stronger on Irish and intra-European routes, and has introduced the 737-800 series planes which give 27 per cent higher capacity and a greater profit margin than easyJet's fleet of 737-700s. This partly explained easyJet's decision to buy a fleet of Airbus A319 aircraft, of similar capacity to the 737-700 but at two-thirds of the price.

In mainland Europe, easyJet generally flies to main airports, which are more popular but more expensive, whereas Ryanair prefers more remote, lower-cost destinations. It lost a European court action which held that subsidies for flying to Charleroi airport in

Belgium were unfair. Both airlines are well managed, with easyJet losing the edge in marketing flair and communication to Michael O'Leary's aggressive and attention-demanding tactics as well as lower ticket costs. Both airlines use the same highly successful business model and provide essentially the same product.

EasyJet and Ryanair have shown that a low-cost operation, managed in a highly entrepreneurial way based on price-led competition, can open up new markets and generate significant profits whilst flying people from point to point as efficiently as the more expensive airlines which have not been able to create new low-cost operations to match them. Having transformed the European short-haul air industry, the question was which one would establish itself as the low-cost leader, and the answer is clearly Ryanair.

Questions on the low-cost airline case study

- How attractive do you think the low-cost airline sector is for new entrants? If you were considering starting a new airline in the sector, what would be your strategy? Where do you think there is the greatest potential for growth?
- Both easyJet and Ryanair have proved able to grow more quickly than corporate ventures and to dominate the sector. What are the reasons for their success? Using the 'practical theory' model in Chapter 7 (Table 7.3), 'what works', why and how for these airlines?
- If you compare easyJet and Ryanair, there are many points of similarity. What do you think are the most important differences between them? How are these likely to affect their longer-term development?
- Why have the corporate ventures not been more successful to date?
- Consider the three types of strategy – opportunity, resource and relational – in Table 7.5. Which airlines would you consider are using each type of strategy?
- What lessons and conclusions can you draw from the case of this sector, which could be useful to learn from generally or in other market sectors?

chapter 9

where do we
go from here?

chapter contents

introduction

The purpose of this final chapter is to explore the future of entrepreneurship, developing conceptual ideas and practical approaches from academic, practical and personal perspectives, and to stimulate thinking about the opportunities and implications these raise.

The learning goals of the chapter will enable you to:

- reflect on your learning from the book through reading and applying the opportunity-centred approach
- assess the emerging issues in entrepreneurship and the implications for you, in personal, career and academic dimensions
- review your career goals and develop an entrepreneurial career plan.

The outcome from the chapter is to help you in planning your entrepreneurial career by reviewing and using the key learning points from the book. It closes with a challenge to the reader: what are you going to do to create your own entrepreneurial future?

The chapter includes a reflection on the Opportunity-Centred Entrepreneurship approach and its contribution to theory and learning, and its implications for entrepreneurial practice. A number of emerging themes are proposed as being significant for the future development of entrepreneurship in terms of practice, policy and research. These include the role of science and technology entrepreneurship and innovation; the importance of an inclusive, international and multicultural approach to entrepreneurship as a means of democratic, economic and social empowerment; the future of social enterprise as this becomes part of the mainstream; the need for environmentally sustainable forms of entrepreneurship; the challenge of entrepreneurial thinking to corporate and public sector organisations; the vital importance of female entrepreneurship; the crucial role of learning and education in entrepreneurial development; and the necessity of a lifelong approach to entrepreneurial development. These themes will shape the future environment for your entrepreneurial career.

opportunity-centred entrepreneurship in context

This is a reflection on Opportunity-Centred Entrepreneurship and its contribution to entrepreneurial theory, learning and practice

This book has aimed to increase your awareness, skills and readiness to act in entrepreneurial ways. It puts the human experience of entrepreneurship at its heart, by focusing it as a real-world learning process. You will have your own views on how useful this has been for you. So the approach concentrates on personal and social development, in the wider context of family, community, work and life experience. It emphasises that entrepreneurship is a path open to everyone, because the skills and approaches are capable of being learned. It offers a focus, a way of working, questions to ask and tools to use. It is a joined-up approach to entrepreneurship.

We can go further than this and suggest that enterprising behaviour is a normal and everyday aspect of human life. People are inherently curious about problems, opportunities and possibilities. We like playing, whether this is playing with people, with ideas, with tangible objects and technology, or with pictures and music. Just as everyone is inherently creative, everyone has the latent capacity for enterprise.

However, to develop and make use of this, we have to recognise that people have powerful and sometimes disempowering formative experiences in society. Families, communities, educational and government systems and employers have very strong formative influences which can encourage or discourage creativity and enterprise, sometimes by exercising repressive control. So whilst individuals have choices and are responsible for taking or not taking enterprising choices, the social worlds within which we live influence and enable or constrain these choices in many ways. Therefore there is much more to becoming an enterprising or opportunity society than simply encouraging individual enterprise. The concepts behind Opportunity-Centred Entrepreneurship need to be adopted above the level of the individual, by educational institutions, business support and government agencies. These issues will be addressed in the next section.

It is significant that major movements in management thinking and practice have often been accompanied by the development of accompanying tools, language and defined practices. If we think of such movements as total quality and the related Kaizen movement, strategic management, business process re-engineering and knowledge management, they have been implemented and enacted with the help of defined or 'best practice' methods. Whether we agree that the movements themselves and the tools used have been effective is another matter, but there is a body of knowledge and practice available for use. Entrepreneurship and entrepreneurial management are notably different, in lacking an acknowledged base of knowledge and practice. If you read the leading texts on the subject you will find a rich assortment of theory, many case studies, some decision-making frameworks usually derived from a financial base, and one recurring tool – the business plan. This is an area in which educators and writers on entrepreneurship have so far largely failed to develop a useful and sound methodology for the discipline. Surely there is more to entrepreneurial practice than the business plan?

So it is proposed that one important contribution that Opportunity-Centred Entrepreneurship makes is to provide a process and a set of tools. They are not the only tools, but they are a start. The process and tools may not be ideal for every situation, but they are flexible and can be added to. Some of the tools, such as the opportunity mapping and sensemaking approaches, have been gathered and adapted from other sources outside entrepreneurial practice. Others, such as the opportunity assessment tool, have been developed and tested over several years. People can use these as a starting point and adapt them for their own needs and situation. The result can be systemic improvement in the way that entrepreneurial opportunities are developed and implemented because there is now a framework and methodology which we can use.

Continuing the journey: emerging and future challenges in entrepreneurship

Part of the fascination of entrepreneurship is that it is a dynamic and continually evolving area of practice and study. Increasing numbers of students are conducting research studies and dissertation projects at final year undergraduate, postgraduate and doctoral levels. There are a growing number of research conferences and academic journals dedicated to small business management, entrepreneurship, enterprise education and related issues. The volume of research and scholarship in the field is ever-increasing and it is therefore important that this is directed towards the important, complex and challenging issues faced by entrepreneurs, policymakers, researchers, teachers and others. This next session summarises eight of the emerging trends which are creating fresh challenges for society as well as presenting emerging business opportunities for entrepreneurs. These can also offer topics for independent study, enabling you to gain in-depth understanding of these emerging issues. They are:

- innovation
- entrepreneurship as inclusion or exclusivity
- international entrepreneurship
- sustainable enterprise
- diversity and multiculturalism
- women's enterprise
- beyond legal capitalism to the informal and criminal economy
- education and learning.

Several of these have arisen within the book so far, and they are included here, both to provide guidance, ideas and suggestions for students considering dissertation research topics related to entrepreneurship, and to indicate the major challenges and sources of opportunities which we face in continuing to develop entrepreneurial activity.

Innovation

Innovation will continue to be a significant driving force in entrepreneurship. There will be a continuing convergence of ideas and technology which anticipate or respond to demand and economic and social forces. The role of science, technology and knowledge in stimulating, enabling and exploiting innovation will continue to grow. The next decade will see major new areas of technological possibility enter the market, including new bio and genetic technologies, aspects of nanotechnology, and many other science and research-based innovations. There is also increasing convergence of areas of science and technology which had been separate, for example bio, nano and computing technology, which hold the potential to create new industries.

The challenge will be to develop and exploit these in ways that both create wealth and meet social needs. There are, as set out in this section, many economic, social and resource-based challenges which require entrepreneurial innovation to develop new technologies, for example in energy, water, climate change, health, agriculture and transportation. There is some danger of a 'closed system' of research laboratories in universities and industry feeding large corporations which exploit new products in limited ways to secure their own positions. The high-cost industrial economies, primarily the United States and EU, remain dominated by the interests of major corporations in many ways. The speed and productivity of innovation is slower in Europe than the United States, and there are real challenges for entrepreneurs in gaining access to emerging technologies and working with researchers and corporate organisations to create new products, ventures and business models.

It is clear that the 'clock speed' of innovation is increasing, as it becomes ever more capital and knowledge intensive, whilst growing competition for advantage in many markets means that the speed of movement between opportunity recognition and introduction of new technology accelerates. This means that the development of innovation in processes as well as products and services has accelerated, and the organisation of innovation must become more effective. If one organisation can innovate through close partnerships with its suppliers and distributors and enter the market before another which is less well organised, it clearly has a major advantage. The ability of Dell to innovate more quickly and at lower cost to the customer than competitors in the computer market is one example of this.

The Internet has transformed the way we do business, enabling many new business opportunities and models to be created. This will continue as access, speed and online technology develop whilst costs of access fall. Innovation in online technologies will continue to make all kinds of business opportunities available to worldwide markets. The rise of wireless technology and truly portable handheld devices for the mass market will drive continuing innovation and demand.

Entrepreneurial working is increasingly challenging the ways in which corporate and public sector organisations in particular function. It is easy for them to stifle innovation, yet they often control the resources which are essential for innovation. Finding new ways of innovating between organisations, for example at a regional level in the Leuven–Aachen–Eindhoven technology triangle, is essential for competitive development of new technologies. Public sector organisations such as regional governments need to facilitate not stifle innovation, as is being achieved in the Helsinki region through its regional development organisation, Culminatum.

Entrepreneurship as economic inclusion or exclusivity

Entrepreneurship is based in large part, as outlined in Chapter 2, on capitalist growth theory, which results in the temporary dominance of the most successful economic model. This gives rise to the dominance of a US-based model of entrepreneurship, largely serving US economic interests, which we can term 'the bison in the living room'. This bison is large, dominant, and unaware of the destructive effects it can unwittingly cause on the environment around it. So far it has been very successful but its suitability for worldwide existence is questionable, and it may even become a threatened species. Its existence is founded on the following assumptions.

- It is based on the notion of individual enterprise and self-enrichment through the investment of personal effort in conditions of uncertainty.
- It assumes and makes fundamental decisions on dynamics of investment, risk and return within the paradigm of capitalist economic growth.
- Its goal is normally continuous growth in scale, turnover, sales and profitability.
- It operates on a resource-consumption model of 'capture and exploit', with waste or sub-optimal use of natural, physical, human and other resources being of secondary or no concern.
- It is blind to the consequences of its actions on the wider ecology of the world economy, societies, resources and environment, and takes no responsibility for these.
- It assumes that its government will use its powerful position to provide business advantage rather than equity, by dominating and changing or ignoring legal, trading and environmental agreements to protect its interests.
- It assumes competition to achieve market domination is inherently good, except by foreign entrants to its own markets.

These statements summarise the US model of the entrepreneurial business. The late Peter Drucker (1993) long argued the need for the US economy to progress from this form of entrepreneurship. It has been, and continues to be, a highly successful model, and the aim is not to criticise the United States for its economic success, because one could be just as critical of the European failure to develop a model of enterprise which is compatible with the goals of economic and social inclusion of the EU. The purpose of this section is not to undermine or challenge, but rather to make two suggestions. One is that the current US model is not the only or even the best model of enterprise for every situation, for although it is culturally privileged, other forms exist and are necessary. This is tricky, because its mindset is dominance rather than co-existence. The other suggestion is that the US model itself must evolve if it is to survive the growing economic challenges from India and China. This is less difficult, because entrepreneurs who enact the model are quite capable of recognising the need for change when it serves their own interests.

Theoretically and practically, there is a need to move beyond the paradigm of entrepreneurship defined by the United States and adopted as the mainstream by western economies. The US model is one that tends towards economic exclusivity and domination: Boeing, Microsoft and other multinational corporations embody this. European political leaders, for example in the UK, talk of an inclusive model of 'enterprise truly for all' and recognise the economic and social imperative of an inclusive model, but they are a long way from realising this. It is increasingly recognised in developing countries that the challenge of creating wealth, employment and greater social equality in these economies must come from an inclusive approach to enterprise. However we do not yet have an inclusive model for entrepreneurship, and a challenge and opportunity for researchers and practitioners is to learn from the practices of enterprises around the world and to develop new or adapted models of enterprise which can be used in different contexts.

Potentially, entrepreneurship is a popular force which opens up the prospect of business activity, independence and ownership to a wide range of the population, thereby underpinning democratic participation in developing and post-socialist countries. However there is a need for plurality and inclusivity to be achieved through different types of enterprise being formed and supported. It is quite likely that the basis for inclusive models of entrepreneurship can be found by studying, for example, such cases as the family-owned medium-sized businesses termed the *mittelstand* in Germany; the collaborative business networks in Emilio-Romagna; or the rural village enterprises and new production models in the wine-producing areas of South Africa. The practices of distributed ownership, collaborative resource use and production, and shared rewards within an economic and social ecology need to be understood and documented. This suggests an international approach, which leads to the next issue.

International entrepreneurship

Not only the future of entrepreneurship is international; we are already there, and global entrepreneurship is the reality. This provides challenges as well as opportunities. The rapidly growing economies of China and India are stimulating and benefiting from the entrepreneurship of their own populations, as well as becoming increasingly attractive to external investors and partners. They are moving up the 'value chain' and producing products and services with higher value-added in knowledge and technology which increasingly challenge US and European producers in their domestic markets.

This economic growth is providing challenges at both national and international levels which can be expected to increase. The modernisation of the Chinese economy is creating massive growth in demand for resources such as electricity, coal, oil, steel and other commodities. It is already clear that as China continues to grow, accompanied by other Southeast Asian economies, the US model of consumption capitalism will not be sustainable because resources such as oil are finite and cannot be discovered and pumped fast enough to meet demand, the peak of oil production has been reached, and the environmental consequences, especially climate change, are not sustainable. The projected increase in the world population of 50 per cent or 3 billion extra people by 2050, primarily in developing economies, will place huge strain on the world economy and on resources to feed, house, employ and support this population.

This is the nub of the problem for entrepreneurship, and one that researchers, innovators and entrepreneurs must focus on to find new approaches and solutions. In principle, the entire population of the world is entitled to develop entrepreneurial skills and opportunities and cannot be denied that right, but this has major consequences. The way to achieve widespread participation in enterprise in changing economies is a vital topic for exploration. The case of 'free market' reforms in the post-Soviet Russia in the early 1990s quickly resulted in a kind of 'robber baron' capitalism as major industries and rights to natural resources such as gas were captured by a self-enriching oligarchy. This shows how simplistically applying the US model of enterprise in a different context can have unexpected social and economic consequences.

For the majority of potential entrepreneurs in the developing world, enterprise will mean moving initially into some form of 'necessity entrepreneurship' as a route out of poverty. For those in failed or despotic states without free markets or support for new businesses or trading activities, such as Myanmar, North Korea and Zimbabwe, that is probably impossible without a change in government. But for millions of others it is clear that neither state intervention, multinational investment or other solutions are to hand and enterprise is one of the few options available; therefore the challenge to develop inclusive models of enterprise is imperative.

However, economic growth increases resource use, which can quickly become unsustainable, especially in combination with population growth. This is not only about oil and carbon-based energy sources, serious though that situation is. The changing world climate, resulting from the carbon-based economy, also increases demand for water as a resource, with the effects being felt worldwide, from Nevada and California to Africa and India. So whilst one strategy to assist in African development is to improve agricultural practices and increase food production, this is impossible without water. There is already severe tension between Egypt and other African countries about access to and use of Nile water. These are geopolitical questions which cannot be dodged by entrepreneurship researchers and practitioners, for they arise from entrepreneurial activity, and present challenges which entrepreneurs and innovators have the responsibility and opportunity to try to overcome.

Sustainable enterprise

Therefore the next challenge for entrepreneurship is to develop models of entrepreneurial activity which are sustainable: environmentally, ecologically, socially and economically. They cannot be dependent for growth and continuity just on competition for and consumption of scarce and limited resources. Access to resources is vital for entrepreneurs, yet we must move on from the 'use it up' to a 'use it again' model for the world economy to be able to support its increasing population. One place for researchers and entrepreneurs to start is to connect with environmentalists. There has been significant progress in environmental awareness, resource conservation and waste recycling, especially in some mainland European countries, since the 1990s. Waste dumping of recyclable resources is reducing and new industries are being created to provide advice and services in energy generation and conservation, ecologically friendly building and waste recycling. It is not the whole solution but the limits have certainly not been reached.

There is scope for continuing innovation to achieve sustainable enterprise based on renewable resources, and these forms of enterprise offer significant scope for creating new knowledge, wealth and employment worldwide. There is an urgent need to develop 'lean resource' methods of business which make minimal demands on non-renewable resources, just as companies have been able to develop 'lean production' methods. Distribution and transportation are resource-intensive and often wasteful, offering scope for cost and resource reduction through smarter technologies. Water, energy and material conservation and recycling are clearly areas of rapidly growing importance which we cannot afford to ignore, yet where new value can be created. There is even scope for developed societies to learn from the scavenging practices of the acutely poor people in developing economies who eke out a living by finding recyclable resources from waste dumps, including waste exported from the UK. Can innovation provide more efficient and dignified methods of screening waste to reclaim recyclables?

Diversity and multicult;ıralism

Diversity and multiculturalism are inevitable outcomes from an international and inclusive approach to entrepreneurship. This must be welcomed as a positive advantage, yet also brings challenges which need to be resolved. Multiculturalism offers multiple perspectives, the potential for conflict arising out of misunderstanding or competing ideologies, and the need for dialogue, negotiation and shared understanding. The case of Leicester demonstrates the point.

In the 1960s and 1970s, Leicester was an unremarkable British provincial city, dependent on a textile and garment industry which was destined to decline, and with a middle-ranking football team and University. However it became an attractive destination for immigrants from India and East Africa, initially to work in the textile industry. Over the next three decades, Hindu and Moslem communities became established in inner-city Leicester. Tensions with the indigenous English population arose over employment, housing, education and racial issues, which led to urban disturbances in the early 1980s, a period during which the local economy declined.

Since then, the renaissance of Leicester has been increasingly the story of its ethnic enterprises. Both Indian communities have established business networks, with visible retail presences, Belgrave Road for example developing a national cluster of Indian costume jewellery businesses and Narborough Road becoming a destination for curry houses and restaurants. Away from the vibrant shopfronts, progress has had a lower profile yet arguably been more significant. An increasing number of businesses are Indian-owned, and as the textile industry declined the proportion of printing, service and professional businesses has increased, with a growing number being higher value-added firms. A group of young women who felt excluded from economic and social opportunity formed their own network, the Peepul Centre, which has become a major force for social and community enterprise and renewal. Increasingly, the economic growth, cultural activity and enterprise is driven by ethnic entrepreneurs, who have put Leicester on the cultural map.

Leicester is not unique, but the lessons it offers are that ethnic and cultural diversity creates new ideas and possibilities, whilst presenting challenges and possible conflict which need to be defused through tolerance, building trust and mutual understanding.

How can entrepreneurship be encouraged in ethnically diverse yet economically deprived areas? Public and government agencies need to be sensitive yet bold in promoting equality of opportunity and seeking participation across the community. Enterprise needs to be seen and supported as a means of engaging people and groups in self and collective expression and improvement. Community support networks need to be recognised as valid and useful, and offered public support where they can reach people who feel excluded from mainstream public and private services. We can conceptualise this as a collective learning experience, in which Leicester has become much more enterprising by developing inclusive approaches to enterprise which work.

Women's enterprise

The Leicester experience is one in which ethnic minority women play an increasingly important part, and it is recognised in many societies that increasing their contribution to entrepreneurial activity is vital, for women and for society; the question is how. There is growing interest in both theoretical exploration and practical development of female entrepreneurship on a worldwide basis. Historically, women have been less active than men in formal entrepreneurship, if this is measured by the statistics of business ownership or the GEM report. However, this understates the informal roles which women have played in businesses owned by men or in family and village enterprises. Also, there have been powerful forces to discourage and constrain their participation in business in many societies. Generally these are diminishing, with a few 'hardline' exceptions, such as Saudi Arabia.

How can female entrepreneurship be developed? There are at least three reasons why this is a vital area both for academic study and for practical action. First, entrepreneurship can provide women with independent income, by helping to alleviate poverty or dependence and increasing the lifestyle choices they can make for themselves and their families. The significance of this in developing economies should not be underestimated as a potential contribution to their economic and social empowerment.

Second, as levels of education for women increase, their capabilities, ambitions and expectations of career roles also grow. Levels of female graduates in the UK and other developed countries continue to increase. Whilst at present female rates of entrepreneurial participation in most age groups are just over half those for men, these are also increasing. However, the availability of jobs to meet women's career aspirations and preferences is not keeping pace with this development in all societies, and for an increasing number, self-employment and entrepreneurship will be a better career option at certain stages in their careers. For women with family responsibilities, for example, running their own business is an option they may be able to manage more flexibly and with greater reward than a part-time job. However support measures for mid-career female entrepreneurship need to be explicitly addressed, for example through education and training for women who are considering or preparing to start business ventures (Diamond, 2003).

The third reason is that the types of business created by women are often qualitatively different from those started by men. They will see different opportunities, have different ideas, and use their skills and social contacts in different ways, contributing to a greater diversity of business activity. The inclusive new business models and approaches to enterprise which are needed are very likely to originate from female entrepreneurship. The real progress made in social enterprise has resulted in large part from the networking and collective action of enterprising women. An example of this is Banmujer, the Women's

Development Bank of Venezuela. This was formed in 1999 by Nora Castaneda and a network of women's groups. They had found that conventional banks were reluctant to lend money to women who wanted to start businesses but had no assets to guarantee the loans. State-funded, all its employees are women and it makes loans to women who work as part of a group who co-operate on business projects. Through its network of field advisors, the bank also provides business, financial, legal and health advice. Examples such as this show how female and social entrepreneurship are moving into the mainstream and changing the nature of mainstream business activity.

Beyond legal capitalism to the informal and criminal economy

Every human activity has a shadow-side, a negative and destructive aspect which is one we usually prefer to ignore. Since entrepreneurship is a natural form of social activity, what is the shadow-side? The answer is criminality, and immoral and unethical behaviour. As Rehn and Taalas (2004) argue, we cannot ignore the role of criminality in entrepreneurship. They propose that the study of entrepreneurship operates within an 'unconscious legalism' and that we should consider that entrepreneurship, which they define as the enactment of social networks, can operate outside the legal-market nexus. Historically, entrepreneurs have operated at the margins of, or outside, the law at certain times in most societies. To pretend otherwise is to opt for a sanitised and artificially wholesome narrative of entrepreneurial history. In the nineteenth century, British merchants traded in slaves and opium, activities which were legal at the time but which had known moral consequences. These trades are now illegal but human and narcotic trafficking continue to be major activities worldwide. The activities have not changed fundamentally, simply the legal frameworks. Conversely, entrepreneurship was illegal in Eastern bloc socialist societies, yet 'black market' enterprise flourished. When the socialist system collapsed, entrepreneurship was legalised. This strengthens the case for viewing enterprise as a fundamental aspect of human social behaviour, in which the relationship with socially imposed legal frameworks changes over time.

Entrepreneurship is not in itself a moral concept, being neither 'right' nor 'wrong', good nor bad. It is too simplistic to say that 'what is legal is entrepreneurial, and what is illegal is criminal and therefore not entrepreneurial', although this argument is politically more convenient than the alternative position: that entrepreneurial activity may take place either within or outside the legal framework, and therefore there are entrepreneurial activities which will be illegal and hence criminal in some societies at certain times. Entrepreneurs often do not like legal frameworks, seeing them as restrictive, yet they are vital in creating conditions for trade and commerce. However, the essential point is that there are types of entrepreneurial activity of which society approves because they are morally acceptable, and there are other types of activity which are disapproved because they are ethically undesirable, or just plain wrong. This argument may be uncomfortable, because it forces us to accept that the slave and drug traders, together with other profit-opportunists operating outside the law, are entrepreneurs of a kind. The distinction we have to make is about the entrepreneur's moral responsibility for the choices which he or she makes, and that we have entrepreneurs who choose to behave ethically, in ways which society approves, or unethically, because society proscribes their activity. Therefore the important distinction is between ethical and unethical entrepreneurial behaviour.

In all countries there is a significant amount of economic activity taking place in what is termed the 'informal' or 'grey' economy. Not all of the business activities are illegal; there are legitimate trades being practised such as car sales and repairs, building work and many other activities by 'get-rich-quick merchants', but the people performing them are not registered as businesses or self-employed, and the transactions take place outside the legal and fiscal systems. These are informal and technically illegal, so workers, customers and suppliers have no legal safeguards against fraud or defective goods or services. Beyond the informal sector is the criminal economy, where the activities themselves are illegal, including theft, smuggling, narcotic trading, violence and so on. One problem with this sector of the economy is that the informal and criminal do not simply run in parallel but converge and intermingle.

In societies which have poor legal enforcement, or where the legal system is oppressive from a business perspective, informal and criminal enterprise will flourish. The business environment in those countries will be unattractive for legal entrepreneurs and as a result the formal economy will not grow. The situation in Zimbabwe in 2005, when the Mugabe government demolished the shanty towns where thousands of people operated informal businesses to survive in a failed economy, is an outstanding example. Where criminal or political organisations have established networks of illegal businesses, such as in Southern Italy and in parts of Northern Ireland, they tend to intimidate and place legitimate businesses at a disadvantage. The judgement we have to take is that, although people running these organisations are demonstrating entrepreneurial skills (amongst others), the informal and criminal enterprises do not help, but rather undermine, social and economic progress in societies which have sound legal frameworks for enterprise.

The challenge and opportunity for entrepreneurship researchers, policymakers and prac-titioners is how to reduce the informal and develop the formal enterprise sector. We need to understand better the similarities and distinctions between entrepreneurial and criminal behaviour and how people can progress from informal to formal activity. From a social perspective it might seem desirable to close down the criminal enterprise networks, but this is much easier said than done. However from an academic perspective it would be useful to gain insights into how they operate and the lessons which can be learned from them.

Education and learning

Education and learning for entrepreneurship will remain a live issue because all seven of the above challenges depend on the effectiveness of the entrepreneurial learning process. So education and learning are vital for innovation, socially inclusive entrepreneurship, international and sustainable entrepreneurship, multicultural and female enterprise, and movement from informal to formal business activity to progress. Entrepreneurial learning and research are means of facilitating the changes and transformations which are needed. That is not to say that there is one 'best way', but that the knowledge of what works in one environment can be exchanged and shared with others.

Enterprising learning has an increasing role in school education, throughout the curriculum. It offers a holistic way of developing abilities and habits of independence, self-efficacy, creativity, innovating and organising across and between subject areas. In this way, enterprising learning can enable students to apply knowledge in intersubjective ways, embracing sciences, technology, sports, arts and humanities. Students need to 'feel the enterprising experience', and for this to happen the learning environment, teaching and learning methods and capabilities of teaching staff must all evolve to provide transforma-tive, enabling learning experiences. Technology can be used much more effectively to facilitate interactive entrepreneurial learning.

The challenge is to make enterprise education a means of achieving social change, enabling marginalised groups such as students who have become alienated from formal education, those with learning difficulties or from migrant communities, to engage with learning experiences through which they connect practical skills, creativity and self-development into purposeful activity, enabling and inspiring them to see what they can do and who they can become. This is not just rhetoric. There are many school and community projects doing just this, as the UK enterprise in schools pathfinder projects have shown, at http://www.teachernet.gov.uk/.

Enterprising learning must be lifelong; as the section on entrepreneurial careers shows, demographic change means it is inevitable that increasing numbers of people will need to become entrepreneurs at different stages in their lives. We can also point to many successful experiences of entrepreneurs becoming involved in the learning process, as guest speakers, role models, coaches and trainers. So there is scope for continued innovation, research and challenge in researching and developing enterprise education.

Key ideas for entrepreneurship research and student projects

These broad issues are all significant in relation to entrepreneurial practice, in policy at all levels from regional to international, and in academic research. They all offer potential for practical action as business opportunities as well as for independent study, for example for an entrepreneurial studies research or dissertation project. However this requires investigation and identification of a specific problem or question, which the following activity is intended to help identify.

activity

- Which of the eight issues in the previous section interest or affect you most? How could they affect you in future?
- Select one (or a combination of more than one) of these issues which you find most interesting or relevant to your own situation – for example, 'female and multicultural entrepreneurship'.
- What do you think are the questions, problems and 'hot topics' you think need to be explored in relation to this issue?
- What problem or question could you investigate for either a coursework project, such as a dissertation, or an independent investigation to identify possible opportunities? What would be the personal, academic and practical benefits from investigating this?

developing an entrepreneurial career

This section moves from considering major issues of entrepreneurial future concern and opportunity to the very specific and personal concern of your own entrepreneurial future, which will be affected by at least some of these macro-level trends. The aim is to help you to plan your entrepreneurial career. It brings together the themes of previous chapters and prompts you to reflect on these key questions:

- What goals do you want to achieve, and why?
- How will you accomplish your goals?
- What is your personal value, and how can you increase this?
- What do you need to learn in order to achieve your goals, and how will you gain this learning?

The aim is to encourage reflective thinking about your learning from the book, and to help you to create career plan for yourself which you can then go forward and make happen. If you have already prepared a plan, this section will give you an opportunity to reflect on it with some fresh insights. Here are some reasons why you, as an aspiring entrepreneur or enterprising person, should have a career plan:

- A plan puts you in control; you decide and direct where you want to go.
- You are therefore much more likely to achieve your goals.
- A career plan is your personal business plan; your entrepreneurial career is your core business and a plan will help you to develop and manage it proactively and effectively – you will 'make your own luck' rather than hoping to 'get lucky'.
- Planning enables you to create new possibilities and to think through how to achieve them.
- You can judge whether opportunities which arise help you to achieve your career goals.
- The plan can help you to increase and maintain your individual value in all senses – personal, business, and financial.

A model of entrepreneurial career pathways

Conventionally, careers have been considered as pathways with a series of roles and progressions which include working largely as an employee. However for many people their career routes have included periods of self-employment and entrepreneurship. As working lives become more fragmented and people seek greater self-direction, we need to look at how entrepreneurial options can be chosen at different career stages. Schein (1993) proposed a career model with ten major stages, from childhood to retirement, and eight 'career anchors' or preferred career options, of which five could include aspects of entrepreneurial management: entrepreneurial creativity; autonomy and independence; pure challenge; lifestyle; and general managerial competence.

The demographic profile of the UK and other OECD countries displays an ageing population, in which more people will need to develop entrepreneurial capability to find new opportunities for economic activity or extending their working lives. This need for lifelong entrepreneurship is increasing as economic changes require an increasing proportion of the existing working population, from a broad social and demographic background, to be able to develop entrepreneurial skills at any stage of their career, and especially as they get older and employment opportunities may be less available.

The UK GEM report for 2005 provides valuable statistics which indicate the scale of entrepreneurship at different career stages. The GEM survey uses the age ranges 16–24, 25–34, 35–44, 45–54 and 55–64. The age bands between age 16 (the earliest age of joining the formal workforce in the UK) and 34 are considered to be ones of education and 'early career' formation and development, whilst the age ranges 35–44 and 45–54 define mid-career entrepreneurship, and over 55 can be considered to be 'third age'. Total entrepreneurial activity (TEA) is highest in the 35–44 age group, at 7.9 per cent of the population, including 10 per cent of males and 5.5 per cent of females. This age group shows the highest level of confidence in opportunity availability and confidence in personal skills, which diminish slightly in the 45–54 age range, with potential entrepreneurs in these age ranges most likely to be qualified at first degree, A-level or vocational qualification levels (Harding et al, 2006).

Whilst younger age groups may be more likely in future to take entrepreneurial action, it is the groups in mid-career which are most likely to do so at present and constitute the largest proportion of the population engaged in entrepreneurial activity, whilst the proportion of the population in the 35–55 age group is growing more rapidly than the 16–34 age group. The lower proportion of female entrepreneurship indicates the need for continuing support and encouragement to enable women to develop their entrepreneurial potential, especially in mid-career. These findings are reinforced by Labour Market Survey analysis which identified that most of the increase in self-employment in the UK during 2002–3 could be attributed to the 35–49 and older age groups, with the proportion of self-employment in relation to the workforce increasing

example

Case study: Home Stagers®

Tina Jesson, founder of Home Stagers®, completed an interior design course and found that by applying the principles to her own property she was able to increase the sale price and overcome the problem of negative equity. From this simple but effective beginning in 1995, she went on to establish Home Stagers as the UK's only nationally recognised home-styling and property-presentation business.

The approach is simple but highly effective. A hard-to-sell house is appraised by a trained stylist and ways of restyling it, through design, redecoration, changing furnishings, fixtures and lighting, are proposed within an agreed budget. Once these are completed, the property is offered for sale. Tina's research showed that every £100 spent on presentation in this way is more effective in selling a property than a £1000 reduction in the selling price.

Tina became a successful home stylist in the late 1990s and soon demonstrated that demand for her service existed, but she has achieved much more than this since establishing the Home Stagers brand in 2001. The concept of home styling was assisted by popular TV 'home makeover' programmes, and Tina has turned this into a successful business with defined service standards and an accredited training programme for home stylists, which is run by The British Academy of Home Stagers. People who wish to become stylists can be trained and licensed to operate as a sole trader within the Home Stagers Network, and to train people from overseas to set up their own business and develop the network in their own country. In this way a national and even international service is being provided with common service standards. The network also reaches out to estate agents, and a constantly updated website and monthly e-mail magazine ensure that Home Stagers stays at the centre of the property styling business.

www.homestagers.co.uk

in line with age. The greatest increases in business activity were reported in financial and property services and construction (Macaulay, 2003).

Mid-career entrepreneurship can be especially significant in the lives of women, for family as well as career reasons. Increasingly we find examples such as Tina who are establishing innovative and ambitious business ventures which enable them to meet a market gap in a new way.

Table 9.1 sets out five generic career stages, from education to 'third age' and suggests typical events and entrepreneurial options which may occur in each of these.

TABLE 9.1 **Entrepreneurial career stage model**

Career stage	Typical events	Entrepreneurial questions and options
Late career/ third age Age 55+	Seniority Retirement Develop wider interests Divest from own business or hire succession management	How to use existing contacts, expertise and resources? How to extend economic activity? Self-employment, lifestyle business Develop portfolio of interests Social or community enterprise Advisor, coach or non-executive roles
Mid-career Age 35–54	Career advance and responsibility Marketable skills and expertise Reassess career direction Unachieved aspirations Redundancy Parenting or caring Career break/return to work Changes in family relationships	How to achieve successful career transition? How to identify and develop opportunity based on existing skills and experience? Leave employment to start new business Return to work or start own business Consultancy Management buy-in or buy-out Create spin-out venture Join or lead innovation project or venture team Grow existing or family business
Early career Age 25–34	Establish career direction Develop skills and experience in corporate, profession or small business Professional or technical training/development Expand social and work-related networks – social capital Child rearing Accumulate personal resource	How to choose independence over employment? Learn entrepreneurial capabilities from experienced people Start own business Creative innovation at work Team member in innovation project, start-up or spinout venture Continue to work full or part time or freelance

TABLE 9.1 continued

Career stage	Typical events	Entrepreneurial questions and options
Initiation into working life Age: 16–24	Early work experience Development of social networks Quest for independence Exploration and personal growth Partnering, possible marriage	How to develop skills, interests and social contacts into enterprising projects? Small-scale ventures with friends Graduate start-up
Education and early life Age: 5 up to 21	Vocational, further or higher education/training Academic or vocational choices and specialisation Family influences	How to turn interests and needs into earning opportunities? Enterprise education Participation in family business Enterprise in personal interests

Source: Rae, 2005c.

- Which career stage are you in at present?
- Which of the events relate to your own experience?
- Which of the entrepreneurial questions and options are most relevant or interesting for you, now and in the future?

Planning your entrepreneurial career

Before starting this activity, there are some resources which it will be helpful to have available which arise from the work you have done in Chapter 3. Table 9.2 lists them.

TABLE 9.2 **Personal development exercises from Chapter 3**

Chapter 3 Personal enterprise	Entrepreneurial learning model: – Personal and social emergence – Contextual learning – Negotiated enterprise Personal values, goals and motivations Drawing your learning map Assessing fit between ideas and personal goals Personal orientation to risk and uncertainty Entrepreneurial and management capabilities (toolkit) Leadership and entrepreneurial teamwork Mapping your personal networks Review exercise

You will revisit much of this information in developing your career plan and you may find that a lot of the thinking is already there, especially in the review exercise. The planning process will help you to think it through, bring it together, and decide what you want to do and how to make it a reality.

The career planning process has five headings, shown in Figure 9.1. Each of these five headings is explored through questions which are intended to prompt you to think through each aspect and to help you to develop your career plan around it.

Select the format you prefer for your career plan: this could be a mind map, a table plan (there is a format in the toolkit), or whatever approach works best for you.

You will find that there are many interconnections between the headings of the plan. The five headings given here are a suggestion, and you can develop your own if you prefer. It could be, for example, that you create financial, learning and venture plans which lock into the career plan. In each of the five sections, start to develop your career plan, based on the work you have already done and on the further thinking which you do in response to the questions posed.

Goals and motivations

Even if you do not have goals and prefer to take life as it comes, it can be helpful to consider what your goals might be. In Chapter 3 we explored personal goals, values and motivations quite deeply. Revisit this thinking and reflect on it:

● What you now consider your motivations to be?
● What values are most important to you?
● Do you have a personal vision for your future? What is this?

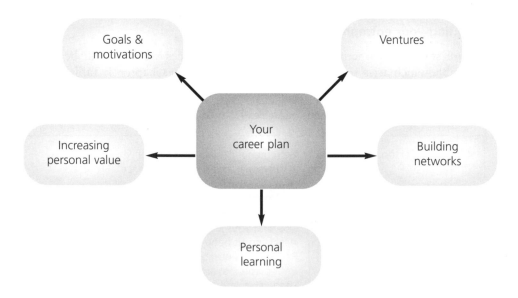

FIGURE 9.1 **Your career plan**

- Do you have goals for: (as appropriate)
  - business
  - career
  - personal growth
  - family
  - social life?
- For each of these goals, think about how you will measure or assess when you have achieved it.

Increasing personal value

An important theme of this book is developing both personal and social value to create new opportunities. As an approach to your career, it is about creating and growing your personal value over your lifetime. Your value takes a number of different forms: your self-esteem and value to others as a person, the value created by applying your capabilities, know-how and reputation, your financial value, and so on; the list could be much longer. Personal enterprise involves self-reliance and increasing personal assets which provide security, choices and independence. The key point here is to assess your current value, under the headings which are most important to you, and to decide how and to what level you want to increase your value.

- How do you assess your own self-worth?
- What do you consider is your greatest value to other people?
- From the exercises in Chapter 3, think back and consider what you would assess your personal value to be in terms of your:
  - capabilities
  - know-how
  - personality.
- How do you consider you can use these qualities most effectively to develop your career?
- In what ways do you aim to increase or develop these qualities further?

Now consider the financial aspects, a vital measure for most entrepreneurs.

- What is your total net financial worth? You can work this out by estimating the value of your main assets, such as any property, business equity, investments and savings, pension plan, valuable possessions and ready cash. Then deduct your liabilities: debt, student loan and fee repayments, mortgage and so on.
- Are you satisfied with this value?
- At present day values, to what figure do you aim to increase your net assets, and by when? If you plan to retire at a given age, how much personal wealth do you aim to generate by then? How many times can you aim to multiply your present value? The younger you are, the higher the multiple of your current wealth this can be.
- How much of your personal wealth would you invest in your own business venture, given the risks and potential returns?
- What is your current annual income, after tax and deductions?
- How satisfied are you with this figure, which is the current financial value placed on your work?

- To what figure do you aim to increase this next year? In two years? In ten years? Again, use present day values for this.

Think of these questions as helping you develop your personal business plan, by considering financial targets which quantify your goals.

Ventures

In Chapters 4–6 you developed ideas around possible opportunities, assessed their potential for venturing and as investment propositions, and developed a venture plan. Consider how far your successful involvement in entering, growing and exiting a venture has the potential to accomplish your goals and realise your personal value.

Think about your personal expectations in terms of goals, motivations and financial targets, and the optimum route to achieving these.

- If you continue to do what you are currently doing, will this enable you to achieve your aspirations?
- If the answer is 'yes' then possibly you do not need to continue with this exercise. If the answer is 'no', then continue below.
- My aspirations will be best achieved through:
    - a salaried career role in an organisation
    - becoming a manager with an equity share in a business
    - investing in an existing business, with or without a management role
    - creating and growing my own business
    - improving the returns from what I do now
    - another option not described above.

The best options will differ at different stages of a career. For example, the first option may not seem very entrepreneurial. However for a younger person at the start of their career it may be the best way of building up experience, capabilities, contacts and financial resources to prepare for an entrepreneurial move after a few years.

Whichever option you have chosen, you need to plan for it. If you are seeking a management role with an equity stake, unless that can be achieved in your current organisation you will need to search for a suitable opportunity. If you are looking to acquire or invest in an existing business, again you need to decide on your investment criteria and to start searching.

If you intend to create your own venture, then researching and preparing a venture plan, as outlined in Chapter 6, is essential.

If the option of improving the returns from what you do now is the one you have chosen, this suggests that you work in a business which is either your own or you share in the profits in some way. It is likely that you need to identify opportunities from which your business can unlock value. Revisit Chapters 4–5 to look at how you can identify and exploit such opportunities. Aim to identify at least one project which is a sound investment proposition, and develop a plan to exploit it.

Personal learning

None of this can be realised without effective learning; applying what you have already learned, as well as learning new capabilities and developing new ideas.

Look at the goals you have set yourself, and the ventures you plan to run which will achieve your goals. Then look at your self-assessment of your entrepreneurial management capabilities and review which you completed in Chapter 3.

You should to consider these questions:

- Does your learning up to this point provide you with all the personal capabilities and knowledge you will need to accomplish the opportunity you are planning?
- What further learning, experience and development do you therefore need?
- Looking at your personal goals overall, does your current learning provide you with all the capabilities and knowledge you will need to achieve them?
- What further learning do you think you need in order to achieve your goals?

List your areas for personal learning and development. For each of them, think about:

- What do you need to learn – to develop your capabilities, knowledge, experience, understanding?
- Why is the learning important, and what could the consequences of 'not learning' be?
- When do you need to learn it by; what are your priorities?
- How can you gain the learning you need?
- Based on these questions, what are your learning goals?

Planning your learning and development

Since learning is such an integral aspect of entrepreneurial achievement, these suggestions are included to help you develop additional ideas and options for developing the learning aspects of your career plan. It includes three types of learning methods:

- *Active*: learning through experience and practice.
- *Social*: learning from others.
- *Formal*: theoretical learning.

Active learning

This is opportunity or problem-based learning. In establishing a new venture, you are faced with a set of novel problems and decisions to which you might not have immediate solutions. Insights can be gained from formal courses and from other people, but even after being guided by these, you must decide and act for yourself. Most learning in starting and growing a venture is active, and the new venture creation process is a powerful source of learning.

The results of your decisions and actions, whether successful or unsuccessful, need to be reviewed and learned from. It is important to try and discover 'what works' for you – remember the practical theory grid in Chapter 7? Iterative trial and error learning is often used where you could have found by investigation that 'expert' or well proven approaches to the problem already exist.

Experimenting and 'playing with ideas', for example developing a strategy or a new product, generate new insights through discovery learning. This is a powerful process. By working towards a reasonably you can try out defined goal, different approaches and combinations, going round the learning loop several times until a workable approach is found. Sometimes there are unexpected outcomes from the discovery process, leading to new possibilities.

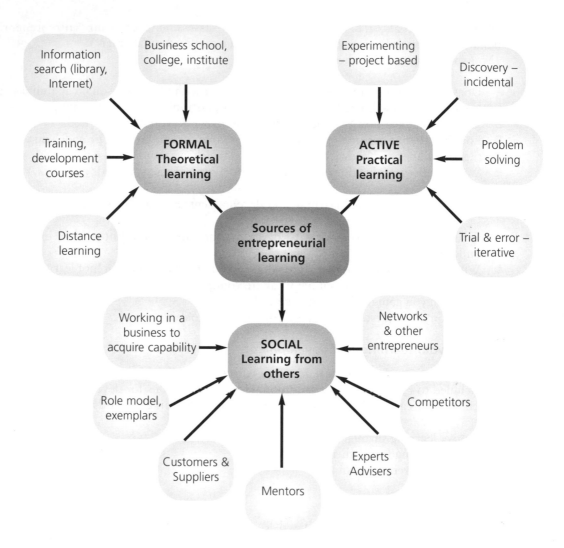

FIGURE 9.2 **Entrepreneurial capability: sources of learning**

Learning from others

Learning is, for most people, a social process, and this transfer of experience can take many different forms. Early in their careers, many future entrepreneurs develop their core capabilities through working in organisations where they are able to gain the training and experience which enables them to form or acquire a venture later in their career. Getting into dynamic businesses where you can learn quickly from exceptional people can be a strong early career move. Finding a growing small business to work in can be a good career start for a graduate, since working for an entrepreneurial manager or director can be a highly formative, inspirational and sometimes frustrating process.

Networks of business contacts, including other entrepreneurs, industry experts, customers, suppliers and competitors, can be valuable sources of ideas and experiences.

Gaining access to such sources of expertise can also be a learning process in relationship building. Finding out how suppliers and customers operate, and exploring ways of integrating more closely with them, is a rich source of ideas for adding value, as outlined in Chapter 3.

Expert advisers such as accountants, bankers, lawyers, scientists, academics and business advisers can be highly valuable to the entrepreneur as a way of gaining access to expert-based learning. However you need to judge the relevance of the advice to your own situation, and its likely efficacy. No adviser has all the (right) answers and you need to assess whether they really understand the business opportunity and your problem or are simply offering generalised solutions.

Formal learning

Academic and short courses together with books and e-learning mean that there is a tremendous resource of learning media readily available. The complexity faced by businesses and the need to reduce the risks of failure mean that some formal business training is a sensible option for the new entrepreneur.

Developments in e-learning and Internet technology are broadening access to entrepreneurship education, making it easier for people to learn what they need part time whilst working or running a business, and overcoming geographical, time and other barriers. The convergence between entrepreneurship, business education and technology makes it easier for the entrepreneur to combine the active learning they gain from starting and growing their business with formal learning to develop their capability. The use of e-mail and desktop video conferencing make global contact and learning relationships much easier, using technology to access an enriched range of learning with a network of other people.

Finally, information searches to access existing knowledge are becoming ever more important. The ease of access to information through the Internet and related sources such as online libraries, databases and newsgroups makes speedy access to the best available information possible. Books and media features on entrepreneurs and business ventures are also useful sources of knowledge: see the list of reference resources.

Building networks

In Chapter 3 you drew a map of your relationships and contacts, and considered how your network could help you in a venture. In planning your career, how could people in your existing network be of help to you, for example by:

● investing or providing other resources
● buying from you or supplying you
● opening access to people, knowledge, resources
● helping you learn and develop, e.g. as a mentor?

Your network forms an important resource, and like any investment it will be more valuable if well managed. So in addition to thinking about its current uses, think about:

● How can you sustain your network of contacts to promote their future co-operation? Who could be your future customers and investors? Who are the contacts you wish to develop?

● How can you grow your network: do you need to develop more contacts in specific domains, such as industry contacts and potential investors?

We have now completed the five headings of the career plan. Take time out to develop your own career plan in your chosen format. You may find that this takes several attempts; it is important that you believe in the plan which you create, and that you are fired up to go out and turn into reality.

Seven suggestions for managing your career plan

1. Think of your plan as a dynamic agenda which evolves and changes as you learn and progress.
2. Reward yourself for your successes; use each achievement as a motivator to spur you on to greater challenges.
3. Encourage yourself to learn continuously and work at capabilities which you need to develop, engaging less favoured as well as your preferred ways of learning.
4. Find someone who can help you as your mentor, such as an experienced entrepreneur who is prepared to listen and coach you through critical moments.
5. Check regularly how you are progressing against your goals and the plan – review what works for you and what does not, and update your plan and personal theory.
6. Learn from achievements, setbacks and failure: analyse why they happened, what you could have identified earlier and how to act differently in future.
7. Keep moving forward and enjoy your entrepreneurial life; search constantly for opportunities, evaluate them, plan how they can be exploited, and act on those you judge to be the best prospects.

so what are you going to do?

The aim of the book has been to increase your entrepreneurial interest, knowledge, skills, confidence and ambition. The book is the same for everyone, yet every reader will read it in different ways and gain different insights in relation to their unique personal journey. This final activity asks you to reflect on your learning from the book, and to consider how you can use this, and what you are going to do as a result.

activity

● Take a few minutes to review your overall learning from reading and working through this book.
  ● What are the main learning points you have gained?
  ● How have your ideas developed?
● How could you use what you have learned, for example:
  ● for academic study and coursework, projects or dissertation?
  ● to initiate or develop your career?
  ● to identify and act on an opportunity?
● What action will you take?

entrepreneurial and management capabilities

The aim of this section in the toolkit is to enable you to identify your existing capabilities in the key entrepreneurial and management capabilities listed below and mentioned in Chapter 3. This section will help you to:

● identify existing capabilities
● identify the strengths and limitations you bring to a venture and a team
● plan your learning in those capabilities you need to develop.

The first part covers the entrepreneurial capabilities, including personal organisation, which applies to both sets of capabilities. It is suggested that you work through this first. It is connected with Chapter 3.

The second part covers the management capabilities. It is suggested that you work through this in connection with Chapter 7.

Entrepreneurial capabilities

Personal organisation
Investigating opportunity
Applying innovation
Strategic venture planning
Market development

Management capabilities

Leading and managing people
Managing organisation and operations
Managing finance and resources
Responsible management: social, legal
    environmental and ethical responsibility

Entrepreneurial
capabilities

Management
capabilities

Personal organisation	Leading and managing people
Investigating opportunity	Managing organisation and operations
Applying innovation	Managing finance and resources
Strategic venture planning	Responsible management – social, legal,
Market development	environmental and ethical responsibility

entrepreneurial and management capabilities: self-assessment

In this section you are asked to assess your own level of entrepreneurial capability. This information will then be useful to you in the following sections, which take you through forming and leading entrepreneurial teams, networking, and considering your learning and development needs.

The six clusters of personal, interpersonal and entrepreneurial capabilities are set out in the following table. Read through each cluster in turn and ask yourself:

- Have I ever demonstrated experience in doing this? How practised am I?
- How capable am I? What example or evidence could I give of my capability?
- How confident am I in my ability?
- Assess your level of capability as follows:
  - 4 – I am highly capable in this, fully confident of my ability.
  - 3 – I am quite capable with some successful experience which I could develop.
  - 2 – I have quite limited capability and experience and would need quite a lot of practice to become competent.
  - 1 – I have no experience of this and cannot claim capability, would need to develop – but everyone has to start somewhere!
- Write your score for each statement in the column on the right margin (you can photocopy this or download a worksheet if you prefer not to write on the book).

Entrepreneurial capabilities

Cluster	Entrepreneurial capabilities	Assessment
Personal organisation	<ul><li>Set and plan to achieve personal and business goals</li><li>Take personal responsibility for the outcomes and consequences of my actions</li><li>Plan and use time productively to achieve my goals</li><li>Apply energy and dynamism to achieve results effectively</li><li>Apply self-awareness of personal strengths and limitations to achieving goals</li><li>Seek creative and effective ways of solving problems and meeting needs</li><li>Manage stress and pressure which may result from uncertainty and investment of effort</li></ul>	
	Total score out of 28	
Interpersonal interaction	<ul><li>Grow and maintain networks of social and industry contacts</li><li>Find out what is important to people and understand their perspectives</li><li>Influence and persuade people to understand, accept and trust my point of view</li></ul>	

Cluster	Entrepreneurial capabilities	Assessment
Interpersonal interaction	• Negotiate and conclude agreements with people • Lead individuals and groups to achieve common goals • Coach and provide feedback to people on their behaviour and performance	
	Total score out of 24	
Investigating opportunity	• Identify and investigate the potential value of new opportunities • Investigate and develop options for exploiting opportunities • Identify resources which could be connected to exploit opportunities • Assess, evaluate and select the opportunities which offer greatest potential	
	Total score out of 16	
Applying innovation	• Identify new possibilities and apply creative thinking to initiate new products, services and processes • Connect needs, resources, knowledge and technologies to create new products, services and processes • Develop innovations which can be applied to solve customer problems and meet actual and potential needs • Ensure innovations can be produced to meet customer requirements and expectations	
	Total score out of 16	
Strategic venture planning	• Propose a strategic vision and strategic plan for the future development and growth of a venture • Prepare a credible business proposal to gain support from and identify the benefits to investors, partners, customers and other stakeholders • Define a realistic business model which will enable a venture to meet customer requirements and create value from the opportunity • Identify and plan the resources needed for the launch and development of a venture: what will be required, when and potential sources	

Cluster	Entrepreneurial capabilities	Assessment
Strategic venture planning	● Identify and assess the strengths and weaknesses of competitors and differentiate a venture from these in ways customers will value ● Identify the critical factors for success of a venture and integrate these into the venture strategy and business model so that they can be achieved	
	Total score out of 24	
Market development	● Identify markets, segments and their characteristics ● Find out actual and emerging customer needs, preferences and decision-making criteria ● Develop and implement marketing plans to communicate and sell to target customers ● Contact, meet, present to, negotiate with and sell to customers ● Set targets and monitor performance for sales ● Review and evaluate the effectiveness of marketing plans	
	Total score out of 24	
	Final score out of 132 Divide your score by 132 and multiply by 100 to give a percentage	

Now review your self-assessment.

Please bear in mind that this self-assessment is just that. It is based on your recollection and scoring of your feeling of capability and confidence in these areas. It does not predict future performance but it can help guide your future development.

So if you are a student with limited work experience you may have scored quite strongly in the personal and interpersonal clusters, but much lower in some of the other clusters where you do not yet have practical experience. However by completing the exercises in Chapter 4, you may already be developing capabilities in opportunity investigation and market development. Other capabilities can be developed by completing the practical exercises in Chapters 5 and 6.

A designer, engineer or IT specialist may have scored well under applying innovation, but lower in the clusters which involve more business skills. A manager in a large or public sector organisation may have scored well in the strategic venture planning but lower in opportunity investigation and market development; conversely a marketeer would do well in this area.

Only an experienced entrepreneur and manager is likely to score highly in all clusters!

What to do next?

Rank the clusters by score, from highest to lowest.

Which of the six are your top two?
These capabilities are distinctive strengths, for you to use and to develop further. They are likely to be your important contributions to an entrepreneurial team.

Which of the six are your middle two?
These capabilities are potential strengths, which can and need to be developed further, through practice, study, experience and learning from experts.

Which of the six are your lowest two?
These capabilities are limitations or weaknesses. This may be because of lack of opportunity to practise and gain experience in your career so far. Or it may result from choices you have made about subjects, career options, or from feeling your strengths lie in other areas. Some understanding and practical ability will be needed in these areas for you to be effective in entrepreneurial working. However the choice you will need to make is how far you want to develop these capabilities, or alternatively how far you can compensate for them by relying on your strengths by seeking to work with others who have complementary skills to your own. You can consider this in planning your development at the end of this chapter.

management capabilities

Complete the management capabilities self-assessment in the same way by reflecting on each statement in the table:

● Have I ever demonstrated experience in doing this? How practised am I?
● How capable am I? What example or evidence could I give of my capability?
● How confident am I in my ability?
● Assess your level of capability as follows:
    4 – I am highly capable in this, fully confident of my ability.
    3 – I am quite capable with some successful experience which I could develop.
    2 – I have quite limited capability and experience and would need quite a lot of practice to become competent.
    1 – I have no experience of this and cannot claim capability, would need to develop – but everyone has to start somewhere!
● Write your score for each statement in the column on the right margin.

Management capabilities

Cluster	Management capabilities	Assessment
Leading and managing people	● Develop and communicate a clear mission, direction and core values for the organisation which everyone can relate to their work ● Ensure effective, clear and regular two-way communications with everyone in the organisation ● Develop and implement effective human resource management systems (e.g. for employment and performance management) which meet organisational and statutory requirement ● Ensure every manager in the organisation is aware of his/her responsibilities for managing people effectively ● Ensure all employees have access to development and training opportunities to meet organisational, personal and statutory requirements	
	Total score out of 20	
Managing organisation and operations	● Create an organisation structure able to support achievement of the business goals ● Define key responsibilities within the organisation and ensure these are filled ● Define and implement the key processes to provide the product or service effectively, efficiently and in line with customer expectations ● Define and introduce performance measures to monitor effectiveness, efficiency and quality ● Introduce and maintain systems and methods to continuously improve performance, cost and quality	
	Total score out of 20	
Managing finance and resources	● Plan the financial requirements of the business to meet its business goals ● Plan and monitor financial performance of the business against key targets ● Plan to meet investor and lender requirements for their interest in the business ● Develop systems to plan and monitor (one score): ● break-even, viability and profitability overall and of individual products, services and key accounts or operations	

Cluster	Management capabilities	Assessment
Managing finance and resources	● resource requirements and liabilities of contracts are identified and can be met ● investment and working capital requirements ● cash flow ● debtor and creditor payments and timescales ● Ensure statutory financial reporting requirements are met, e.g. accounting, taxation and VAT	
	Total score out of 20	
Responsible management	● Display sensitivity to stakeholder interests, concerns and expectations of the business ● Identify legislative and statutory requirements for the business and monitor evidence of compliance with these ● Maintain dialogue with community and media organisations to ensure people in the business are aware of their interests and respond effectively to them ● Ensure the business develops and implements appropriate policies and practices in relation to social, environmental and ethical responsibility, equality of opportunity and diversity	
	Total score out of 16	
	Final score out of 76 Divide your score by 76 and multiply by 100 to give a percentage	

Now review your self-assessment.

Please bear in mind that this self-assessment is just that. It is based on your recollection and scoring of your feeling of capability and confidence in these areas. It does not predict future performance but it can help guide your future development.

Only an experienced and versatile manager is likely to score highly in all clusters!

What to do next?

Rank the clusters by score, from highest to lowest.

Which of the four is your highest?
This capability is a distinctive strength, for you to use and to develop further. It is likely to be your important contribution to a management team.

Which of the four are your middle two?
These capabilities are potential strengths, which can and need to be developed further, through practice, study, experience and learning from experts.

Which of the four is your lowest?
This capability is a limitation or weakness. This may be because of lack of opportunity to practise and gain experience in your career so far. Or it may result from choices you have made about subjects, career options, or from a feeling that your strengths lie in other areas. Some understanding and practical ability will be needed in these areas for you to be effective in managerial working. However the choice you will need to make is how far you want to develop this capability, or alternatively how far you can compensate for them by relying on your strengths or by seeking to work with others who have complementary skills to your own. You can consider this in planning your development.

Overall, out of the ten clusters of capabilities, which were your highest three?
Are these primarily entrepreneurial or managerial?
It is important to seek opportunities to use these. These are likely to be the main contributions you can make to a venture team and will help to define your role in the team.

Which clusters show moderate strength, which you think you can develop further?
Plan how you can find ways of achieving this.

Which clusters showed least strengths? These may in part be due to lack of experience, but lack of aptitude is also likely to be a factor. You may need and be able to develop them to some extent, and it would be in your interest to do this. But be aware that you have limitations in these areas and you will need to find and work with people who have greater skill in these areas and whom you trust.

career plan

what I want to achieve

Goals and motivations

● My Personal Vision for the future is:

● These are the values which are most important to me:

● These are my Life Goals for:
  ● Business

  ● Career

  ● Personal growth

  ● Family

  ● Social life

Include when each goal is to be achieved and how success will be measured

Increasing my personal value

● My value to myself and to others is based on:

● These are the ways in which I aim to build on my personal qualities to develop my career further:

Financial value

By when

● I aim to increase the value of my total net financial assets to:

● I aim to increase my annual financial income to:

How I will achieve my goals

These are my plans for how I will achieve each of my goals:

Personal learning

These are my goals for learning, through which I will be able to achieve my life goals:

Include in each plan how you will gain the learning, by when, and who will help your learning

Signed:_____Date: _____

opportunity assessment questionnaire

Use the questionnaire overleaf to assess your opportunity.

- Answer the questions on each dimension.
- Where possible, use factual data to answer the questions.
- Total the scores for each dimension and plot these onto the scoring pentagon at the end of the questionnaire.
- Join the plotting points to show its profile.
- What does the profile suggest about the potential for exploiting this opportunity? (See notes following the questionnaire).

Name or type of venture: --

1. Investment

How much of the available financial assets does the venture require?	All	5
	Above 75%	4
	Above 50%	3
	Above 25%	2
	Below 25%	1
	None	0
How much of the human capital available does the venture require?(Includes time, commitment, expertise, knowledge, and skills.)	All	5
	Above 75%	4
	Above 50%	3
	Above 25%	2
	Below 25%	1
How much external financial investment is required as a percentage of the total funding required?	All	5
	Above 75%	4
	Above 50%	3
	Above 25%	2
	Up to 25%	1
	None	0
Does the venture rely on credibility or reputation being invested (for example through a recognised brand name, franchise, partnership, joint venture or accreditation)?	Essential	5
	Significant	4
	Moderate	3
	Low	2
	None	0
Total points		

2. Risk

What proportion of the investment could be realised through sale of tangible assets with resale value?	All	0
	Above 75%	1
	Above 50%	2
	Above 25%	3
	Up to 25%	4
	None	5
Have all the essential elements on which the venture depends been tested and proved to be predictable and reliable (consumer behaviour, marketing, process technology, suppliers, etc.)?	Completely untested	5
	Largely untested	4
	Partly unproven	3
	Significantly proven	2
	Completely predictable	1

How far do the people who will run the venture have proven skills, experience and track record in all its essential elements?(Includes marketing, finance, operations, technology)	Few elements	5
	Some elements	4
	Most elements	3
	All significant elements	2
	All elements	1
Have all the essential elements on which the venture depends been tested and proved to be predictable and reliable (consumer behaviour, marketing, process technology, suppliers, etc.)?	Completely untested	5
	Largely untested	4
	Partly unproven	3
	Significantly proven	2
	Completely predictable	1

3. Return

What is the net profit margin the venture is expected to make?	21+%	5
	16–20%	4
	11–15%	3
	6–10%	2
	Less than 5%	1
What is the anticipated return on investment each year, once the venture is in profit?	21+%	5
	16–20%	4
	11–15%	3
	6–10%	2
	Less than 5%	1
What is the anticipated growth in the value of the investment per year, after the first year (for example, value of equity or assets such as intellectual property or real estate)?	31+%	5
	21–30%	4
	11–20%	3
	6–10%	2
	Less than 5%	1
How quickly will positive cash flow be reached?	Within 3 months	5
	Within 6 months	4
	1 year	3
	18 months	2
	2 years	0
Total points		

4. Impact of change

How far does the venture create or find a new market, identify unmet demand, or meet customer requirements in a new way?	Opens a completely new market	5
	Serves an underdeveloped market with little competition	4
	Extends an existing market	3
	Meets customer requirements in a new way	2
	Serves an existing market	1
Does the venture apply innovation to offer customers new benefits or meet their needs more effectively (by creating a new product or by using new technology or production processes etc.)?	Highly innovative	5
	Significant innovation	4
	Moderate innovation	3
	Some innovation	2
	Little innovation	1
Does the venture use a new distribution method to communicate with and sell to customers (for example, online, Internet, SMS text, digital media)?	Totally new	5
	Significantly changed	4
	Moderately changed	3
	Little changed	2
	Unchanged	1
Will the venture lead to significant change in the structure of the industry, e.g. for competitors and suppliers?	Radical change	5
	Significant change	4
	Moderate change	3
	Little change	2
	No change	1
Total points		

5. Time

Will the project start:	Significantly in advance of competitors	5
	Slightly in advance of competitors	4
	At same time as competitors	2
	Later than competitors	1
How quickly will the project start to produce a return on the investment?	More than 2 years	5
	1–2 years	4
	6–12 months	3
	3–6 months	2
	Within 3 months	1

For how long will the venture continue to produce a return on the investment?	Indefinitely	5
	5–10 years	4
	2–5 years	3
	1–2 years	2
	Up to 1 year	1
How likely is the project to create additional profitable opportunities during its lifespan (e.g. spin-off business, new products, product extensions, new markets, market extensions)?	A series of high-return opportunities identified	5
	Moderate-return opportunities identified	4
	Strong potential for future opportunities	3
	Future opportunitieshighly likely	2
	Limited future potential	1

Scoring pentagon

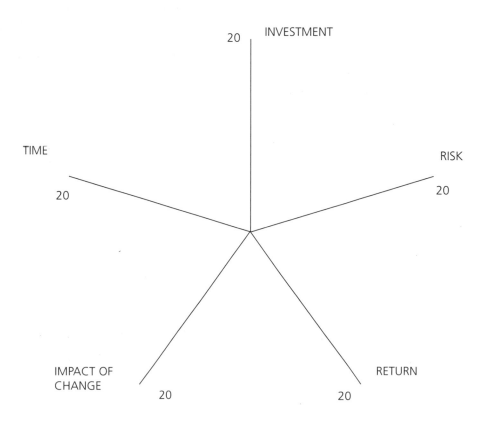

Interpreting the profile

Use the questions below to analyse the profile and consider ways in which the venture could be re-configured to improve its prospects.

- Is the profile aggressive: a large profile showing greater risk, higher reward, bigger investment, larger-scale change and medium to longer timescales? This will require a high level of entrepreneurial management capability. Do you – or your team – possess this?
- Is the profile defensive: a tightly grouped profile with lower degrees of investment, risk, reward, change and short to medium timescales? This may suggest an over-cautious approach which will provide modest rewards. How can its potential be enhanced?
- Can the investment required be reduced, or more of it obtained from other investors?
- Is it an attractive investment, and to what type of investor? Will you invest your own money?
- What factors give rise to the degree of risk, and can any of these be reduced, for example through an incremental approach to finding 'what works' such as market or product testing, research, planning, finding people with the right experience?
- Is the projected return proportionate to the degree of risk?
- Does the impact of change in the venture increase its risk, and if so can this be reduced without detracting from the venture's competitive advantage?
- Can the venture achieve greater results through applying more innovative approaches?
- Can more value-adding spin-off services be created from the venture to enhance its earnings and lifetime?
- Can the timescales be altered, for example to bring forward the start of earnings, and to extend the earning lifetime of the venture?
- Can the value of the venture be increased over its lifetime?

opportunity selection model

Opportunity selection model

High-value opportunity	Market	Low-value opportunity
Able to access market of growing size and value	Market growth	Limited growth potential in smaller markets
Known, identifiable customers in defined market sector	Customer base	Limited or non-specific customer base
Customer reliance on product increasing over time	Customer reliance and convergence	Customers not reliant on product, divergent from their needs
Trust and open relationships with clients; compatible practices	Customer interaction	Adversarial customer relationships; lack of fit
Long-term partnerships within strong supplier and technology networks	Partnering and networks	One-off relationships within weak networks
Unique advantages and strengths apparent in relation to competitors	Competition	Undifferentiated from competitors, forced to compete on price

High-value opportunity	Innovation	Low-value opportunity
Able to lead the market using prior experience	Innovation leadership	Learn as you go along to catch up
Application solves a problem informed by customers' needs	Innovation related to customer needs	Application does not solve customers' real problem
Differentiated technology; optimal performance and cost benefits	Technology differentiation	Undifferentiated technology; marginal performance and cost improvement
Strong IP protection with clear ownership and control, hard to copy	Intellectual property	Weak or no IP protection – can be copied
Opportunity to be first to market	Speed to market	Follower to market
Implementation feasible; challenges can be overcome	Feasibility of implementation	Difficult to implement with many obstacles

Opportunity selection model

High-value opportunity	Strategy	Low-value opportunity	High-value opportunity	People	Low-value opportunity
Have a strategy to create and grow business	Business growth	Limited purpose and scope to build a business	CEO shows leadership in innovation	CEO leadership	CEO not an innovative leader
Multiple strategic and exit options	Strategic options	Single or limited exploitation options	Management team skilled, compatible and motivated to achieve	Management team effectiveness	Team lack management skills, fit and motivation
High value creation from high profit margin and cash generation	Value creation	Low perceived value and profit margin	Able to use prior experience and knowledge of industry	Contextual experience	No pre-knowledge of industries or technology
Superior business model	Innovative business model	No advantage over existing business models	Able to recruit experienced people from within industry	Staff capability	Experienced and capable staff not available

Opportunity selection model

High-value opportunity	Investment	Low-value opportunity	High-value opportunity	Learning	Low-value opportunity
High return and profitability in relation to investment	Investment reward	Low financial return for investment	Independent control of business direction	Independent control	Not in full control of the business
Attractive to potential investors with growing equity value	Investor attraction	Unattractive to investors offering limited increase in equity value	Personal vision and confidence in business potential	Personal vision	Self doubt and lack of scope to succeed
Acceptable risk of loss in worst case scenario	Risk	Unacceptably high downside risk	Able to reduce margin between success and failure	Incremental learning	Unable to reduce margin of effectiveness
Commercially viable with predictable break-even and cash flow	Viability and cash flow	Unpredictable cash flow, unlikely to achieve viability	Intuition, knowing the right thing to do	Intuition	Does not feel right – bad past experience
Long-term opportunity and income stream	Timescale	Short-term timeframe and rapid exit strategy	Able to practise ethical framework and values	Ethics	Non-ethical exploitation

Scoring

- Mark an X in the box on each factor (paired set of statements) which most closely matches your business opportunity.
- Under each cluster (group of four or six factors), count how many factors have been marked in the left-hand (high-value) box.
- Give each 1 point.
- Give no points for factors marked in the right-hand (low-value) box.
- Write the number in the box below.

Market	Innovation
6 factors total:	6 factors total:
Strategy	People
4 factors total:	4 factors total:
Investment	Learning
5 factors total:	5 factors total:
30 factors Total for all 6 clusters:	

Scoring guideline

Score

0–7	Likely to be a low-value opportunity with limited return, if all have aspects been explored suggest disregarding it.
8–15	Moderate-value opportunity, can aspects with growth potential be developed?
16–24	Worthwhile opportunity, needs careful analysis to improve weak areas and raise the value potential
25–30	Strong potential for a high-value opportunity; beware of over-optimism. Explore in detail the weak areas, potential competition and feasibility; plan to implement

Whatever the score, look carefully at the low-value clusters (scoring half or less) and explore how these could be increased.

Write the cluster score on the diagram overleaf:

Ways of increasing opportunity value:

Market

Innovation

Strategy

People

Investment

Learning

venture planning template

PRESENTING YOUR VENTURE PLAN

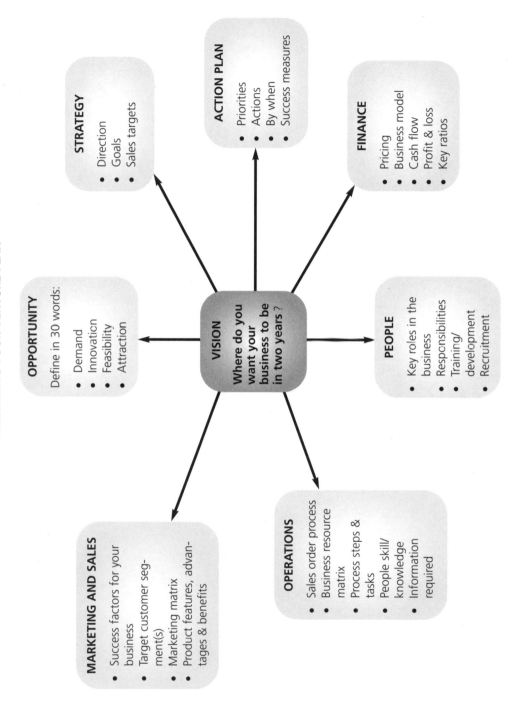

STRATEGY
- Direction
- Goals
- Sales targets

ACTION PLAN
- Priorities
- Actions
- By when
- Success measures

FINANCE
- Pricing
- Business model
- Cash flow
- Profit & loss
- Key ratios

OPPORTUNITY
Define in 30 words:
- Demand
- Innovation
- Feasibility
- Attraction

VISION
Where do you want your business to be in two years ?

PEOPLE
- Key roles in the business
- Responsibilities
- Training/ development
- Recruitment

MARKETING AND SALES
- Success factors for your business
- Target customer seg- ment(s)
- Marketing matrix
- Product features, advan- tages & benefits

OPERATIONS
- Sales order process
- Business resource matrix
- Process steps & tasks
- People skill/ knowledge
- Information required

BUSINESS MODEL

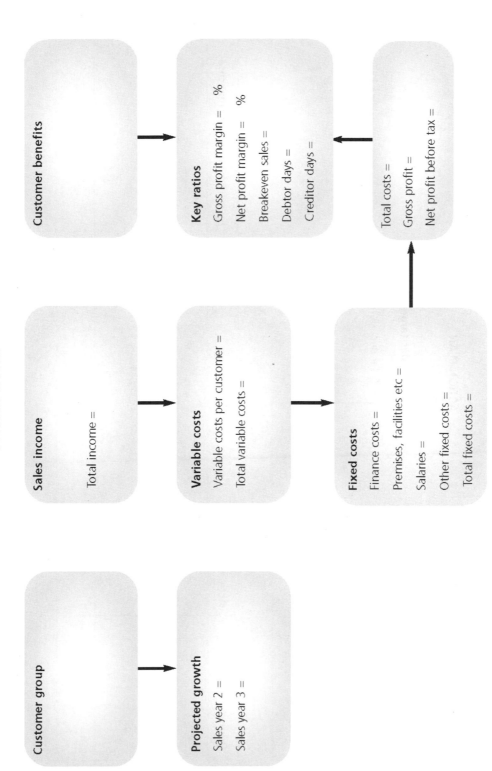

Customer benefits

Key ratios

Gross profit margin =   %

Net profit margin =   %

Breakeven sales =

Debtor days =

Creditor days =

Total costs =

Gross profit =

Net profit before tax =

Sales income

Total income =

Variable costs

Variable costs per customer =

Total variable costs =

Fixed costs

Finance costs =

Premises, facilities etc =

Salaries =

Other fixed costs =

Total fixed costs =

Customer group

Projected growth

Sales year 2 =

Sales year 3 =

ACTION PLAN

Business goals

1.

2.

3.

Sales target

Product or market segment	Months			
	3	6	9	12
1.				
2.				
3.				

Priority	Actions to do	By when	By whom	Success measure

INFORMATION TO SUPPORT VENTURE PLAN

Section	Worksheet	Other
Vision		
Strategy		
Opportunity		
Marketing & sales		
Finance		
Operations		
People		
Other		

The Business Action Plan you present should include:

1. Business planner mindmap – overview.
2. Business model.
3. Action plan.
4. Information to support it.

finance planner

1. cash flow projection

The cash flow projection is simply a forecast of when cash payments are expected to be received or paid out from the business. What actually takes place will be recorded in the cash flow statement and compared with the projection.

It is important to be realistic in your assumptions about timing of cash receipts and payments. New and small businesses live or die by their cash flow and managing cash flow is critical to business health, as the more positive the cash position is at the end of the month the less the business has to borrow or use an overdraft. A cash flow is different from a Profit and Loss statement, as it records accounting transactions when they actually occur.

The next page shows a typical format for a cash flow forecast.

TYPICAL FORMAT FOR A CASH FLOW FORECAST

Monthly cash flow forecast 1 Jan to 31 Dec

	Jan	Feb	Mar	Apr	May	June	July	Aug	Sept	Oct	Nov	Dec
Opening balance A												
Receipts												
Cash from sales												
Cash from debtors												
VAT net receipts												
Other receipts												
Sale of assets												
Capital												
Total receipts B												
Payments												
Suppliers												
Wages/drawings												
PAYE/NIC												
VAT net payments												
Tax payments												
Rent												
Rates												
Light heat power												
Phone												
Fees												
Interest												
Other												
Total payments C												
Closing bank balance												
A+B-C												
Cumulative												

Cash flow terms

Cash from sales	Cash for sales of products
Cash from debtors	Invoiced goods sold on terms
VAT	Value added tax collected on all sales
Other receipts	Any other income
Sale of assets	Proceeds from the sale of an asset
Capital	Amount of money invested in the business
Payment to Suppliers	Goods or services bought in
Wages/drawings	PAYE system for wages
PAYE/NIC	National insurance contributions
VAT net payment	Paid to VAT office each period
Tax payments	Corporation Tax on company profits
Rent	Cost of premises

2. profit and loss forecast

A profit and loss (P&L) forecast shows the level of profit (or loss) which the business is expected to produce at the end of the accounting period. A P&L forecast is different from a cash flow as it is drawn up on an accounting rather than cash basis.

On the next page is an example of a P&L statement for a business for a 12-month period broken down by months. It show the income, cost of goods, gross profit, expenses, net profit before interest and tax.

Interpreting the figures is important. This takes time and experience, but understanding the P&L as a live accounting tool can help you to manage the business much more effectively.

TYPICAL FORMAT FOR A PROFIT AND LOSS STATEMENT

Monthly profit and loss account   1 Jan to 31 Dec

	Jan	Feb	Mar	Apr	May	June	July	Aug	Sept	Oct	Nov	Dec
Sales (A)												
less cost of sales												
Purchases												
Labour												
Other direct costs												
Total (B)												
Gross profit (C: take B from A)												
less overheads												
Rent and rates												
Heat light power												
Phone												
Professional fees												
Depreciation												
Employee costs												
Other overheads												
Drawings												
Interest												
Total (D)												
Plus misc. income (E)												
Net profiT (F)												
BALANCE												
C+E-D												

Profit and loss terms

Sales (A)	Sum of all income from product sold
Cost of sales:	
Purchases (B)	Costs of goods/services bought in
Labour (B)	Employment costs of people in the business
Direct costs (B)	Costs incurred in production of product
Overheads	
Rent and rates (D)	Amortised over the year
Light/power(D)	Actual costs of services used
Phone (D)	As above
Misc Income (E)	Any other income received
Profit:	A − B = C Gross Profit − D + E = F Net profit

3. balance sheet forecast

A balance sheet for your business will show what the business is owed (debtors) and what it owes (creditors) on a specific day, for example a forecast at 12 months from the start of trading.

Typical format for a balance sheet forecast:

Balance Sheet Forecast (on 31st December 2005)
Assets   £
1. Fixed Assets
  Freehold property
  Leasehold property
  Office Equipment
  Vehicles
  Plant / machinery
  Other equipment
Total fixed assets (A)
2. Current Assets
  Cash in hand and at bank
  Stock
  Debtors
Total current assets (B)
TOTAL ASSETS   (A+B)

Capital and Liabilities
3. Capital
  Shareholders'/prop capital
  Profit and Loss
TOTAL CAPITAL (C)

4. Medium-term liabilities
  Loans
5. Current Liabilities
  Overdraft
  Tax payable
  Creditors
Total liabilities (D)
TOTAL CAPITAL & LIABILITIES (C+D)

Balance sheet terms

Fixed assets	Permanent assets (e.g. property, plant and equipment)
Current assets	Cash/debtors (money owing to business)/stock
Capital	The shareholders' funds invested in the business
Liabilities	Loans/overdraft/tax payable/creditors owed by the business

4. key financial ratios for the business

Gross margin	Gross profit as a percentage of sales
Gross margin	$= £150,000 / £500,000 * 100$ = 30 per cent
Net margin	Net profit as a percentage of sales
Net margin	$= £50,000 / £500,000 * 100$ = 10 per cent
Break-even sales (revenue)	Fixed costs divided by gross margin
Break-even (SR)	$= £100,000 / 0.3$ (30 per cent) $= £333,333$
Break-even sales (volume)	Fixed costs divided by total selling price less variable cost
Break-even (SV)	$= £100,000 / (£10 - £7)$ = 33,333 units
Margin of safety	Margin of safety revenue as a percentage of actual sales
Margin of safety	$= £166,667 / £500,000 * 100$ = 33 per cent

The importance of break-even analysis (B/E)

- B/E defines minimum sales level required for the business to be viable.
- It is used to assess financial viability of new products/services and to assess customer profitability, and enables more effective business decisions to be taken.
- A break-even calculation on any business can be applied at any point, providing the split between income, fixed and variable costs is known.
- B/E analysis can also be used to work out if a contract or order is worthwhile.
- Knowing the B/E position makes it possible to track the performance of the business daily, weekly, or monthly, to ensure it is making money.
- B/E can be used to assess the extra sales needed to employ an additional member of staff, an important decision for a small business. Here are performance ratios for employing people in the business:

$$\frac{\text{Sales turnover}}{\text{No. staff}} = \text{sales per person} \qquad\qquad \frac{\text{Net profit}}{\text{No. staff}}$$

$$\frac{500,000}{5} = 100,000 \text{ per person} \qquad\qquad \frac{20,000}{5} = 4,000$$

$$\frac{\text{Employment costs}}{\text{Gross margin per cent}} \times 100 = \text{sales needed to employ an extra person}$$

$$\frac{20,000 \times 100}{60} = £33,333$$

$$\frac{\text{Sales-input costs}}{\text{No. staff}} = \text{value added/person} \qquad \frac{75,000}{3} = 25,000$$

further reading

Chapter 1

Birley, S. and Muzyka, D. (2000) *Mastering Entrepreneurship* (2nd ed.). FT/Prentice Hall, London.
Bridge, S., O'Neill, K. and Cromie, S. (2003) *Understanding Enterprise, Entrepreneurship and Small Business* (2nd ed.). Palgrave Macmillan, London.
Deakins, D. and Freel, M. (2005) *Entrepreneurship and Small Firms* (4th ed.). McGraw Hill, Maidenhead.
Global Entrepreneurship Monitor (GEM website www.gemconsortium.org).

Chapter 2

Burns, P. (2001) *Entrepreneurship and Small Business*. Palgrave Macmillan, London.
Beaver, G. (2002) *Small Business, Entrepreneurship and Enterprise Development*. Pearson Education, Harlow.
Binks, M. and Vale, P. (1990) *Entrepreneurship and Economic Change*. McGraw-Hill, Maidenhead.
Gray, C. (1998). *Enterprise and Culture*. Routledge, London.
Hébert, R. and Link, A. (1988) *The Entrepreneur: Mainstream Views and Radical Critiques*. Praeger, New York.
Kirby, D. (2005) *Entrepreneurship*. McGraw-Hill, Maidenhead.
Schumpeter, J. (1934) *The Theory of Economic Development*. Harvard University Press, Boston, Mass.
Sexton, D. and Landström, H. (eds) (1999) *The Blackwell Handbook of Entrepreneurship*. Blackwell, Oxford.
Shane, S. (2003). *A General Theory of Entrepreneurship: The Individual–Opportunity Nexus*. Edward Elgar, Cheltenham.
Timmons, J.A. (2003) *New Venture Creation: Entrepreneurship for the 21st Century* (6th ed.). McGraw-Hill International, Dubuque, Iowa.

Chapter 3

Bolton, B. and Thompson, J. (2000) *Entrepreneurs: Talent, Temperament, Technique*. Butterworth-Heinemann.
Fletcher, D. (2002) *Understanding the Small Family Business*. Routledge, London.
Kaplan, J. (2003) *Patterns of Entrepreneurship*. Wiley, Hoboken, N.J.

Chapter 4

Buzan, T. and B. (2003) *The Mind Map Book*. BBC Books, London.
Lumsdaine, E. and Binks, M. (2005). *Entrepreneurship, Creativity, and Effective Problem Solving: Keep on Moving!* E&M Lumsdaine Solar Consultants, Hancock, Mich.
Southern, M. and West, C. (2002) *The Beermat Entrepreneur: Turn Your Good Idea Into a Great Business*. Pearson Prentice Hall, London.
Drucker, P. (1985) *Innovation and Entrepreneurship*. Heinemann, London.
Morgan, G. (1993) *Imaginization: The Art of Creative Management*. Sage, Thousand Oaks, Calif.

Chapter 5

Allen, K.R. (1999) *Launching New Ventures: An Entrepreneurial Approach* (2nd ed.). Houghton Mifflin, Boston, Mass.
Burns, P. (2004) *Corporate Entrepreneurship*. Palgrave Macmillan, London.
Chaston, I. and Mangles, T. (2002) *Small Business Marketing Management*. Palgrave Macmillan, London.
McKnight, T.K. (2004) *Will It Fly? How to Know if Your New Business Idea Has Wings ... Before You take the Leap*. FT/Prentice Hall, London.

Chapter 6

Timmons, J.A. (2003) *New Venture Creation: Entrepreneurship for the 21st Century* (6th ed.). McGraw-Hill International, Dubuque, Iowa.
Mullins, J. (2003) *The New Business Road Test: What Entrepreneurs and Executives Should Do Before Writing a Business Plan*. FT-Prentice Hall, London.
Barrow, C., Barrow, P. and Brown, R. (2001) *The Business Plan Workbook*. Kogan Page, London.
Record, M. (2000) *Preparing a Winning Business Plan*. How To Books, Oxford.
Shepherd, D.A. and Douglas, E.J. (1999) *Attracting Equity Investors,* Sage, Thousand Oaks, Calif.
Stutely, R. (2001) *The Definitive Business Plan* (2nd ed.). FT/Prentice Hall, London.
Timmons, J.A., Zacharakis, A. and Spinelli, S. (2004) *Business Plans that Work*. McGraw-Hill, Maidenhead.
Williams, S. (2004) *Lloyds Small Business Guide*. Penguin, Harmondsworth.

Chapter 7

Hashemi, S. and B. (2002) *Anyone Can Do It: Building Coffee Republic from our own Kitchen Table*. Capstone, Mankato, Minn.
Price, R. (2006) *Annual Editions: Entrepreneurship*. McGraw-Hill, Maidenhead.
Shepherd, D.A. and Shanley, M. (1998) *New Venture Strategy*. Sage, Thousand Oaks, Calif.
Weick, K. (1995) *Sensemaking in Organizations*. Sage, Thousand Oaks, Calif.
Wickham, P.A. (2003) *Strategic Entrepreneurship: A Decision-Making Approach to New Venture Creation and Management*. Pearson: Harlow.
Woods, C. (2004) *From Acorns ... How To Build Your Brilliant Business From Scratch*. Pearson, London.

Chapter 8

Dees, Gregory J. (2001) *Enterprising Nonprofits: A Toolkit for Social Entrepreneurship*. Wiley, New York.
Björkegren, D. (1996) *The Culture Business: Management Strategies for the Arts Related Business*. Routledge, London.
Lash, S. and Urry, J. (1994) *Economies of Signs and Space*. Sage, London.
Leadbeater, C. and Oakley, K. (1999) *The Independents: Britain's New Cultural Entrepreneurs*. Demos, London.
Leadbeater, C. (1997) *The Rise of the Social Entrepreneur*. Demos, London.

Chapter 9

Moore, D. and Holly Buttner, E. (1997) *Women Entrepreneurs: Moving Beyond the Glass Ceiling*. Sage, London.

Schein, E. (1993) *Career Anchors: Discovering Your Real Values*. Pfeiffer, San Francisco, Calif.

Schon, D.A. (1983) *The Reflective Practitioner*. Temple Smith, London.

Spinosa, C., Flores, F. and Dreyfus, H. (1997) *Entrepreneurship, Democratic Action and the Cultivation of Solidarity*. MIT Press, Cambridge, Mass.

Steyaert, C. and Bouwen, R. (1997) Telling Stories of Entrepreneurship: Towards a Narrative-contextual Epistemology for Entrepreneurial Studies. In R. Donckels and A. Miettinen (eds), *Entrepreneurship and SME Research*, pp. 47–62. Ashgate, Aldershot.

references and bibliography

Aldrich, H. and Zimmer, C. (1986) Entrepreneurship through Social Networks. In D. S. Sexton and R.W. Smilor (eds), *The Art and Science of Entrepreneurship*, pp. 3–23. Ballinger, Cambridge, Mass.

Allen, S. and Truman, C. (eds) (1993) *Women in Business: Perspectives on Women Entrepreneurs*. Routledge, London.

Ancona, D. (2005) *Leadership in an Age of Uncertainty*. MIT Leadership Center Research Brief, MIT, Cambridge, Mass.

Argyris, C. and Schon, D. (1978) *Organizational Learning*. Addison-Wesley, Boston, Mass.

Baines, S. and Robson, L. (2001) Being Self-employed or Being Enterprising? The Case of Creative Work for the Media Industries. *Journal of Small Business and Enterprise Development*, 8(4), pp. 349–62.

Baines, S. and Wheelock, J. (1998) Working for Each Other: Gender, the Household and Micro-business Survival and Growth. *International Small Business Journal*, **17**(1), pp.16–35.

Bandura, A. (1986) *Social Foundations of Thought and Action: A Social Cognitive Theory*. Prentice-Hall, Upper Saddle River, N. J.

Baucus, D. and Sherrie, E. (1994) Second-career Entrepreneurs: A Multiple Case Study Analysis of Entrepreneurial Processes and Antecedent Variables. *Entrepreneurship: Theory and Practice*, Winter, **19**(2), pp. 41–72.

Baumard, P. (1999) *Tacit Knowledge in Organizations*. Sage, London.

Baumback, C. and Mancuso, J. (1987) *Entrepreneurship and Venture Management*. Prentice-Hall, Upper Saddle River, N.J.

Beaver, G. (2002) *Small Business, Entrepreneurship and Enterprise Development*. Pearson Education, Harlow.

Berger, P. and Luckmann, T. (1967) *The Social Construction of Reality*. Allen Lane, London.

Bhidé, A. (1999) Developing Start-up Strategies. In W. Sahlman, H. Stevenson, M. Roberts and A. Bhidé (eds), *The Entrepreneurial Venture* (2nd ed.), pp. 121–37. Harvard Business School Press, Boston, Mass.

Binks, M. and Vale, P. (1990) *Entrepreneurship and Economic Change*. McGraw-Hill, Maidenhead.

Bird, B. (1988). Implementing Entrepreneurial Ideas: The Case for Intention. *Academy of Management Review*, **13**(3), pp. 442–53.

Bird, B. and Jelinek, M. (1988) The Operation of Entrepreneurial Intentions. *Entrepreneurship Theory and Practice*, **13**(2), pp. 21–9.

Birley, S. (1986) The Role of Networks in the Entrepreneurial Process. *Journal of Business Venturing*, Winter, **1**, pp. I07–17.

Birley, S. and Stockley, S. (2000) Entrepreneurial Teams and Venture Growth. In D. Sexton and H. Landström (eds), *The Blackwell Handbook of Entrepreneurship*, pp. 287–307. Blackwell, Oxford.

Björkegren, D. (1996) *The Culture Business: Management Strategies for the Arts Related Business*. Routledge, London.

Blackburn, R. and Mackintosh, L. (1999) *The Entrepreneurship Potential of People in the Third Age: A Case of Over Expectation?* Paper presented at Small Business and Enterprise Development Conference, University of Leeds, March 1999.

Bloch, S. (2005) Complexity, Chaos, and Nonlinear Dynamics: A New Perspective on Career Development Theory. *Career Development Quarterly*, March, **53**, pp. 194–207.

Bolton, J. E. (1971) *Small Firms: Report of the Committee of Inquiry on Small Firms*; HMSO, London.

Boyd, N. and Vozikis, G. (1994) The Influence of Self-efficacy on the Development of Entrepreneurial Intentions and Actions. *Entrepreneurship Theory and Practice*, **18**(4), pp. 63–77.

Bridge, S., O'Neill, K. and Cromie, S. (2003) *Understanding Enterprise, Entrepreneurship and Small Business*. Palgrave Macmillan, Basingstoke.

Brockhaus, R. (1980) Risk Taking Propensity of Entrepreneurs. *Academy of Management Journal*, **23**(3), pp. 509–20.

Brockhaus, R. (1982) The Psychology of the Entrepreneur. In C. Kent, D. Sexton and K. Vesper (eds), *Encyclopedia of Entrepreneurship*, pp.39–57, Prentice-Hall, Upper Saddle River, N.J.

Bruner, J. (1990) *Acts of Meaning*. Harvard University Press, Cambridge, Mass.

Burns, P. (2001) *Entrepreneurship and Small Business*. Palgrave Macmillan, London.

Burns, P. (2004) *Corporate Entrepreneurship*. Palgrave Macmillan, London.

Burgelman, R. (1983) Corporate Entrepreneurship and Strategic Management: Insights from a Process Study. *Management Science*, **29**, pp. 1349–64.

Buzan, T. and B. (2003) *The Mind Map Book*. BBC Books, London.

Cantillon, R. (1755) *Essai sur la nature du commerce en général*. Edited by H. Higgs (1934), Macmillan, London.

Carland, J.W., Carland, J-A. and Carland, W. (1995) *A Model of entrepreneurship: The Process of Venture Creation*. www.sbaer.uca.edu/docs/proceedings/95sbi.

Carr, P. (2000) *The Age of Enterprise*. Blackhall Publishing, Dublin.

Carr, P. and Beaver, G. (2002) The Enterprise Culture: Understanding a Misunderstood Concept. *Journal of Strategic Change*, **11** (Special Collection for Warwick Business School), pp. 105–13.

Casson, M. (2003) *The Entrepreneur, An Economic Theory*. Edward Elgar, Cheltenham

Centre for Education and Industry (2001) *Independent Research into Learning for Enterprise and Entrepreneurship*. University of Warwick, Coventry.

Chandler, G., Dahlqvist, J. and Davidsson, P. (2002) *Opportunity Recognition Processes: A Taxonomy and Outcome Implications*. Paper presented at the Babson/Kaufman Entrepreneurship Research Conference, Wellesley, Mass.

Chell, E., Harworth, J. and Brearley, S. (1991) *The Entrepreneurial Personality: Concepts, Cases and Categories*. Routledge, London.

Churchill, N. and Lewis, V. (1983) The Five Stages of Business Growth. *Harvard Business Review*, **61**(3), pp. 30–50.

Clark, B.R. (1998) *Creating Entrepreneurial Universities: Organizational Pathways Of Transition*. IAU Press/Elsevier, Oxford.

Cope, J. (2005) Toward a Dynamic Learning Perspective of Entrepreneurship. *Entrepreneurship: Theory and Practice*, **29**(4), pp. 373–98.

Cope, J. and Watts, G. (2000) Learning by Doing: An Exploration of Critical Incidents and Reflection in Entrepreneurial Learning. *International Journal of Entrepreneurial Behaviour and Research*, **6**(3), pp. 104–24.

Corbett, A. (2005) Experiential Learning Within the Process of Opportunity Identification and Exploitation. *Entrepreneurship: Theory and Practice*, **29**(4), p. 473.

Corbett, A.C. (2002) Recognizing High-tech Opportunities: A Learning and Cognitive

Approach. *Frontiers of Entrepreneurship Research*. Paper presented at the Babson/Kaufman Entrepreneurship Research Conference, Wellesley, Mass.

Creative Industries Task Force (2001) *The Cultural Industries Mapping Document*. DCMS, London.

Curran, J. (2000) What is Small Business Policy in the UK for? Evaluation and Assessing Small Business Policies. *International Small Business Journal*, 18(3), pp. 36–51.

Davidsson, P., Delmar, F. and Wiklund, J. (2002) Entrepreneurship as Growth: Growth as Entrepreneurship. In M. Hitt, R. Ireland, S. Camp, and D. Sexton (eds), *Strategic Entrepreneurship: Creating a New Mindset*, pp. 328–42. Blackwell, Oxford.

Davidsson, P., Low, M. and Wright, M. (2001) Editor's Introduction: Low and MacMillan Ten Years On: Achievements and Future Directions for Entrepreneurship Research. *Entrepreneurship Theory and Practice*, 25(4), pp. 5–15.

De Geus, A. (1988) Planning as Learning. *Harvard Business Review*, Mar/Apr, 66(2), pp. 70–4.

De Geus, A. (1997) *The Living Company*. Nicholas Brealey, London.

Deakins, D. and Freel, M. (1998) Entrepreneurial Learning and the Growth Process in SMEs. *The Learning Organization*, 5(3), pp. 144–55.

Deakins, D. and Freel, M. (2006) *Entrepreneurship and Small Firms*. McGraw-Hill, London.

Dees, Gregory J. (2001) *Enterprising Nonprofits: A Toolkit for Social Entrepreneurship*. Wiley, New York.

Department for Education and Skills (2003) *The Future of Higher Education*. HMSO, London.

Department for Education and Skills and Davies, H. (2002) *A Review of Enterprise and the Economy in Education*. HMSO, London.

Department of Culture, Media and Sport (1999) *The Cultural Industries: White Paper*. DCMS, London.

DCMS Creative Industries Task Force, (2001). *The Cultural Industries Mapping Document*. DCMS, London.

DCMS, (2004). *Creative Industries Toolkit*. www.dcms.gov.uk.

Department of Trade and Industry (1998) *Our Competitive Future: Building the Knowledge Driven Economy*. DTI, London.

Devins, D. and Gold, J. (2002) Social Constructionism: A Theoretical Framework to Underpin Support for the Development of Managers in SMEs? *Journal of Small Business and Enterprise Development*, 9(2), pp. 111–19.

Dewey, J. (1934) *Art as Experience*. In J.A. Boydston (ed.) (1991) *The Collected Works of John Dewey*. Southern Illinois University Press, Carbondale.

Diamond, K. (2003) *Female Entrepreneurship: Developing Worldwide*. Keynote address at 48th International Council for Small Business World Conference, Belfast, June 2003.

Drucker, P. (1985) *Innovation and Entrepreneurship*. Heinemann, London.

Drucker, P. (1993) *Post-Capitalist Society*. Butterworth-Heinemann, Oxford.

Du Gay, P. (1997) *Production of Culture: Cultures of Production*. Sage, London.

Dutta, D. and Crossan, M. (2005). The Nature of Entrepreneurial Opportunities: Understanding the Process Using the 4I Organizational Learning Framework. *Entrepreneurship: Theory and Practice*, 29(4), pp. 425–49.

European Commission (2000) *European Charter for Small Enterprises*. European Commission, Brussels.

Festinger, L. (1957) *A Theory of Cognitive Dissonance*. Stanford University Press, Stanford, Calif.

Fiet, J. (2001) The Theoretical Side of Teaching Entrepreneurship. *Journal of Business Venturing*, **16**(1), pp. 1–24.

Fiet, J. and Migliore, P. (2001) The Testing of a Model of Entrepreneurial Discovery by Aspiring Entrepreneurs. Paper presented at the Babson/Kaufman Entrepreneurship Research Conference, Wellesley, Mass.

Fletcher, D. (2000) Family and Enterprise. In S. Carter and D. Jones-Evans (eds), *Enterprise and Small Business: Principles, Practice and Policy*, pp.155–65. Addison-Wesley Longman, Harlow.

Fletcher, D. (2002) *Understanding the Small Family Business. Routledge*, London.

Forrest, P. (2004) *The Observed Characteristics of Successful Businesses*. The National Business Awards White Paper, Quest Media, London.

Forrest, P. and O'Connor, M. (2004) *The Barriers to Success ... and How They Are Overcome*. The National Business Awards White Paper, Quest Media, London.

Gaglio, C.M. and Taub, R.P. (1992) Entrepreneurs and Opportunity Recognition. In N.C. Churchill, J.A. Hornaday, B.A. Kirchhoff, O.J. Krasner and K.H. Vesper (eds), *Frontiers of Entrepreneurship Research*. Babson College, Wellesley, Mass.

Gaglio, C.M. and Katz, J. (2001) The Psychological Basis of Opportunity Identification: Entrepreneurial Alertness. *Journal of Small Business Economics*, **16**(2), pp 95–111.

Garavan, T.N. and O'Cinneide, B. (1994) Entrepreneurship Education and Training Programmes: A Review and Evaluation – Part 1. *Journal of European Industrial Training*, **18**(8), pp. 3–12; Part 2: **18**(11), pp. 13–21. MCB University Press.

Garnsey, E. (1998) A Theory of the Early Growth of the Firm. *Industrial and Corporate Change*, 7, pp. 523–36.

Gartner, W. (1989) 'Who Is an Entrepreneneur' is the Wrong Question. *Entrepreneurship Theory and Practice*, **13**(4), pp. 47–67.

Gartner, W., Carter, C. and Hills, G. (2003) The Language of Opportunity. In C. Steyaert and D. Hjorth (eds), *New Movements in Entrepreneurship*, pp. 103–24. Edward Elgar, Cheltenham.

Gartner, W., Shaver, K. and Gatewood, E. (2000) *Doing It for Yourself: Career Attributions of Nascent Entrepreneurs*. Paper presented at the Babson/Kaufman Entrepreneurship Research Conference, Wellesley, Mass.

Gavron, R., Cowling, M., Holtham, G. and Westall, A. (1998) *The Entrepreneurial Society*. IPPR, London.

Gibb, A. (1987) *Enterprise Culture: Its Meaning and Implications for Education and Training*. MCB University Press, Bradford.

Gibb, A. (1993) The Enterprise Culture and Education. *Entrepreneurship Theory and Practice*, **11**(3), pp. 11–34.

Gibb, A. (1996) Entrepreneurship and Small Business Management: Can we Afford to Neglect them in the Twenty-first Century Business School, *British Journal of Management*, 7, pp. 309–21.

Gibb, A. (2000) Corporate Restructuring and Entrepreneurship: What can Large Organisations Learn from Small? *Enterprise and Innovation Management Studies*, **1**(1), pp. 19–35.

Gibb, A. (2001) *Creating Conducive Environments for Learning and Entrepreneurship*. Address to the conference of the Entrepreneurship Forum, Naples, 21–24 June 2001.

Gibb Dyer, W. Jr (1994) Toward a Theory of Entrepreneurial Careers. *Entrepreneurship Theory and Practice*, **19**(2), pp. 7–21.

Guth, W. and Ginsberg, A. (1990) Introduction to the Special Issue. *Strategic Management Journal*, **11**, pp. 5–15

Gorman, G., Hanlon, D. and King, W. (1997) Some Research Perspectives on Entrepreneurship Education, Enterprise Education and Education for Small Business Management: A Ten-year Literature Review. *International Small Business Journal*, **15**(3), pp. 56–77.

Gray, C. (1998) *Enterprise and Culture*. Routledge, London.

Greene, P.G. and Brown, T.E. (1997) Resource Needs and the Dynamic Capitalism Typology. *Journal of Business Venturing*, **12**, pp. 161–73.

Grégoire, D., Déry, R. Béchard, J.-P. (2001) *Evolving Conversations: A Look at the Convergence in Entrepreneurship Research*. Paper presented at the Babson/Kaufman Entrepreneurship Research Conference, Wellesley, Mass.

Greiner, L. (1972) Evolution and Revolution as Organisations Grow. *Harvard Business Review*, **7–8**(72), pp. 37–46.

Hall, S. (1997) *Representation: Cultural Representations and Signifying Practices. Sage*, London.

Hamilton, E. (2004) *Socially Situated Entrepreneurial Learning in Family Business*. Paper presented at Institute for Small Business Affairs national conference, Newcastle, 2–4 November 2004.

Hannon, P. (2004) *Making the Journey from Student to Entrepreneur: A Review of the Existing Research into Graduate Entrepreneurship*. National Council for Graduate Entrepreneurship, Birmingham.

Hansemark, O. (1998) The Effects of an Entrepreneurship Programme on Need for Achievement and Locus of Control of Reinforcement. *International Journal of Entrepreneurial Behaviour and Research*, **4**(1), pp. 28–50.

Harding, R. (2006) *Global Entrepreneurship Monitor, UK National Report for 2005*. London Business School, London.

Harding, R., Brooksbank, D., Hart, M., Jones-Evans, D., Levie, J., O'Reilly, M. and Walker. J. (2006) *Global Entrepreneurship Monitor, United Kingdom 2005*. London Business School, London.

Harrison, R. and Leitch, C. (2005) Entrepreneurial Learning: Researching the Interface between Learning and the Entrepreneurial Context. *Entrepreneurship Theory and Practice*, **29**(4), pp. 351.

Hartshorn, C. (2002) *Learning from the Life-world of the Entrepreneur*. Paper presented at the Cambridge-MIT Institute Innovative Learning Methods workshop, University of Durham, March 2002.

Hatch, M-J. (1997) *Organization Theory: Modern Symbolic and Post Modern Perspectives*. Oxford University Press, Oxford.

Heartfield, J. (2000) *Great Expectations: The Creative Industries in the New Economy*. Design Agenda, London.

Hébert, R. and Link, A. (1988) *The Entrepreneur: Mainstream Views and Radical Critiques*. Praeger, New York.

Hench, T. and Sandberg, W. (2000) *'As the Fog Cleared, Something Changed': Opportunity Recognition as a Dynamic, Self-organizing Process*. Paper presented at the Babson/Kaufman Entrepreneurship Research Conference, Wellesley, Mass.

Hill, J. and McGowan, P. (1999) Small Business and Enterprise Development: Questions about Research Methodology. *International Journal of Entrepreneurial Behaviour and Research*, **5**(1), pp. 5–18.

Hills, G. (1995) *Opportunity Recognition by Successful Entrepreneurs: A Pilot Study*. Frontiers of Entrepreneurship Research, Babson College, Wellesley, Mass.

Hills, G., Lumpkin, G. and Singh, R. (1997) *Opportunity Recognition: Perceptions and Behaviors of Entrepreneurs*. Paper presented at the Babson/Kaufman Entrepreneurship Research Conference, Wellesley, Mass.

Hills, G. and Shrader, R. (1998) *Successful Entrepreneurs' Insights into Opportunity Recognition*. Paper presented at the Babson/Kaufman Entrepreneurship Research Conference, Wellesley, Mass.

Hills, G., Shrader, R. and Lumpkin, G. (1999) *Opportunity Recognition as a Creative Process*. Paper presented at the Babson/Kaufman Entrepreneurship Research Conference, Wellesley, Mass.

Hisrich, R. (1988) Entrepreneurship: Past Present and Future. *Journal of Small Business Management*, October, pp. 1–4.

Hitt, M., Ireland, R., Camp, S. and Sexton, D. (eds) (2002) *Strategic Entrepreneurship: Creating a New Mindset*. Blackwell, Oxford.

Hjorth, D. and Steyaert, C. (eds) (2004) *Narrative and Discursive Approaches in Entrepreneurship*. Edward Elgar, Cheltenham.

Hofer, C. and Bygrave, W. (1992) Researching Entrepreneurship. *Entrepreneurship Theory and Practice*, **16**(3), pp. 91–100.

Holmes, T. and Cartwright, S. (1994) Mid-career Change: The Ingredients for Success. *Employee Relations*, **16**(7), pp.58–72.

Honig, B. (2001) Learning Strategies and Resources for Entrepreneurs and Intrapreneurs. *Entrepreneurship Theory and Practice*, **26**(1), pp. 21–35.

ICSB (2004) *Advancing the SME agenda*: conference magazine, International Council for Small Business 49th World Conference, Johannesburg, 2004.

Jack, S. and Anderson, A. (1999) Entrepreneurship Education within the Enterprise Culture. *International Journal of Entrepreneurial Behaviour and Research*, **5**(3), pp. 110–25.

Johannisson, B., Alexanderson, O., Nowicki, K. and Senneseth, K. (1994) Beyond Anarchy and Organization: Entrepreneurs in Contextual Networks. *Entrepreneurship and Regional Development*, **6**, pp. 329–356.

Jones, O. and Tilley, F. (2003) *Competitive Advantage in SMEs*. Wiley, New York.

Kanter, R. (1983) *The Change Masters*. Allen & Unwin, London.

Kanter, R.M. (1988) When a Thousand Flowers Bloom: Structural, Collective, and Social Conditions for Innovation in Organizations. *Research in Organizational Behavior*, **10**, pp. 169–211.

Kaplan, J. (2003) *Patterns of Entrepreneurship*. Wiley, Hoboken, N.J.

Katz, J.A. (1994) Modelling Entrepreneurial Career Progressions: Concepts and Considerations. *Entrepreneurship: Theory and Practice;* **19**(2), pp. 23–40.

Kirzner, I. (1973) *Competition and Entrepreneurship*. University of Chicago Press, Chicago.

Kirzner, I. (1997) Entrepreneurial Discovery and the Competitive Market Process: An Austrian Approach. *Journal of Economic Literature*, **35**, pp. 60–85.

Koestler, A. (1964). *The Act of Creation*. Hutchinson, London.

Kupferberg, F. (1998) Humanistic Entrepreneurship and Entrepreneurial Career Commitment. *Entrepreneurship and Regional Development*, July–September, **10**(3), p. 171.

Lam, S.K.S. (1999) *Portraits of Successful Entrepreneurs and High Flyers: A Psychological Perspective*. Ashgate, Aldershot.

Lamont, L.M. (1987) What Entrepreneurs Learn from Experience. In C. Baumback and J. Mancuso (eds), *Entrepreneurship and Venture Management*, pp. 360–7. Prentice-Hall, Upper Saddle River, N.J.

Lash, S. and Urry, J. (1994) *Economies of Signs and Space*. Sage, London.

Laukkannen, M. (2000) Exploring Alternative Approaches in High-level Entrepreneurship: Creating Micro-mechanisms for Endogenous Regional Growth. *Entrepreneurship and Regional development*, **12**(1), pp. 25–47.

Lave, J. and Wenger, E. (1991) *Situated Learning: Legitimate Peripheral Participation*. Cambridge University Press, Cambridge.

Leadbeater, C. (1997) *The Rise of the Social Entrepreneur*. Demos, London.

Leadbeater, C. and Oakley, K. (1999) *The Independents: Britain's New Cultural Entrepreneurs*. Demos, London.

Leadbeater, C. and Oakley, K. (2001) *Surfing the Long Wave: Knowledge Entrepreneurship in Britain*. Demos, London.

Levie, J. (1999) *Enterprising Education in Higher Education in England*. Department for Education and Employment, London.

Long, W. and McMullan, W.E. (1984) *Mapping the New Venture Opportunity Identification Process*. Paper presented at the Babson/Kaufman Entrepreneurship Research Conference, Wellesley, Mass.

Low, M. and MacMillan, I. (1988) Entrepreneurship: Past Research and Future Challenges. *Journal of Management*, **35**, pp. 139–161.

Lumpkin, G. and Lichtenstein, B. (2005). The Role of Organizational Learning in the Opportunity-Recognition Process. *Entrepreneurship: Theory and Practice*, **29**(4), pp. 451–72.

Lumpkin, G.T., Hills, G.E. and Shrader, R.C. (2004) Opportunity Recognition. In H.P. Welsch (ed.), *Entrepreneurship: The Way Ahead*, pp. 73–90. Routledge, London.

Lumsdaine, E. and Binks, M. (2005) *Entrepreneurship, Creativity, and Effective Problem Solving: Keep on Moving!* E&M Lumsdaine Solar Consultants, Hancock, Mich.

Macaulay, C. (2003) *Changes to Self-employment in the UK: 2002 to 2003*. Office for National Statistics, London.

Mallon, M. and Cohen, L. (2001) Time for a Change? Women's Accounts of the Move from Organizational Careers to Self-Employment. *British Journal of Management*, **12**, pp. 217–30.

Manimala, M. (1992) Entrepreneurial Heuristics: A Comparison Between High Pl (Pioneering-lnnovative) and Low Pl Ventures. *Journal of Business Venturing*, 7, pp. 477–504.

Margerison, C. (1991) *Making Management Development Work*. McGraw-Hill, Maidenhead.

McClelland, D. (1961) *The Achieving Society*. Van Nostrand, Princeton, N.J.

Menzies, T. (2003) *21st Century Pragmatism: Universities and Entrepreneurship Education and Development*. Paper presented at 48th International Council for Small Business conference, Belfast.

Minniti, M. and Bygrave, W. (2001) A Dynamic Model of Entrepreneurial Learning. *Entrepreneurship Theory and Practice*, **25**(3), pp. 5–16.

Mitchell, R. (1997) Oral History and Expert Scripts: Demystifying the Entrepreneurial Experience. *International Journal of Entrepreneurial Behaviour and Research*, **3**(2), pp. 122–39.

Mitchell, R., Brock Smith, I., Morse, E., Seawright, C., Peredo, A. and McKenzie, B. (2002) Are Entrepreneurial Cognitions Universal? Assessing Entrepreneurial Cognition Across Cultures. *Entrepreneurship Theory and Practice*, **26**(4), pp. 9–32.

Mitchell, R., Busenitz, L., Lant, T., McDougall, P., Morse, E. and Brock Smith, J. (2002)

Towards a Theory of Entrepreneurial Cognition. *Entrepreneurship Theory and Practice*, **27**(2) pp. 93–104.

Mitton, D. (1989) The Compleat Entrepreneur. *Entrepreneurship Theory and Practice*, **13**(3), pp. 9–19.

Mitton, D. (1997) *Entrepreneurship: One More Time – Non-cognitive Characteristics that Make the Cognitive Clock Tick*. Paper presented at the Babson/Kaufman Entrepreneurship Research Conference, Wellesley, Mass.

Moore, D. and Holly Buttner, E. (1997) *Women Entrepreneurs: Moving Beyond the Glass Ceiling*. Sage, London.

Morgan, G. (1993) *Imaginization: The Art of Creative Management*. Sage, Thousand Oaks, Calif.

Mumford, A. (1995). *Effective Learning*. Institute of Personnel and Development, London.

OECD (1998) *Fostering Entrepreneurship*. OECD, Paris.

Ogbor, J. (2000) Mythicising and Reification in Entrepreneurial Discourse: Ideology – Critique or Entrepreneurial Studies. *Journal of Management Studies*, **37**(5), pp. 605–37.

Parker, S. (2004) *Learning about the Unknown: How Fast do Entrepreneurs Adjust their Beliefs?* Paper presented at 49th ICSB World Conference, Johannesburg.

Pedler, M. (1997) Interpreting Action Learning. In J. Burgoyne and M. Reynolds (eds), *Management Learning: Integrating Perspectives in Theory and Practice*, pp. 248–264. Sage, London.

Penrose, E. (1959) *The Theory of the Growth of the Firm*. Blackwell, Oxford.

Pitt, M. (1998) A Tale of Two Gladiators: 'Reading' Entrepreneurs as Texts. *Organization Studies*, **19**(3), pp. 387–414.

Pittaway, L., Robertson, M., Munir, K., Denyer, D. and Neely, A. (2004) Networking and Innovation: A Systematic Review of the Evidence. *International Journal of Management Reviews*, **5–6**(3–4), pp. 137–68.

Politis, D. (2005). The Process of Entrepreneurial Learning: A Conceptual Framework. *Entrepreneurship: Theory and Practice*, **29**(4), p399–424.

Porter, M. (1996) What is Strategy?. *Harvard Business Review*, **74**(6), pp. 61–78,

Rae, D. and Carswell, M. (2000) Using a Life Story Approach in Researching Entrepreneurial Learning: The Development of a Conceptual Model and its Implications in the Design of Learning Experiences. *Education and Training*, **42**(4/5), pp. 220–28.

Rae, D. and Carswell, M. (2001) Towards a Conceptual Understanding of Entrepreneurial Learning. *Small Business and Enterprise Development*, **8**(2), pp. 150–8.

Rae, D. (1999) *The Entrepreneurial Spirit: Learning to Unlock Value*. Blackhall, Dublin.

Rae, D. (2000) Understanding Entrepreneurial Learning: A Question of How? *International Journal of Entrepreneurial Behaviour and Research*, **6**(3), pp. 145–9.

Rae, D. (2001) EasyJet: A Case of Entrepreneurial Management?, *Strategic Change*, **10**, pp. 325–36.

Rae, D. (2003a) *Entrepreneurial Identity and Capability: The Role of Learning*. PhD thesis, Nottingham Trent University.

Rae, D. (2003b) Opportunity Centred Learning: An Innovation in Enterprise Education? *Education and Training*, **45**(8/9), pp. 542–9.

Rae, D. (2004a) Entrepreneurial Learning: A Practical Model from the Creative Industries. *Education and Training*, **46**(8–9), pp. 492–500.

Rae, D. (2004b) Practical Theories from Entrepreneurs' Stories: Discursive Approaches to

Entrepreneurial Learning. *Journal of Small Business and Enterprise Development*, **11**(2), pp. 195–202.

Rae, D. (2004c). *How Does Opportunity Recognition Connect with Entrepreneurial Learning?* Paper presented at: International Council for Small Business 49th World Conference, Johannesburg, June 20-23, 2004

Rae, D. (2005a) Cultural Diffusion: A Formative Process in Creative Entrepreneurship? *International Journal of Entrepreneurship and Innovation*, **6**(3), pp. 185–92.

Rae, D. (2005b) Entrepreneurial Learning: A Narrative-based Conceptual Model. *Journal of Small Business and Enterprise Development*, **12**(2), pp. 323–35.

Rae, D. (2005c) Mid-career Entrepreneurial Learning. *Education and Training*, **47**(8–9), pp. 562–74.

Raffo, C., O'Connor, J., Lovatt, A. and Banks, M. (2000) Attitudes to Formal Business Training amongst Entrepreneurs in the Cultural Industries: Situated Business Learning through 'Doing with Others'. *Journal of Education and Work*, **13**(2), pp. 215–30.

Rehn, A. and Taalas, S. (2004) Crime and Assumptions in Entrepreneurship. In D. Hjorth and C. Steyaert (eds), *Narrative and Discursive Approaches in Entrepreneurship*, pp. 144–59. Edward Elgar, Cheltenham.

Reuber, R. and Fischer, E. (1993) *The Learning Experiences of Entrepreneurs*. Paper presented at the Babson/Kaufman Entrepreneurship Research Conference, Wellesley, Mass.

Revans, R. (1980) *Action Learning: New Techniques for Managers*. Blond and Briggs, London.

Reynolds, P., Hay, M. and Camp, S. (1999, 2001, 2002) *Global Entrepreneurship Monitor*. http://www.gemconsortium.org, USA.

Rickards, T. (1988) *Creativity and Problem Solving at Work*. Gower, Aldershot.

Rotter, J. (1966) Generalized Experiences for Internal Versus External Control of Reinforcement. *Psychological Monographs*, 80: no. 609.

Runco, M. and Albert, R. (1990) *Theories of Creativity*. Sage, Thousand Oaks, Calif.

Schein, E. (1978) *Career Dynamics: Matching Individual and Organizational Needs*. Addison-Wesley, Boston, Mass.

Schein, E. (1993) *Career Anchors: Discovering Your Real Values*. Pfeiffer, San Francisco, Calif.

Schon, D.A. (1983) *The Reflective Practitioner*. Temple Smith, London.

Schumacher, E.F. (1974) *Small Is Beautiful: A Study of Economics as if People Mattered*. Abacus, London.

Schumpeter, J. (1934) *The Theory of Economic Development*. Harvard University Press, Cambridge, Mass.

Schwandt, T. (1998) Constructivist, Interpretivist Approaches to Human Inquiry. In N. Denzin and Y. Lincoln (eds), *The Landscape of Qualitative Research*, pp. 221–59. Sage, Thousand Oaks, Calif.

Scott, A.J. (1999) The Cultural Economy: Geography and the Creative Field. *Media,Culture and Society*, **21**(6), pp. 807–17.

Shane, S. (2003) *A General Theory of Entrepreneurship: The Individual-opportunity Nexus*. Edward Elgar, Cheltenham.

Shane, S. and Venkataraman, S. (2000) The Promise of Entrepreneurship as a Field of Research. *Academy of Management Review*, **25**(1), pp. 217–26.

Sharma, P. and Chrisman, J. (1999) Toward a Reconciliation of the Definitional Issues in the Field of Corporate Entrepreneurship. *Entrepreneurship Theory and Practice*, **23**(3), pp. 11–27.

Shepherd, D. and Krueger, N. (2002) An Intentions-based Model of Entrepreneurial Teams' Social Cognition. *Entrepreneurship Theory and Practice*, **27**(2), p. 167.

Shorthose, J. (2000) The Ecology of the Creative Community in Nottingham's Lace Market. In R. Aubrey and H. David (eds), *Greater Nottingham in the 21st Century: Reflections on the Future*, pp 223–8. Nottingham Trent University.

Shotter, J. (1993) *Conversational Realities: Constructing Life through Language*. Sage, London.

Shotter, J. (1995). The Manager as a Practical Author: A Rhetorical-responsive, Social Constructionist Approach to Social-organizational Problems. In D-M. Hosking, H.P. Dachler and K.J. Gergen (eds), *Management and Organisation: Relational Alternatives to Individualism*, pp. 125–47. Avebury, Aldershot.

Spinosa, C., Flores, F. and Dreyfus, H. (1997) *Entrepreneurship, Democratic Action and the Cultivation of Solidarity*. MIT Press, Cambridge, Mass.

Starr, J. and Fondas, N. (1992) A Model of Entrepreneurial Socialization and Organization Formation. *Entrepreneurship Theory and Practice*, **17**(1), pp. 67–75.

Stevenson, H. and Jarillo, C.(1990) A Paradigm of Entrepreneurship: Entrepreneurial Management. *Strategic Management Journal*, **11**, pp. 17–27.

Steyaert, C. and Bouwen, R. (1997) Telling Stories of Entrepreneurship: Towards a Narrative-contextual Epistemology for Entrepreneurial Studies. In R. Donckels and A. Miettinen (eds), *Entrepreneurship and SME Research*, pp. 47–62. Ashgate, Aldershot.

Steyaert C. and Hjorth, D. (eds) (2003) *New Movements in Entrepreneurship*. Edward Elgar, Cheltenham.

Storey, D. (1994) *Understanding the Small Business Sector*. Routledge, London.

Timmons, J. (1999) *New Venture Creation: Entrepreneurship for the 21st Century*. McGraw-Hill, Boston, Mass.

Timmons, J. (2002) *New Venture Creation: Entrepreneurship for the 21st Century*. *McGraw-Hill,* Boston, Mass.

Timmons, J., Smollem, L. and Dingee, A. (1985) *New Venture Creation*. Irwin, Homewood, Illinois.

Tucker, R. (2002) *Driving Growth Through Innovation: How Leading Firms Are Transforming Their Futures*. Berrett-Koehler, San Francisco, Calif..

Ucbasaran, D., Westhead, P. and Wright, M. (2001) The Focus of Entrepreneurial Research: Contextual and Process Issues. *Entrepreneurship Theory and Practice*. **25**(4), pp. 57–80.

Van de Ven, A.H. (1993) The Development of an Infrastructure for Entrepreneurship. *Journal of Business Venturing*, **8**, pp. 211–30.

Venkataraman, S. 1997. The Distinctive Domain of Entrepreneurship Research: An Editor's Perspective. In I. Katz and R. Brockhaus (eds), *Advances in Entrepreneurship, Firm Emergence, and Growth*, vol. 3. pp. 119–38. JAI Press, Greenwich, Conn.

Vesper, K (1980) *New Venture Strategies*. Prentice-Hall, New Jersey.

Wallas, G. (1926) *The Art of Thought*. Harcourt-Brace, New York.

Watkins, D. and Stone, G. (1999) *Entrepreneurship Education in UK Higher Education: Origins, Development and Trends*. Paper presented at Enterprise and Learning conference, University of Paisley, November 1999.

Watson, T.J. and Harris, P. (1999) *The Emergent Manager*. Sage, London.

Watson, T.J. (1995) Entrepreneurship and Professional Management: A Fatal Distinction. *International Small Business Journal*, **13**(2), pp. 34–46.

Weick, K., (1979). *The Social Psychology of Organizing*. Addison-Wesley, Boston, Mass.

Weick, K. (1995) *Sensemaking in Organizations*. Sage, Thousand Oaks, Calif.

Weinrauch, D. (1980) The Second Time Around: Entrepreneurship as a Mid-career Alternative. *Journal of Small Business Management*, **18**(1), pp. 25–32.

Wenger, E. (1998) *Communities of Practice: Learning, Meaning and Identity*. Cambridge University Press, Cambridge.

Westhead, P. and Wright, M. (1998) Novice, Portfolio, and Serial Founders: Are They Different? *Journal of Business Venturing*, **13**, pp173–204.

Wickham, P. (2004) *Strategic Entrepreneurship*. Pearson, Harlow.

Williams, S. (1999) *Lloyds Small Business Guide*. Penguin Books, Harmondsworth.

Wolff, N. (2001) *Managing the Downside while Maximizing the Upside: Real Options Reasoning to Entrepreneurial Learning*. Paper presented at the Babson/Kaufman Entrepreneurship Research Conference, Wellesley, Mass.

Young, J. and Sexton, D. (1997) Entrepreneurial Learning: A Conceptual Framework. *Journal of Enterprising Culture*, 5(3), pp. 223–48.

Journals

Academy of Management Journal (Publisher: Academy of Management) (ABI)

Academy of Management Review (Publisher: Academy of Management Review) (ABI)

Entrepreneur Magazine (Publisher: Entrepreneur Media Inc.)

Entrepreneurship and Regional Development (Publisher: Taylor and Francis)

Entrepreneurship: Theory and Practice (Publisher: Baylor University) (ABI)

International Journal of Entrepreneurship and Innovation (Publisher: IP Publishing)

International Journal of Entrepreneurial Behaviour and Research (Publisher: MCB)

International Small Business Journal (ABI)

Journal of Business Venturing (Publisher: Elsevier) (ABI)

Journal of Small Business and Enterprise Development (Publisher: Emerald) (online)

Journal of Small Business Management (Publisher: West Virginia University and ISCB) (ABI)

Small Business Reports (ABI)

Small Business Forum (ABI)

Small Business Economic Trends (ABI)

Strategic Management Journal (Publisher: Wiley) (online)

UK Venture Capital Journal (Publisher: Securities Data Publishing)

Websites

www.babson.edu/entrep/fer/ Babson College US – Frontiers of Entrepreneurship research website, latest research on entrepreneurship

www.businessbureau-uk.co.uk/ Useful small business resources, information and advice.

www.businessadviceonline.org/ Small Business Service/Business Link website

www.bizmove.com/starting.htm The Small Business Knowledge Base. This is a large, well structured US-based resource.

www.centreforenterprise.co.uk Regional centre for enterprise - resources and discussion on enterprise education, research and practice.

www.derby.ac.uk/cem/links. Centre for Entrepreneurial Management web links

www.entreworld.org/ Kauffman Foundation for Entrepreneurship: US information on business start and growth

www.gemconsortium.org/ Global Entrepreneurship Monitor – essential international research report on entrepreneurial development

www.entrepreneur.com/ US business start-up website

www.inc.com Based on Inc. Magazine for entrepreneurs and small business owners, this site includes articles from the latest issue plus a searchable archive of about 4000 items

www.managers.org.uk Institute of Management website useful for its Management Link directories of management skills and management sources

http://peerspectives.org/ 'Entrepreneurial Edge' US information on business growth

www.toolkit.cch.com US business owners toolkit

www.businesszone.co.uk UK-based small business information

www.clearlybusiness.com Usable Barclays Bank owned site

www.enterweb.org sources on entrepreneurship – mainly European

www.smallbusinessportal.co.uk UK small business research portal

www.prowess.org.uk womens enterprise support website

www.innovateur.co.uk useful resource site for science and technology innovators and entrepreneurs

www.entrepreneur.com US 'Entrepreneur' magazine website

http://entrepreneurship.mit.edu Entrepreneurship Center at MIT

www.europa.eu.int/comm/enterprise/entrepreneurship European Director General Enterprise website

www.innovation.gov.uk UK government innovation site

www.ost.gov.uk UK government office for science and technology

www.patent.gov.uk Patent Office site useful for intellectual property information

www.zeromillion.com Business Idea and Opportunity Evalution

Social and not for profit entrepreneurship websites

www.ashoka.org Ashoka social enterprise network

www.changemakers.net Changemakers social enterprise network

www.drucker.org Peter Drucker Foundation for Non-profit Management

www.socialentrepreneurs.org US National Center for Social Entrepreneurs

www.sse.org UK School for Social Entrepreneurship

www.globalideasbank.org Global Ideas Bank

index